THE RUHLEBEN FOOTBALL

"The real Escape to V

– Sports Journalists' Association

ALSO BY PAUL BROWN

SAVAGE ENTHUSIASM:
A HISTORY OF FOOTBALL FANS
"A very decent, impeccably sourced primer on what has happened to fans down the ages" – *When Saturday Comes*
"A splendid new book by an always exemplary researcher" – Sports Journalists' Association

THE VICTORIAN FOOTBALL MISCELLANY
"One of the greatest books ever written about football since Charlie Buchan put down his pen!" – Danny Baker
"Hugely entertaining" – *When Saturday Comes*

ALL WITH SMILING FACES:
HOW NEWCASTLE BECAME UNITED, 1881-1910
"Fantastic... charts the club's early years and meteoric rise in the Victorian and Edwardian eras" – *Newcastle Chronicle*
"I loved it!" – Ant McPartlin, Twitter @antanddec

NON-FOOTBALL

THE ROCKETBELT CAPER: A TRUE TALE OF
INVENTION, OBSESSION AND MURDER
"A delight to read. Genuinely stranger than fiction. Recommended" – *Popular Science UK*
"Has all the markings of a Hollywood blockbuster, and is a bizarrely unforgettable read" – *The Crack*

THE RUHLEBEN FOOTBALL ASSOCIATION

How Steve Bloomer's Footballers Survived a First World War Prison Camp

Paul Brown

Goal Post

Published in 2020 by Goal Post
An imprint of Superelastic
County Durham, UK
www.superelastic.co.uk

ISBN-13: 978-0-9955412-3-8

A CIP data record for this book is
available from the British Library.

This is a work of non-fiction. Everything between
quotation marks comes from memoirs, diaries, letters,
newspaper articles and other historical documents.

If you enjoy reading this book please consider leaving a
review on your favourite book store or reader website.

www.stuffbypaulbrown.com

"If we run now, we lose more than a match."
– Pelé, *Escape to Victory*, 1980

Contents

"Where the Boche Interns British Citizens: A Bird's-Eye View of the Camp at Ruhleben" by GF Morrell, from The Graphic, 22 April 1916 / In Ruhleben, Sladen, 1917 / Flickr API / Internet Archive / Wikimedia

Prologue

A Great International Match

The old forward paused for breath with his hands on his hips. He wore an untucked blue-and-white striped jersey with the cuffs of its long sleeves riding up on his forearms. Knickerbockers billowed around his knees and dark socks were pulled up over his calves. Straggling bootlaces were wrapped multiple times around his ankles. His thinning hair was swept back from a widow's peak and his pale face was reddened by the cold. Puffs of his breath clouded in the air. As the game resumed, he broke into a jog.

It had been two decades since he had made his debut for England, scoring two goals in his hometown of Derby. Then he had played in front of swaying terraces and heaving grandstands packed with an excited crowd drawn from the terraced streets and chimneyed factories that spiralled around the town's football ground. Now he was surrounded by ragged fellow prisoners who had left their ramshackle barracks to huddle along the touchlines on a field that was surrounded by armed guards and ringed by barbed-wire fences.

The blue-and-whites pursued the sodden brown football up the muddy field in a gallop of leather boots. Their opponents, the all-whites, were stretched across the middle of the pitch like a washing line pegged with laundry.

Unable to get through, the blue-and-whites went around. A pass out wide found an advancing winger. His twisting run sent a defender stumbling onto his backside in the dirt. Then came the cross, looped high into the box, drawing out the goalkeeper and falling perfectly for the old forward. He met the ball with his head and, with a subtle flick, guided the leather caser between the posts. *"Goal!"*

A cheer of delight rippled through the crowd. There were several thousand spectators bunched together four and five deep around the touchlines. Almost everyone, it seemed, had come out to watch the game. Many of them had a great interest in football, others less so. But for every one of them, their hardships plain to see, this was a welcome spectacle and distraction. And, by any measure, this was a top-drawer match featuring some of Britain's most famous players. It was, as billed, "A Great International Match". What price would those back home pay to watch such a game? And what price to see such a goal?

The blue-and-whites shook hands and patted each other on the backs, while the all-whites returned to their positions. The game resumed. The players were older than might have been remembered, but they were recognisable to any football fan who had clicked through the turnstiles to watch them back in Britain or had read about them and seen their portraits in the sporting pages of the newspapers. These were some of the game's most famous names.

There was Fred Pentland of Middlesbrough and England, the clever and pacy winger with a knack for a killer cross. There was Jack Cameron, the Scotland international and Tottenham Hotspur player-manager, the astute, goalscoring pivot of his team. There was Sam Wolstenholme, another England international, of Blackburn

Rovers, plus Jack Brearley of Everton and Tottenham, and Edwin Dutton of Newcastle United. And, standing clear above all of them in terms of fame and ability was the old forward, Derby County's record goalscorer, England's greatest match-winner and the very best player of his generation – Steve Bloomer.

Bloomer had always been a slender figure, and the past few months had hardly fattened him up. Meagre rations had thinned his limbs and slightened his build, just as they had sapped his strength and drained his energy. There were dark lines under his eyes. Bloomer was 41 years old – still young by modern standards, but not by the standards of the day, and certainly not by the standards of professional football. But he could still play, and he remained the focus of attention on the pitch. He didn't run around as much as he used to, but he controlled the game with calls and gestures and clever touches and bursts of his once-famed speed.

For the spectators, Bloomer and the other footballers were close enough to touch. And, more than that, the footballers were a part of their community, living among them and sharing their experiences and misfortunes. They lined up next to these footballers at roll call, stood next to them around the water standpipe and queued behind them for food rations. They ate with them, talked to them and slept beside them. Some of them got to play football with them. And those that didn't get to play at least got to watch. These famous names were comrades, companions and friends.

The pleasures of football brought a reassuring warmth to spectators as a cold drizzle blew across the plain. The football pitch was marked out on a large oval playing field, big enough for four such pitches, although much of it was a boggy marsh. Surrounding the field was a cinder and sand racetrack, ringed with rails. Beyond the track was an eight-foot wire fence. The fence posts were sharpened to jagged points with barbed wire strung along the top. Guards stood at the fences in spiked helmets or *pickelhauben*, with rifles and fixed bayonets.

At the side of the field, along the home stretch of the racetrack, were the old grandstands, where more spectators congregated to watch the action. And next to the grandstands were the red-brick barracks, where the men lived and ate and survived, and the guardrooms, where their captors lived. Two more fences surrounded the camp and separated the men from freedom.

This was Ruhleben, a former racetrack-turned-prison camp, located to the west of Berlin, Germany. The camp was set on low-lying land part-encircled by a bend in the River Spree. To the south was a railway line, which ran to central Berlin, just seven or eight miles away. To the north was the Spree and beyond that the Spandau arsenal and munitions works, its tall black chimneys spewing smoke into the air.

In the camp, the game continued. More goals were scored, and the crowd applauded. The guards watched keenly from their posts, and even the German officers were enthralled by the action. Trains rattled along the railway and barges passed by on the river. Flocks of birds flapped across the cold, grey sky. For a moment, all of those present could experience a taste of normality, even if nothing about their situation was normal.

Outside, beyond the guards and barbed-wire fences, Europe was at war. This was the Great War for Civilisation, a cataclysmic conflict that was shaping history and changing the world. The war was out of sight but never out of mind. The prisoners read news of the Marne, Ypres and Gallipoli and felt frustrated, useless and hopeless. Many of them wanted to be released not so they could return to their families but so they could head to the battlefronts and "show the Hun a thing or two". But for now they were stuck on this cold, open plain. And so they played football.

There were eight professional footballers in Ruhleben, plus several amateurs who had played the game at a decent level. Numerous others had played football at school or university, for their village or works teams, or with friends in the streets or the fields. There were around 4,500 men in the camp, and almost 500 of them participated in organised football matches. Thousands of others became spectators and supporters. Most would not see home or their families for the long duration of the war. They were prisoners, but football – for a short while – made them feel like that were not. It offered them enjoyment, camaraderie and an escape from the reality of their situation.

"An epic story of the triumph of the British spirit of sportsmanship in a German prison camp!" proclaimed one newspaper when it published an account of the Ruhleben footballers. The importance of football to the prisoners could not be overstated. One of the footballers, Everton's Wattie Campbell, said the game helped break the monotony of camp life and "carried away thoughts of home for a while". It was absolutely essential for maintaining the prisoners' physical well-being and mental health. Football, he said, "kept us alive".

1

Bloomer to Germany

How is it you score so many goals?" an interviewer once asked Steve Bloomer. There had been 422 of them for Derby County, Middlesbrough and England. "It is because I shoot so often," replied Bloomer, in typically straightforward fashion. He lived and breathed goals, and it was no surprise to anyone who had followed his career that he continued to score them in Ruhleben. *"Bloomer Still Scoring,"* read one newspaper headline, published in 1915, several months into his incarceration in Germany. *"Bloomer Sticks to Football,"* said another. By his own account, football was all he knew. For Bloomer and the thousands of prisoners he inspired, stuck in a desperate prison camp amid a devastating war, football was their escape.

Bloomer was the greatest goalscorer of his generation. He was football's biggest star during the game's flourishing Victorian and Edwardian boom times, and he helped drive its remarkable growth with every goal he scored. Bloomer began his career during the early years of professionalism when Football League matches might attract four or five thousand fans. By the time he finished playing, League matches could be watched by ten times that many and the FA Cup Final by more than 100,000. Bloomer was recognised and respected, and loved or feared, by millions of football fans around the country who read in newspapers about his exploits, saw his photograph on cigarette cards and queued at the turnstiles to watch him play.

Part of Bloomer's appeal was that he was an everyman, a working-class hero who rose to prominence during an era in which association football shifted away from its public school roots and became the game of the people. He was an ordinary man with extraordinary abilities who had worked in the same jobs and lived on the same streets as many of those who watched him play. Jimmy Catton, the editor of the *Athletic News*, called Bloomer "a son of the people, a type of the plebeian". Catton, the most prominent football writer of the late-Victorian and Edwardian periods, regarded Bloomer as England's greatest goalscorer and a player without equal.

Despite his fame and popularity, Bloomer was something of an enigma. Few observers could put their fingers on exactly what it was that made him so good, and the man himself offered few clues. It was often said that Bloomer didn't look like a footballer. He was too slight of build, too pale in countenance, too languid in demeanour. "The star did not look the part," said footballer-turned-journalist Ivan Sharpe, who played with him at Derby. "Bloomer was called 'Paleface'. In the dressing room, his limbs lacked the ruddy glow of the players around him. His build was slim, yet he was master of them all."

There is no film footage of Bloomer in action, only a handful of photographs and sketches that offer indications of his brilliance. But his goalscoring statistics and the written accounts of those who saw him play leave no doubt that he was a footballing phenomenon who helped shape the game we know today. "He was a famous figure," wrote Sharpe, "one of the most arresting figures of all, in the 1890s and the early seasons of the 20th century, when the game's popularity was being clinched by the feats of players who, it seems, will remain among the greatest of all time."

Bloomer was born in Cradley, in the Black Country, on 20 January 1874. His father, Caleb, was a puddler in an iron foundry, toiling in the heat and fumes at the face of the furnace. His mother, Mareb, died of pleurisy when Bloomer was 13. By then, the family had moved to Derby, and Bloomer – one of six children – was working as an apprentice blacksmith. After his mother's death, Bloomer went to work with his father at the iron foundry. Bloomer was a striker at the foundry, pounding hot iron with a forging hammer. He was also a striker at football – although that term wouldn't be used to describe a forward for several decades – and was banging in goals at a prodigious rate for Derby's junior teams. He claimed to have once scored 14 goals in a single game, for Derby Swifts in a 22-2 victory.

His tough working background gave him something of a physical edge over his peers, and he was generally stronger and quicker than his opponents – even if he didn't look it. Bloomer's unhopeful appearance saw him written off in his first turnout in a Derby County shirt, in a trial match at the age of 17. Harry Newbould, later the Derby manager, described Bloomer as "pale, thin, ghost-like, almost ill-looking", and said the Derby fans laughed when they first saw him. But Bloomer impressed enough over subsequent months to earn a professional contract.

One of those impressed by the youngster was Johnny Goodall, the former Preston North End "Invincible", who nurtured Bloomer at Derby and for England. The balding, moustachioed Goodall was something of an anomaly among

Victorian football folk in that he believed football could be taught. Training routines at the time focused on strength and fitness and involved little or no ball work. Goodall thought footballers should train with the ball at their feet, and his standing as an experienced England international allowed him to influence Derby's training regime.

According to Bloomer, Goodall "helped create my gift for scoring". That gift was partly achieved via a unique shooting practice drill using a bowler hat on a stick as a target. Goodall would throw the ball, and Bloomer would volley it, attempting to knock the hat off the stick from various angles and distances. "From constant shooting, I got the knack of hitting – hard – a still or moving ball," said Bloomer. "The suddenness as well as the accuracy and power of my shooting, I suppose, got me many goals, and the secret, if any, was found at practice."

Goodall was proud of how his protégé developed. "I think I can claim that [Bloomer] profited a little from my coaching," he said, "though, of course, he was always a natural player." Bloomer, for his part, said on more than one occasion that Goodall taught him just about everything he knew. "John Goodall was a great tutor, whose advice I always took and always kept in my head," he said. "He was like a father to me."

Bloomer made his debut for Derby in 1892, aged 18. He scored two goals and celebrated with cartwheels. Three years later, aged 21, he made his debut for England and scored another two goals. After the England game, Goodall – who played alongside Bloomer on both his debuts – came over to shake his hand and congratulate him. "But Steve," said Goodall, tapping Bloomer's head, "don't let this get any bigger." "It was an excellent piece of advice from an old and experienced player to an almost raw recruit," recalled Bloomer, "and I believe I took that advice to heart." There would be no more cartwheels.

Although he was a natural goalscorer, Bloomer rarely played at centre-forward. This was because, at Derby and for England, Johnny Goodall had made the centre-forward spot his own. Bloomer's usual position was at inside-right in a then-typical 2-3-5 formation, with two full-backs or defenders, three half-backs or midfielders and five forwards – two outside-forwards or wingers, two inside-forwards and a centre-forward. The main job of the inside-forward was to "back up" or support the centre-forward, and Bloomer created plenty of goals as well as scoring them.

"He had the golden gift of splitting a defence with one arrow-like, pin-pointed pass," said Ivan Sharpe. "Just as he could make this pass while the ball was moving, so he could score with a sudden touch. He scored most of his goals by sudden shooting. His great haul of goals came principally from first-time shots. His was instantaneous marksmanship aimed at beating the goalkeeper's eye. It follows that he could use both feet. And how did he shoot? With power, of course."

Bloomer's feet were real weapons, each packing a potent shot. But he was also noted for the clever and brave use of his forehead in an era when heading the cannonball of a leather caser was a rare skill. He was 5'7" in height, short by modern football standards, but an inch or so above average for the time. For context, Bloomer was taller than Maradona or Messi, and the same height as Pelé – who was also pretty good with his head.

Another weapon in Bloomer's armoury was his pace. In

the parlance of the time, he could "travel". And he was a quick thinker, noted for his one-touch game. This was another attribute coached into him by Johnny Goodall, who insisted he should always think one step ahead and anticipate what he would do with the ball before it reached him. Rather than taking time to trap the ball, Bloomer would intuitively pass or shoot first time. His anticipatory skills gave him a formidable poacher's instinct that allowed him to seemingly always be in the right place at the right time. It was perhaps this instinct that set him apart as "the greatest living English forward" according to West Bromwich Albion's Billy Bassett, who played alongside Bloomer several times for England.

"As an all-round forward he has never had a superior," said Bassett. "As a leader of a team, he was magnificent. He knew something of tactics; he was more than a merely skilful player." According to Bassett, Bloomer had an unmatched ability to be in the right place at the right time. "There is great art in getting into the right position to receive the ball," said Bassett. "It is that, quite apart from his wonderful skill, which makes Bloomer so dangerous. You always knew where to find Bloomer. He would always place himself in the position which was not only most convenient to his partner but also mightily inconvenient to the defending side."

Bloomer regarded this as a natural and vital instinct. "I seemed always to know just where the goal was," he said. "I did not need to look up when shooting or steady up in order to take aim. I was always on the look-out for a chance to dash through and shoot, or to shoot without any preliminaries. This thought never left me during any match. I kept constantly in my mind, wherever I was, the possibility of snatching a goal."

Billy Meredith, the Manchester United and Manchester City winger, who was perhaps the nearest challenger to Bloomer as the biggest star of the time, said Bloomer was "the greatest sharpshooter the game has ever known". "Bloomer was the biggest streak of lightning I have ever seen on a football field," said Meredith. "He was unbeatable, simply unstoppable."

"There is only one Bloomer, and his methods are his own, his style is unique," wrote authors Alfred Gibson and William Pickford in *Association Football and the Men Who Made It*, the authoritative football publication of the era. "He does nothing like anyone else. A man of action, a living force, a strong, relentless, destroying angel."

In Ruhleben, when he wasn't playing football, Bloomer was talking about it. He huddled with pals around the heating pipes in the freezing prison barracks talking about games and goals. When the weather and the guards allowed, they sat in the grandstands overlooking the camp's playing field. Stories were a currency in Ruhleben, traded for entertainment. They filled the camp's dead air and transported the listener far away from that miserable place. Every one of the 4,500 "Ruhlebenites" had stories to tell, but few of them could match the *Boys' Own* adventures of Britain's greatest footballer.

Bloomer's most memorable game, he reckoned when looking back over his celebrated career, was an England-Scotland international played on 2 April 1898, when he was 24 years old. The venue was the recently-expanded Celtic Park, in Glasgow. Bloomer was at inside-right in an England team he regarded as the finest he was ever part of. And the opposition, he thought, was the best Scotland team he had ever seen. There had never been a bigger crowd at an international football match. Almost 60,000 fans crammed into the racked grandstands and banked terraces to watch this most eagerly anticipated of spectacles. It did not disappoint. "The match was sheer science, football craft and skill at its very highest," Bloomer recalled, "and I believe the greatest international I ever played in."

England, in white shirts with the three lions emblem sewn on the breasts, were ahead within the first minute when Fred Spiksley of The Wednesday (later renamed Sheffield Wednesday) pulled the ball back for Freddy Wheldon of Aston Villa to score. Midway through the first half, England doubled their lead as Bloomer took centre stage. Displaying his lightning instinct and thunderous shot, he latched onto a Spiksley cross and fired the brown leather ball high into the Scotland net. "There was a striking silence on the gathered thousands," noted one reporter, as the home fans contemplated a shock defeat.

England led 2-0 at half-time, but things got very interesting a minute into the second half when Scotland pulled a goal back – causing the home crowd to erupt in excitement. The Scots pressed for an equaliser and England pushed back as the game swung from one end of the pitch to the other. The crowd roared and groaned as attacks were launched and shots were blocked, with the vast majority of the patrons of Celtic Park willing Scotland to draw level. But their hopes were dashed midway through the half, again by Bloomer.

Beating the Victorian offside trap (with at least three opposition players between him and the goal-line), Bloomer raced onto a Gilbert Smith through-ball and effortlessly slipped the ball past the goalkeeper to score his second and England's third. It was a typical strike. "You only needed to say 'Steve!' and Bloomer had the ball in the back of the net," said Smith, England's best amateur footballer, as he recalled playing alongside England's best professional.

Scotland fought back but were constantly troubled by the speed of the English forwards, particularly Bloomer. Despite the best efforts of the Scottish players, and the fervent backing of their fans, Bloomer was the two-goal match-winner, and England were 3-1 victors. The England players celebrated the victory with champagne – lots of champagne. Perhaps their coach driver was drinking with them because, on the way back to their hotel for more drinks, he took a corner far too fast and almost overturned the carriage.

After a boozy dinner, the England players left Glasgow at 10.45pm, and Bloomer was back in Derby by the early hours of the morning. It was there that a policeman spotted him staggering along Normanton Road in a very inebriated state and "using bad language". Bloomer was charged with being drunk and disorderly and summoned to court where he was fined 10 shillings. He apologised via his solicitor and promised it wouldn't happen again.

This incident – which was never repeated – did serve to indicate that Bloomer was not quite as strait-laced as he was sometimes portrayed. The drunkenness was curbed, but the bad language was not. Bloomer was renowned for the colourful epithets he would hurl at teammates if they failed to pick him out with a pass or if they missed the target following his hard-worked assist.

Ivan Sharpe said Bloomer could be a "tyrant" who, if things went wrong, would make his feelings very clearly known. “What d’ye call that?” he would explode. “A pass? I haven’t got an aeroplane!” Then, said Sharpe, Bloomer would “stand stock still, strike an attitude by placing his hands on his hips, and fix the offender with a piercing eye”, then “stamp back to his position in a manner intended publicly to demonstrate his disapproval”. “Quite wrong, of course,” said Sharpe. “Not good for the side. Not good for the alleged offender. Not good for the game. But those who knew Bloomer knew that he was really quite harmless, quite a peaceable person, who meant well and got the best out of his players because of his inspiring example, his great unselfishness and his tremendous devotion to the team on the field of play.”

A few months after the win over Scotland, in September 1898, Bloomer was suspended by the Derby committee for “neglect of training and inattention to duty”. This seemed odd, given his dedication to training. Further reports suggested there had been “a great deal of dissent among the players” during a defeat at The Wednesday – probably choreographed by the ever-demanding Bloomer. “To be a prominent international does not necessarily mean that a man can just do as he likes,” commented one local journalist. “In the case of Bloomer, his little eccentricities have been overlooked times without number.”

Sharpe said Bloomer was “a curious personality... but genius runs that way”. Certainly, Bloomer found it difficult to excuse less talented teammates who failed to meet his high standards and was often inclined to bawl them out in public. “My talking?” Bloomer later reflected. “Yes, I talked on the field. Some say I overdid it. Very likely. I was lost in the game. Some say I did not suffer fools gladly. Maybe. But I have made a few men play.”

Despite his obvious brilliance, Bloomer did not always seem to enjoy playing the game. He often appeared sullen and pensive, as if a great weight of melancholy sat on his sagging shoulders. He was deadly serious in his devotion to football and, by his admission, he had little time for anyone who did not share his attitude. His great ability brought extra responsibility and came loaded with the expectations of his team and their supporters. If his team won, it was down to him. If they lost, it was his fault.

There was this burden of pressure, but there was also an apparent sadness in Bloomer, captured in photographs taken of him, and visible in newspaper clippings and on cigarette cards from the time. Victorian and Edwardian portrait photographs rarely showed smiles, partly due to the early camera's long exposure times, and also because portraits were regarded as a serious record rather than a frivolous snap. But photographs of Bloomer seem tinged with melancholy.

Bloomer had experienced tragedy. His mother had died at a young age, and then in 1896 he lost his younger brother Phillip, also a footballer, who had recently made his first appearance alongside Steve in the Derby County first team. Phillip, who was a year younger than Steve, died of peritonitis aged just 21. And then there was the darkest day of Bloomer's football career, 5 April 1902, when the collapse of a stand during a Scotland v England match killed 25 supporters and injured more than 500 more in what became known as the first Ibrox Disaster.

Bloomer was captaining England for the first time on that tragic afternoon. The game kicked off as planned, in front of almost 75,000 fans at Glasgow's recently-expanded Ibrox stadium. But, after nine minutes of play, a section of the west stand collapsed, sending several hundred people tumbling to the ground. Bloomer recalled hearing a loud crash. "I looked about to see what was happening, and then I saw the stand collapsing," he said. A cloud of dust rose into the air, and fans at the front of the stand spilled onto the pitch. But few people away from the immediate vicinity of the collapse realised what had happened.

The incident caused the players to be taken off the field and back to the dressing rooms. And it was in the dressing rooms that the magnitude of the tragedy became clear. "A dreadful sight met my gaze," said Bloomer. "The officials and others were bringing in the killed and injured, and a long procession was to be seen." Some fans were killed instantly by the fall, and others suffered serious injuries, ranging from broken limbs to fractured skulls. Meanwhile, others were stuck under piles of bodies or fallen beams, as police and other fans worked to free them.

It was thought it would be dangerous to allow the crowd to leave while the rescue operation was ongoing, and it was feared panic would be created if fans realised the true extent of the disaster. So, after a stoppage of 20 minutes, it was decided that the game should resume.

The players were distraught. "There were poor injured fellows lying in all directions," said Bloomer. "We had to stride over many men who were lying moaning and groaning with broken legs, arms, etc. It was all too dreadful for description, and I never want to see anything like it again. We all felt so upset that we could not play like we should have done. Each time that I kicked the ball, I felt as though I was kicking one of those poor fellows." The dreadful experience stayed with him for decades, worsened by the guilt of having to continue to play while people died around him. "No one could possibly feel more sorry than I do," he said.

Bloomer won 23 caps for his country, at a time when the international team would typically play only three games a year. He officially scored 28 goals – although he claimed to have scored 30 in a blink-and-you-miss-it era before replays, when press room errors were common and goalscorers were often misidentified. At club level, Bloomer scored 273 league and cup goals for Derby before, in 1906, he was sensationally and controversially transferred to Middlesbrough. He subsequently scored 62 goals in 130 games for Boro. After four years, at the age of 37, he returned to Derby – to a hero's welcome – and scored another 59 goals. In his two spells, Bloomer scored 332 goals in 525 games for Derby County. His overall total of 422 goals came in 678 games for Derby, Boro and England. And they were scored at a time when, according to Ivan Sharpe (writing in the 1950s), "goals had about twice their present scoring value".

The greatest of all of those 422 goals, Bloomer reckoned, was scored for England against Scotland in 1907, in his last-ever international appearance. Memories of the goal differed, and witnesses said Bloomer received the ball anywhere from 25 to 40 yards out. But what happened next was not in dispute. Bloomer struck the ball first time with such force that it shot into the corner of the goal net in the blink of an eye, leaving the goalkeeper stock-still and the spectators open-mouthed. "I drove the ball home like a rocket," Bloomer recalled. "Colin Veitch, who gave me the pass, nearly hugged me to death." Afterwards, Scotland keeper Peter McBride told Bloomer, "I had no more chance of catching that shot than a snowball in Hades."

The story of how this football hero ended up in Germany is one of a player reaching the natural end of his career and refusing to accept it. At the age of 40, Bloomer had lost his place in the Derby first team, making only a handful of appearances during the 1913-14 season. His last was in an FA Cup defeat at Burnley on 31 January 1914. He spent most of the season with the reserves, where he acted as player-coach. It seemed obvious that the best footballer of his generation would have great value as a coach. But opportunities to work in coaching were limited, with British clubs remaining stubbornly resistant to the idea that the game could be taught. Fitness was king, and ball work was generally ignored.

Bloomer thought this was wrong. "It is all nonsense to say a man should not practise with the ball," he said. "There is not enough of it. Men will never master the ball until they do practise properly." He was very clearly influenced by Johnny Goodall, who had moved abroad in 1910 to pursue a coaching career at RC Roubaix in France. The lack of opportunities in Britain, combined with a desire from continental clubs to recruit British coaches, would lead many former players to move abroad. Continental clubs and associations recognised that Britain was the home of football, and were keen to learn about the game from experienced British professionals.

By 1914, Goodall was back in Britain, but several high-profile British players had followed his pioneering footsteps onto the continent at the end of their playing careers. Jimmy Hogan, the former Burnley and Bolton Wanderers player, was coaching Austrian players in Vienna. Hogan would become one of the most influential of all British coaching exports, linking up with Hugo Meisl to build the

Austrian Wunderteam of the 1930s.

Another influential figure was William Garbutt, the former Arsenal and Blackburn Rovers player, who was coaching Genoa in Italy. He would go on to manage Roma, Napoli, Athletic Bilbao and AC Milan. (The terms "coach" and "manager" were somewhat interchangeable, but "manager" suggested a broader influence on the running of the club, including player recruitment, which would previously have been handled by the club secretary and committee.)

Jack Reynolds, formerly of Burton United, Grimsby Town and Watford, was coaching St Gallen in Switzerland. In 1914 he went to Ajax in Amsterdam. He would be associated with Ajax for more than 25 years and lay the foundations for the club's influential Total Football philosophy. Edgar Chadwick, who played with distinction for Everton and Liverpool, was also in the Netherlands as coach of Sparta Rotterdam. Chadwick had previously coached the Dutch national side, and also a German representative team that toured England.

Several more of Bloomer's contemporaries were coaching in Germany, including his friend and former Middlesbrough teammate Fred Pentland, who was in Karlsruhe preparing a German team for the Olympics. Bloomer's former England teammate Fred Spiksley was the coach of 1. FC Nürnberg in Nuremberg, having previously managed TSV 1860 München in Munich. Jack Cameron, the former Scotland, Everton and Tottenham Hotspur forward who had gone on to manage Tottenham, was now the coach of Dresdner SC in Dresden. England, Everton and Blackburn half-back Sam Wolstenholme was coaching for the Norddeutscher Fussball-Verband (North German Football

Association) in Hamburg, and former Everton, Tottenham and Millwall Athletic forward Jack Brearley was the coach of Berlin's Viktoria club.

The former Luton Town player Charles Griffiths, previously the first full-time coach of Bayern Munich, was coaching Stuttgarter Kickers. William Townley, ex-Blackburn Rovers and England, was the coach of SpVgg Fürth. Townley would go on to follow Griffiths at Bayern Munich. For all of these British football pioneers, Germany was a land of opportunity. There was no real indication, certainly before the July Crisis of 1914, of the earth-shattering events that would follow.

So, whether inspired by Johnny Goodall or Fred Pentland or by any of the other former teammates and opponents who had made the move, Bloomer left for Germany in the first week of July 1914. It was a life-changing decision, but he must have felt he had little choice. He needed to earn money, and opportunities at home were scarce. And he undoubtedly still had much to offer to the game. He had clear ideas on coaching, even if those ideas were perhaps not quite as innovative as those of Goodall, Pentland or some of the others. But Bloomer had a huge advantage over all of his contemporaries. He was, in the opinion of almost every respected observer of the era, the greatest footballer who had ever played the game.

The *Derby Daily Telegraph* announced the news under the headline: *"Bloomer's Departure from England"*. Speculation had been rife, the paper said, since it was noticed that Bloomer's name was missing from the list of players retained by Derby County for the following season. It was rumoured that he would sign for Shirebrook FC, champions of the local Central Alliance league. But now all rumours could be set at rest. Bloomer had left for Germany, "having accepted a position as a coach to a Berlin club".

"Bloomer's connection with Derby County extends over 17 years," said the paper. "He is, without doubt, the most brilliant player ever connected with the club, and his wonderful deeds will be talked about in football circles for years to come. He was always the idol of the crowd." And there seemed little doubt he would thrive in Germany. "With his vast experience, Bloomer should make a splendid coach, and his many friends will join in wishing him every success."

2

Trapped in Berlin

Steve Bloomer was arrested on the morning of 5 August 1914. He had been in Germany for less than a month, working as coach of the Berlin Britannia football club. War took him – and much of Europe – by surprise. Tensions had risen following the assassination of Archduke Franz Ferdinand at the end of June, but it seemed implausible that such enlightened, civilised countries as Germany and Britain could get drawn into a serious conflict. Germany's Kaiser Wilhelm II and Britain's King George V were cousins, and the two nations were on close, seemingly-friendly terms. War was simply unthinkable.

Bloomer had travelled to Germany with few worries, other than thoughts for his wife, Sarah, and their daughters, Hetty, Violet and Doris, who were left at home in Derby. The offer of continued employment in the game he loved was too good to turn down. Bloomer had never earned more than £4 a week. He was relatively well-paid for the time but, with five mouths to feed, never had enough to save. To continue to support his family, he had to go where the work was. It would have been tough to leave his wife and daughters behind knowing that the only contact he would have with them would be via letter. The expectation was that he would be away for several months. As it turned out, he was away for several years.

He arrived in Berlin with a suitcase, a lodging room

and no grasp of German. He was 40 years old and still as lean as he had been at 20, although his close-cropped hair was beginning to thin and recede and he no longer had the babyish face of his youth.

Bloomer had been to the continent before. He was part of the Middlesbrough team that visited Prague and Copenhagen in 1907. But he was back at Derby County by the time Middlesbrough went to Berlin to play the Viktoria club in 1911. So he had never been to Germany, and he didn't speak the language. He was alone in an unfamiliar city, with Derby and his family a long way away.

Bloomer's Berlin was barely recognisable in comparison to the city of today. Only a handful of its landmarks remain after years of destruction and reconstruction. The Berlin of 1914 was far grander and more beautiful than the reconstructed version. Like the modern visitor, Bloomer could have strolled around the Tiergarten, gazed up at the Brandenburg Gate and marvelled at the Berliner Dom, all of which still stand despite the tumultuous changes that have surrounded them. But much of the rest of the city was entirely different, filled with grand squares linked by elegant, tree-lined boulevards.

The changes could be best illustrated at Potsdamer Platz, now a drab tourist hub but once the colourful social heart of the city. In 1914, it was Berlin's equivalent of Piccadilly Circus or Times Square, filled with rows of theatres, restaurants and beer palaces, scores of shops, including the high-end Wertheim department store, and some of Europe's finest hotels, including the Hotel Esplanade and the Hotel Excelsior, both since destroyed. With a pre-war population of around two million, Berlin was one of the biggest and most exciting cities in the world and must have represented quite a draw to Bloomer and the other Brits who made it their home.

The Berlin Britannia club was founded in 1892 as BTuFC Britannia 1892 (Berliner Thorball und Fussball Club Britannia 1892 – Thorball was a German term for cricket). Britannia first became known to British football fans in the summer of 1905 when the team made newspaper headlines after being thrashed 10-1 by touring English League champions Newcastle United. By 1914, Britannia was one of ten football clubs competing in the regional Brandenburg Championship. (Germany's national Bundesliga was formed in 1963.)

According to the British press, the Berlin players had a "surprisingly good" knowledge of the game. "Theoretically they have little to learn from their English comrades," wrote one reporter, "but in practical football, the Germans are but infants." Bloomer found the task of coaching them more challenging and less satisfying than he expected. "The job was a fairly good one, and would have been very enjoyable had the members been British," he recalled, "but they were Germans and poor sportsmen, and instead of my work being a joy it was simply work."

He would not be in the job for long. Political tensions were rapidly escalating. The assassination of the Austrian Archduke by Serbian terrorists had led to war between Austria-Hungary and Serbia. Austria-Hungary had the support of Germany, and Serbia had the support of Russia. Germany's Wilhelm II believed that Russia, France and Britain would use the war between Austria-Hungary and Serbia as a pretext to attack Germany, and he took pre-emptive action. On 1 August 1914, Germany declared war on Russia. The course of history was set.

The dramatic news put a swift end to Steve Bloomer's employment at Britannia Berlin. He was called in to see the club's president, Herr Fauber, who told him that the "glorious war" had rendered all private contracts worthless. His contract with Britannia was, therefore, null and void. Bloomer was ordered to sign a disclaimer to that effect and was paid his outstanding salary, plus expenses to cover his journey home. "And now, Mr Bloomer," Fauber told him, "take my tip and get out of Germany as quickly as possible."

Bloomer needed no further encouragement. "Taking the advice to heart, and realising the danger of my position, I went straight away to the station to get a train for home," he said. But there was no way out. Civilians were prevented from boarding trains, which were being requisitioned to send troops to the emerging battlefronts. Perhaps once all the troops were away, he was told, he would be allowed to travel. So he returned to the station on the following day, and the day after, and the day after that. Each time, he was turned away.

By now, Germany had advanced into Belgium and declared war on France. Bloomer described great excitement on the streets of Berlin and "wild scenes" in the city's cafes and beer gardens. "Germany will teach Europe a lesson," locals told him. "The world will see what German militarism can do!" "We will go through Belgium," Bloomer heard one man say, "then take Paris, then Calais, then London. Christmas in London would be nice!"

"I kept fairly quiet," said Bloomer, "and I kept a jolly sight quieter when Britain declared war on Germany." Britain had issued an ultimatum to Germany, ordering the Kaiser to stop his invasion of Belgium. He refused. At 11 pm on 4 August 1914, Britain and Germany went to war. The news provoked a mixed reaction from Bloomer. He was fearful for his safety, but he wanted to see the German war machine stopped and the café and beer garden braggarts silenced. "I didn't say anything, although I smiled to myself," he said. "My position was a delicate one."

On the following morning, Bloomer went straight to the British consulate to request passage out of the country. He was stopped at the door by two policemen, who asked for his name, age and marital status, and queried what he was doing in Berlin. After answering the questions with the assistance of a translator, Bloomer was placed in a room with around a dozen other British men. A sense of dread hung in the air as the men contemplated their fate. Soon a platoon of guards arrived, armed with revolvers and swords. Bloomer and the other Brits were ordered to form a column and were marched through the streets towards a courthouse at Alexanderplatz. They were advised that anyone who tried to escape would be shot.

Alexanderplatz was one of Berlin's busiest squares, bustling with pedestrians, horse-drawn carriages and electric trams. Thousands of people watched the prisoners' conspicuous march to and through the square. "It was rather a lively journey," said Bloomer. "Crowds surged around us. *'Swine Englanders!'* was, I think, the favourite description applied to us, and this was accompanied by loud and prolonged hisses." Other prisoners described being struck with missiles, including apples, potatoes and other assorted rotten fruit and vegetables. Rather than preventing any escape, the armed guards found themselves protecting the prisoners from the unruly crowd.

At the courthouse, Bloomer and the others were brought before a row of magistrates where they were briefly cross-examined and then presented with papers entitling – or ordering – them to remain in Berlin. They would not be allowed to leave the city or the country and would have to report to the police twice a week.

"The next few weeks were very trying," said Bloomer. "One never knew what was to happen. Excitement was at fever pitch. Every German was a red-hot patriot. Their victories were acclaimed in continual outbursts of wild talk and boastings. Men made a point of getting drunk every night and looking for trouble. I assure you that I kept as far away as possible from these scenes and spent most of my time in my lodgings or feeding at a quiet cafe."

But Bloomer found it difficult to keep quiet amid regular provocation. He tried to stay out of the way by spending time back at the football club, where he would potter about doing odd jobs. (In a significant anti-British move, the club would soon drop the "Britannia" part of its name, and rebrand itself as Berliner Sport Verein 1892.) Some club members sought Bloomer out and insulted him by making "unfavourable references to England". Bloomer later described the Germans as "rotters to the core". "It was as much as I could do to refrain from 'belting' them," he said.

One man, named Scliezburg, behaved in what Bloomer called "a typically Hunnish manner". One of the club's rooms contained a large map of Europe, on which flags were placed to mark the positions of the advancing German army. When Bloomer was present, Scleizburg would provocatively move the flags closer to Paris and the English Channel. "At these times my fingers would itch to show the Hun what at least one Britisher could do with his bare fists," said Bloomer, "but I always managed to control myself sufficiently to walk out of the room."

Bloomer was prevented from sending letters home, and neither his family nor his many friends and fans had any information regarding his whereabouts or well-being. A snippet of news arrived in Derby in late August via Dr WR Roe, the principal of the Derby Deaf and Dumb Institution. Dr Roe had returned home from Switzerland, passing through France, via Paris, on a train packed with German prisoners of war. Also on the train was Charles Griffiths, the Stuttgarter Kickers coach. Griffiths told Roe he had crossed the border into Switzerland to escape. He had seen Bloomer in Berlin a few weeks earlier, and he understood the football star had already returned to England. This, of course, wasn't the case.

A month later, in September, Bloomer's name was included in a list published in the *Football Players' Magazine* of British ex-professionals whose whereabouts on the continent were unknown. "Where are these coaches?" asked the magazine. Alongside Bloomer on the list were Jimmy Hogan, William Garbutt, Jack Reynolds, Sam Wolstenholme and William Townley. The magazine also named Percy Hartley, of Preston and Huddersfield Town, who was the coach of CS Verviers in Belgium. Also listed were Fred Warburton, formerly of Bury, Swindon Town and Plymouth Argyle, who was at HVV Den Haag in The Hague, and former Bolton Wanderers forward Arthur Gaskell, who was coaching in Moscow. It was noted that Tom Bradshaw, formerly of Leicester Fosse and Preston North End, was "luckier than some of his fellow coaches". Bradshaw had managed to get away from his post in the Netherlands and make it back safely to Preston.

As for Bloomer's pal Fred Pentland, a statement received by the pair's former club Middlesbrough declared that the German Olympic team coach was "not unhappy". "Will you be good enough to let Pentland's friends know that he is treated well in every respect?" said the statement. "He asks me to let his people know that he is not in want of anything but money. He can go about almost as he likes, but he cannot leave Germany."

Another snippet of news arrived in Britain that month via a letter from Jack Brearley, the Berlin Viktoria coach, to his wife. After several failed attempts, Brearley had managed to smuggle the message out with the help of an American at the US embassy. "I hope you and the kiddies are well, but how you are managing I don't know," he wrote. "I only wish I could get back, or at least get out of Germany... I can only hope for the best. Possibly I will have to stay here until the war is over. English people have to report to the police twice-weekly, and when we go, we are never sure of coming back."

"I don't see much of Bloomer," wrote Brearley, who was still fulfilling his duties as a coach. He noted that Viktoria had won 3-2 on the previous day, but said there was very little football being played, and his club had spent all of its cash, leaving him out of pocket. "They are a very shabby lot," he said, "and a worse conducted club it is impossible to imagine". He had been turned out of his lodgings because he couldn't pay his rent, and was staying with one of the players. He was, understandably, fed up. "I don't think the war will last long," he wrote. "Hope not anyhow. It seems years since I saw you. Each week looks like a month or more."

It was not only football coaches who were stuck in this desperate limbo. There were perhaps 10,000 British nationals in Germany, more than half of whom were men of "fighting age" and therefore regarded as "enemy aliens". Many of them were permanent residents, with regular jobs in a host of different industries. Some were working temporarily in Germany when the war broke out. Others were tourists, students, or seafarers. Several were honeymooners. There were music hall artists, circus acrobats and other entertainers. And there were many other sportsmen, including professional golfers, tennis players and jockeys.

There was little assistance available for the stranded Brits. The British consulate closed shortly after the declaration of war. The United States – officially a neutral party – took some responsibility for the protection of the British. The women and children – around 5,000 of them – were gradually allowed to leave, most of them via the Netherlands, but the men had nowhere to go. Families bid long farewells as mothers, sisters and daughters boarded trains and boats, leaving fathers, brothers and sons behind.

Many of the men prevented from leaving Germany were only British on a technicality – of which they might not have been aware. German-born children of British parents and British-born children of German parents were not naturalised Germans unless they had completed a lengthy citizenship process. They might never have spoken a word of English in their lives, but they were technically classed as British and as enemy aliens.

Among the "non-naturalised" Germans was one of Bloomer's Berlin Britannia players, 24-year-old inside-forward Edwin Dutton. Dutton was a slim, baby-faced, clean-shaven chap, with side-parted hair swept across his forehead. Bloomer must have seen something of himself in his youthful new charge. The two men played in the same position and, given their relative similarities, Dutton could hardly have had a better coach than Bloomer. But Bloomer spent only a few weeks with his players before the world tipped on its axis. Thrown together in the chaos that followed, Dutton and Bloomer would have plenty of time to get to know each other.

Dutton was born in Mittenwalde, Germany, to English parents on 8 April 1890. His father ran a sports outfitter's shop in Berlin and was a keen advocate of the burgeoning game of football in the city. Edwin began his playing career as a schoolboy at Britannia before moving to another Berlin club, BFC Preussen. His goalscoring ability led to selection for the German national team in April 1909 for a match against Hungary, at the age of just 18. In the following month, Dutton played for Preussen in an exhibition match against Newcastle United. Preussen lost 2-1, but Dutton made a strong impression.

Newcastle had connections with Berlin through previous tours and via their trainer Jimmy McPherson, who had worked at the Berliner SV club as their fitness man. Dutton and McPherson would become very close but, for now, Dutton was invited to Tyneside for a trial match, in which he excelled. Newspapers reported that Dutton "came over from the Fatherland specially for the game and showed splendid form, shooting with splendid accuracy". The appearance of "a real live German footballer" caused quite a stir. "English players must look out," noted the *Star Green 'Un*. "A German invasion apparently is in sight."

Dutton signed for Newcastle before the 1910-11 season,

but he struggled to break into an excellent side. Newcastle were the FA Cup holders and had won the League three times during the Edwardian period with some of the best players in the club's history. Dutton's efforts weren't helped by injury, which sidelined him during his first few months in England. But by the beginning of 1911, he was a regular in the reserve side, and he played for the first team during a summer tour of his home country, where Newcastle comfortably beat five German teams. Dutton scored six goals on tour, including four in a 7-0 win over Düsseldorfer SC 1899.

He was re-signed by Newcastle for 1911-12, but never played a competitive game for the first team, and ended up back at Britannia. This was particularly frustrating because, during his time on Tyneside, Dutton had fallen in love with Mary McPherson, the daughter of Newcastle trainer Jimmy. Whether Dutton returned to England to see Mary outside of his football seasons or Mary visited him in Germany when she was able, their relationship became a long-distance one conducted between Newcastle and Berlin.

German football was still an amateur or semi-professional pursuit, and Dutton worked in his father's sports shop to make ends meet. But he had been paid to play football, and his time at Newcastle meant Dutton was considered by Steve Bloomer to be a fellow professional footballer. He was also considered a pal. Over the next few years, despite a 16-year age gap, "Ted" would become Bloomer's closest friend. For the time being, the two footballers – one an England international and the other a German international – were trapped in wartime limbo, and stuck in Berlin.

Another footballer stuck in Germany – in Nuremberg – was Bloomer's former England colleague Fred Spiksley. But Spiksley managed to get out, and he had a remarkable tale of escape. Born in 1870, Spiksley was four years older than Bloomer and had been another of English football's greatest players. The skilful and extraordinarily fast winger scored more than 300 career goals. He won the British Home Championship twice with England, and the Football League and the FA Cup with The Wednesday. Spiksley scored a hat-trick on his England debut, against Wales in 1893, then scored another hat-trick on his second England appearance, against Scotland a fortnight later. He also scored both goals in The Wednesday's FA Cup final win in 1896.

After a knee injury ended his playing career, Spiksley became an innovative coach, initially in Sweden with AIK and the Swedish national team, and then in Germany at 1860 München and, by 1914, FC Nürnberg. Spiksley considered Nürnberg to be the biggest club in Germany, and it represented a suitable challenge. The club played in the South German Football Championship, alongside Bayern Munich and SpVgg Fürth – the former and latter clubs of William Townley. Like Bloomer and the others, Spiksley was prevented from leaving Germany following the declaration of war. Unlike Bloomer, Spiksley had his family – a wife and son – with him.

Spiksley said the treatment he and his family received was initially "very fair and courteous", except for one incident in which they were reported and arrested for speaking English on a tramcar. However, on 23 August, Spiksley was re-arrested and thrown into prison as an enemy alien. He was placed in solitary confinement, where he was given just a single piece of black rye bread to eat.

"The treatment we received was terrible," he said. "We were bullied about by the warders, and it seemed as if the officials were having their revenge on us."

Spiksley expected to remain in prison until the end of the war. However, after just a few days, he was taken from his cell and led outside, where his wife and son were waiting for him in a motor car. Spiksley's wife, who had been ordered to leave Germany, had stayed to seek his release. Using the influence of the Nürnberg football club, she approached the US Consul and begged for assistance. Spiksley was released – but he was not quite free.

Spiksley and his family travelled with a fleeing British Consul as far as Landau, near the French border, where they were stopped by frontier guards. Despite their protestations, they were told that the men – Spiksley and the Consul – could not cross. Only men who were certified incapable of military service were allowed to leave Germany. To get a certificate, they would need to be examined by a military doctor. The Consul successfully failed his examination, received his certificate, and was allowed to leave. But the former footballer, still only 44 years old and by his own admission "in perfect condition", would have more difficulty. "I was told to see the doctor in the morning," said Spiksley. "It looked as if I was going to be left behind."

But Spiksley did have a potential way out – courtesy of his dodgy knee. The old football injury caused his kneecap to dislocate when he ran. Ahead of his examination, Spiksley soaked the knee in hot water to soften it up. "When I went in to the doctor, he commenced measuring my muscles, and as he found everything was right, I began to lose heart," said Spiksley. "But then he asked me if I could run." Spiksley stood up, began to run, then pretended his knee had "gone out". He sat down, pushed on his kneecap, and deliberately dislocated it. "Then I stood up on the other leg and put the right knee in and out several times," he said, "and the joints cracked so loudly that the doctor promptly granted me the required certificate."

Spiksley escaped with his family through France and was back in England by September. He had sympathetic thoughts for his fellow Brits still trapped in Germany. "I believe they will soon be sent to some place out in the country and made to dig trenches for the German army," he said. Now that he was free, Spiksley was able to contribute to the war effort, as a munitions inspector. After the war he would return to coaching, enjoying an eclectic career back in Germany, and also in Spain, Switzerland, Mexico and Peru.

In Germany, hopes of escape gradually seeped away as winter approached. Then, in late October, the German press reported that Britain was making life difficult for ex-pat Germans by terminating their employments, dissolving their businesses, and detaining German citizens in internment camps. The British government had taken action to restrict the movements of German nationals and had interned some "enemy aliens", although it hadn't yet ordered the widespread internment of German citizens.

Nevertheless, the reports caused public outrage. The German government subsequently issued an ultimatum stating that unless all German citizens in Britain were released by 5 November, all British citizens in Germany would be rounded up and interned. The ultimatum was ignored.

On the following day, 6 November, Germany ordered the internment of every British man aged between 17 and 55. All were already under police supervision and were swiftly located and arrested. "To tell the truth, I don't think that I was exactly sorry," said Bloomer. "I could not have kept quiet any longer."

The arrested men were advised to bring "two blankets, sheets and so forth", and were taken to local police stations. "The exodus is now proceeding," noted the *New York Times*, which reported that 500 men were arrested in the city of Berlin, and another 500 in the suburbs. A hundred were arrested in Dresden and 80 in Hanover. In Hamburg, 1,400 men were arrested, the majority of them seamen from impounded British ships.

The journalist Israel Cohen was working as a correspondent in Berlin, and he wrote about his arrest. "At seven o'clock on Friday morning", he said, "just as I thought of turning over on the other side, there was a ring on the front door, and shortly after there was a knock at my door. I knew that my time had come." Cohen's landlady, visibly distressed, told him that a gentleman wanted to see him. "I had been expecting him," said Cohen.

"Gut morgen," said the police detective. "I am very sorry, but you probably know why I have come."

"The English are to be interned?" asked Cohen.

"Yes," said the policeman. "So get yourself ready, but there is no hurry."

Cohen washed and packed, had breakfast, and looked at the newspapers – which contained the official notice of internment. Then he was escorted, carrying his bag, umbrella and a parcel of bedding, first to a local police station, and then to the Stadtvogtei municipal prison, where he was locked in a cell. At around one o'clock, the cell was opened, and Cohen was ordered outside among a crowd of hundreds of British men, surrounded by armed and mounted police. The men were ordered to line up in fours and were marched, with their luggage, towards Alexanderplatz. Any man who failed to keep up or stepped out of line was yelled at. Those who stopped to rest or struggled with their bags and parcels were beaten. A crowd gathered to watch, but this time it was quiet and reflective, as the grave reality of the situation dawned. "Among the onlookers were the weeping wives or mothers of some of the prisoners," said Cohen.

At Alexanderplatz station, the prisoners were packed onto waiting trains, which took them west, across the Spree, past the Brandenburg Gate, through the Tiergarten and out of the city centre. "We cast many a yearning glance at the streets below us as the train sped on," said Cohen, "through the city quarters and then past the spacious thoroughfares of Charlottenburg, and we felt the fetters tightening about us."

After travelling for half an hour, the trains arrived at Auswanderer Bahnhof, the "Emigrants' Station", so named because it had previously been used as an arrival point for Russian and Polish immigrants. The prisoners disembarked and were herded along a rough country road, still flanked by armed police who yelled and swore at them. Again the prisoners struggled with heavy bags and packages. A carriage was brought for a handful of men who were too ill to walk. One man, missing an amputated leg, was made to hobble along the uneven road on crutches with the rest of the prisoners.

Ahead of them were tall barbed-wire-topped wooden

fences, then a red-brick wall with large gates, guarded by sentries in spiked helmets. The prisoners were herded into shape and held in place. Among them were Steve Bloomer and Edwin Dutton. Then the wooden gates were opened. Above the gates, a sign read: "*Trabrennbahn Ruhleben.*" "Ruhleben Trotting Track."

3

Arrival at Ruhleben

Bloomer, Dutton and the first convoy of prisoners arrived at Ruhleben at 5 pm on Friday 6 November 1914. The sun had set, and the last remnants of twilight illuminated puddles on the muddy ground. The prisoners stood quietly outside the brick wall that reached up towards the dark, cloud-filled sky. They pulled their jackets and overcoats tightly around them and clutched their bags and parcels with chilled hands. They listened as the guards, with their rifles and bayonets, barked orders from beneath their spiked helmets. *"Halt! Ruhig sein!"* – "Stop! Be quiet!" Then the first few hundred prisoners were marched four-by-four into the camp, and the gates swung shut behind them.

A literal translation of "Ruhleben" is "Quiet Life". The prisoners would laugh about that later. As the sign above the gates attested, it had previously been a *trabrennbahn* or trotting track – a racetrack used for harness racing, where jockeys ride in two-wheeled carts behind trotting horses. It had also been used for flat racing and, in civil times, was an attractive and popular draw for Berlin's well-to-do classes who would pack the grandstands in their summer fineries to bet on high-profile races featuring horses and jockeys from around Europe. But the war – and the weather – had removed any attraction the place might once have had.

Ruhleben was situated on a bend in the River Spree,

seven miles west of the centre of Berlin. To the south was the railway to Berlin. To the north-west, across the river, was Spandau and the billowing chimneys of its industrial munitions works. The racetrack sat on a low, flat plain, reclaimed from the river. The oval track ran around a large field. Heavy autumn rain had turned the overgrown field into a marsh. Puddles had become ponds, and ponds had become lakes. There were six grandstands – three on each length of the track. To the east was a steep brick embankment, an abandoned military rampart known as the Old Fort. Spirit-sucking mud was everywhere, and a cold wind blew sand and dirt across the track and all over its fixtures and fittings. It was a cold, dirty, miserable place, and the introduction to it represented something of a shock for the prisoners, many of whom were traumatised by the experience.

The racetrack had been requisitioned as a prison camp in September when a small number of British, French, Belgian and Russian civilians – arrested as "troublemakers" – were interned. It was reported, for example, that one young Brit was incarcerated for uttering "violent diatribes against the German Army" and threatening to pass "great secrets" to the British press. The French, Belgian and Russian prisoners would eventually be moved elsewhere, and Ruhleben became reserved for prisoners from Britain and the still-wide expanses of the British Empire, including Australia, New Zealand, Canada, India, South Africa, Rhodesia, Egypt, Nigeria and the West Indies.

Efforts to turn the racetrack into a prison camp were rudimentary. Barbed-wire and mesh fences were erected around the stables and the grandstands on the southern side of the racetrack, and a tall wooden fence was built around the outer perimeter of the site to supplement the existing fences and wall. But little else was changed, and Ruhleben remained a (now fortified) racetrack. The grandstands stood empty, littered with weeds and dust. And the oval track, with the saturated field inside it, was deserted. The prison was concentrated at the south-west corner of the site, where the main gate led into a courtyard surrounded by red-brick stables with timber roofs. These stables became the camp's barracks.

The prisoners were ordered to line up in front of the first stable and to keep still and stay quiet. They were at last allowed to drop their heavy baggage to the ground. An electric arc light flickered from a pole in the middle of the courtyard. The camp commandant arrived with his officers, all in grey uniforms and peaked caps, with ranking insignia on their collars. The commandant had an Iron Cross pinned to his chest. He addressed the prisoners in German, telling them that they should blame their own government for their incarceration and that if they obeyed the rules, they would be treated fairly. Many of the prisoners – including Bloomer – did not speak German and could not understand anything of what the commandant said.

Then the registration began, with prisoners taken in groups to a table, where they were ordered to fill in slips of paper with their name, age, occupation, religion, last address, and the number of years they had resided in Germany. Meanwhile, the guards searched the prisoners' luggage. Worried they might have their money confiscated, some prisoners slipped their coins and notes into their socks. Someone made a light-hearted comment, displaying the type of gallows humour that would become a useful coping mechanism in Ruhleben, and several prisoners laughed. "Hold your jaws!" yelled a furious guard. "This is no joke!" But the commandant eased the tension. "Not so rough!" he ordered. "They are not criminals."

Once all of the prisoners were processed, they were led to the stables. Bloomer and Dutton, near the front of the line, went in stable 1. Each stable contained 27 horse boxes, around 10 feet square with heavy sliding doors. Many of them still had straw and manure on the floor from the previous occupants. (One stable still housed the last of Ruhleben's horses, which were moved to a wooden barn.)

The boxes were cold and dark. There was no heating and only dim lighting from two electric bulbs in the stable corridors that barely penetrated the boxes. Each horsebox contained six iron bedsteads, stacked on top of each other to make bunk beds. The back-breakingly heavy bedsteads had been carried from Charlottenburg, around three miles away, by the early arrivals. On each bed was a coarse sack, a straw pillow, and two blankets, which Bloomer said were "about the size and thickness of a napkin".

"The first six in here," shouted a guard, before moving to the next box. Gradually, six men at a time, the 27 boxes were filled. This meant 162 men had beds. Around 200 others were not so lucky. These unfortunates were directed up a narrow wooden staircase on the exterior of the stable into the hayloft. There were no bedsteads or blankets in the loft, only a layer of straw. And there was barely enough room for the men. One prisoner recalled that the haylofts were so packed that it was difficult to raise his arms from his sides.

Later, sacks were distributed, and prisoners in the horseboxes who had two blankets were ordered to give one of them up to their neighbours in the lofts. But there were still not enough sacks or blankets to go around. There was not enough food, either. The men in the first stable – or Barrack 1 – were given a small, rough towel and a pewter bowl containing cocoa and a piece of blood sausage. Later arrivals to other barracks had to make do with the towel and an empty bowl.

The influx of prisoners continued through the night. There were 11 stables, and each was filled in the same way as the first, with six men in each of the 27 horse boxes, and a couple of hundred in the haylofts. It was clear that the Germans had grossly underestimated the number of prisoners, and that Ruhleben's makeshift barracks were wholly unsuitable. As well as being cold, dark and overcrowded, they were dangerously unsanitary. The 350-plus men in each barrack had to share two cold water standpipes, and the toilet facilities, located in an external latrine block, were entirely inadequate. Manure and other detritus that stunk out the stables had to be swept up by hand in the absence of any cleaning equipment.

Each barrack was guarded by three soldiers, with one designated as the head guard. On the first night, as the cold and exhausted prisoners attempted to make themselves as comfortable as possible, the armed guards marched up and down the corridors shouting down any dissent or requests for more blankets and sacks. The prisoners were told to keep quiet and to *"Schlafen gehen!"* "Go to sleep!" But for those in the haylofts, in particular, it was virtually impossible to do that. It took until the early hours of the morning for the men to successfully arrange themselves so that everyone could lie down. And then, at 6.30am, the guards marched back down the corridor in their heavy boots, yelling *"Aufstehen!"* – "Get up!"

In Bloomer's barrack, there were 20 or so tin washbasins, which could be filled with cold water from the two standpipes. The first morning wash was described as "pandemonium" as hundreds of prisoners crowded around the basins, lining up and jostling for space, ready to grab for a basin and a splash of water. No soap was provided, so those who had not brought their own went without. But, in such disordered circumstances, few of the prisoners could claim to have had a good wash and, in such filthy conditions, nothing could stay clean in any case.

The morning light gave the prisoners their first proper look at the camp. The main compound – the stable compound – contained the 11 barracks and the toilet block, plus a guardhouse and administration office, and a building known as the Casino, which was a mess-room for the guards. The adjacent grandstand compound contained the three southern grandstands, with a restaurant and Tea House, from which meals would be ladled out from soup boilers. As more prisoners arrived, the Tea House would double as an extra barrack. Men without a berth also slept in the grandstands until room could be found for them elsewhere. By the end of November, there would be 4,000 men packed into the 11 barracks and the Tea House – more than 330 men on average in each brick and timber building. And what an assorted collection of men they were.

"Really, we were a motley crowd," recalled Bloomer. "Every type of man was represented... There were men who were captured on their honeymoon, jockeys, professional golfers, music hall actors, seafaring men, men on holiday, men on business in Germany, men with businesses of their own in Germany, and even men who did not know a word of English and could only speak German. We were collected together and dumped into stables. No distinction was drawn between class. The lucky ones got a bunk in a horsebox. The unfortunate ones were packed like herrings in the loft above."

After their brief morning wash, the prisoners were ordered to line up for coffee. Holding their pewter bowls, they were marched out of the stable compound, four-by-four, and ushered through a gate into the grandstand compound. A five-minute march past the back of the grandstands brought the prisoners to the Tea House, where they queued for their coffee – or at least a dark liquid masquerading as such – plus a small piece of black bread.

It was a pathetic meal, but the prisoners were so cold and miserable that even bad coffee was taken as a comfort. "We marched back that raw November morning warming our hands against the bowl," recalled Israel Cohen. "The taste of the beverage was repulsive... but it was something hot, and we gulped as much of it down as we could stomach."

After breakfast, the prisoners were lined up for work duties – carrying store items, filling sacks with straw, and moving iron beds. It was tough, physical work, and not all were willing or able to do it. Those who didn't carry out their tasks, or who didn't understand their instructions, were yelled at and shoved by the guards. Between work tasks, the prisoners were busy requesting and bartering for essentials such as blankets and food bowls. But there were not enough to go around. Several hundred prisoners stood queuing for an hour, waiting for a promised batch of towels that never arrived.

Around noon, the men were given watery soup, and in

the evening, more bad coffee. It took over an hour to serve every prisoner in the camp, and those towards the back of line found that their soup was stone cold by the time they received it. It was subsequently suggested that meal times might be staggered to ease the demand. This would also allow those unfortunates who did not have a bowl to borrow one from a fellow prisoner who had already eaten.

Prisoners who had money were able to buy extra food and other essentials from a small canteen run by a German woman behind Barrack 11. A fresh bread roll cost 15 pfennigs (pf) – 15 German pennies – and a fork cost ten pf. For those who were flush with cash, butter for the roll was 45pf, and a piece of ham was 30pf. A more palatable cup of coffee than the Tea House fare cost 15pf. Soap and tobacco were also available, while stock lasted. The prices would go up over subsequent weeks as demand increased and supplies began to dwindle.

The rest of the first day in Ruhleben was filled with *appells* or roll calls, requiring the prisoners to troop back and forward across the grim compound. "We were counted so often that we could not help likening our captors to a miser who was always fingering and checking his golden treasure," said Cohen. "We found the process irksome. It reminded us of our school days."

The prisoners were also presented with the camp rules and regulations. Smoking was prohibited in the barracks, and alcohol and gambling were prohibited anywhere in the camp. Anyone who broke these rules would be confined to a dark cell for 72 hours with nothing but water and a piece of black bread – a wartime staple known as *kommissbrot.*

Any prisoner with more than 20 marks was ordered to surrender their money for safekeeping. This did seem to be a genuine security measure, and those who handed over their cash were allowed to withdraw it from the admin office when required. Prisoners would be allowed to write home, but all messages had to be written on a postcard in pencil and would be vetted by a camp censor.

Both Bloomer and Dutton did almost immediately write home to advise family and friends of their predicaments. Bloomer sent a postcard to his wife in Derby, telling her he had been arrested and imprisoned in an internment camp, and that he was "as well as can be under the circumstances". It was reported that Sarah Bloomer was "overjoyed" to hear from her husband. Dutton wrote to Jimmy McPherson, the Newcastle United trainer, and the father of his beloved Mary, advising that he and Bloomer had been "taken to a concentration camp", where the pair were bedfellows. Dutton advised McPherson that Bloomer was "enjoying good health".

During that first day, prisoners who believed they had been wrongfully imprisoned were told to petition the camp administration in writing. Many did so. One man who secured a quick release was a German journalist who was caught up in the march to Ruhleben while covering the internment and, unable to prove his identity, was bundled through the gate with the British. But for most of the prisoners, a petition for release was, according to Cohen, "a waste of paper and energy, as well as a source of disappointment". Most would end up waiting months, only to receive the same reply: "*Abgelehnt*" – "Rejected".

Amid the roll calls and regulations, the prisoners got to meet the officers in charge of the camp. The camp commandant was *Graf* or Count Schwerin, described by Cohen as "a septuagenarian with white moustache and stooping shoulders, who walked with a shaky step and with the help of a stick". Although he wore an Iron Cross, his fighting days were long gone. In civilian life, Count Schwerin was a wealthy landowner from Mecklenburg-Strelitzgood, north of Berlin. He was a broadly good-natured man who seemed sympathetic to the plight of the prisoners. But he was also incompetent, and entirely unsuited to his task. After the first few days, he was rarely seen, leaving the day-to-day running of the camp to his second in command.

Baron von Taube, who would become known to the prisoners simply as "the Baron", was the *Lageroffizier* (camp officer), and, in Schwerin's absences, the acting commandant. He had been an insurance agent in civilian life and had no experience relevant to managing a prison camp. Like Schwerin, he wore an Iron Cross. (The prisoners joked, as there were so many of them around, it must rain Iron Crosses in Germany.)

Cohen described von Taube as "a man of about 50, tall, well-set, and with a grey moustache of a less imposing character than that of his superior". He was always seen with a cigar clamped between his lips. "We soon began to estimate how many cigars a day he smoked," said Cohen. Von Taube lived in a little house just outside the barbed wire fence with his second wife and a black Pomeranian dog. The Baron and Baroness would often be seen walking the dog together around the camp, and it was said they had come to Ruhleben for their honeymoon.

Von Taube was somewhat moody and unpredictable and could erupt in rage at the slightest provocation. When his temper was aroused, the Baron could be particularly cruel. In part, this seemed to be due to his frustration at being unable to manage the overflowing camp properly. According to Cohen, the Baron's inexperience in administration caused his disposition to swing erratically "between unrelenting severity and the most amiable leniency".

Of the other officers, the most-hated was Lieutenant Rudiger, who dealt with the petitions for release and seemed to revel in rejecting them. Although rarely explosively angry, Rudiger was regarded as particularly cruel. Powell called him "a suavely offensive person, and the incarnation of what the Germans call *schadenfreude*, or delight in the misfortune of others". After the war, Rudiger would be the only Ruhleben staff officer charged with war crimes.

The camp's guards were all reservists, most drawn from the civilian police force. Initially, there were only 36 guards, but this number soon swelled to around 200. While three guards manned each barrack, others patrolled the fences and walls and manned the sentry posts in shifts of two hours on and four hours off. Each wore pointed pickelhaube helmets and boot-length greatcoats and carried rifles – typically Mauser M1898s with fixed bayonets.

The guards were hardly an elite bunch, and they fulfilled their duties with an attitude that existed somewhere between boredom and disinterest. If some of the guards were aggrieved at being allocated such a dull and monotonous posting, others were relieved that they had not been sent to the more dangerous fronts. As the war progressed, it would become clear that they had lucked into something of a cushy position, although for many of them their luck would not last.

In between assemblages, the prisoners mingled in the compound. They were keen to avoid the dirty and overcrowded barracks, and access to the racecourse was forbidden, so they were restricted to the courtyard and the spaces between the barracks. It was bitingly cold, with a freezing east wind sweeping over the plain, so the men kept moving, shuffling from stable to stable and huddling together for warmth.

Perhaps inevitably, some of them began a kickabout. "We had no ball of course," said Bloomer, "but to amuse themselves a number of the chaps made a substitute out of a few rags and, forming themselves into sides, played a keen but unsatisfactory game between two of the barracks. Already there were signs that a number of the men were keen on football."

One of the men who made the rag-ball was Henry Mahoney, an engraver by trade, who was arrested while travelling through Germany towards Russia. Mahoney was billeted in the hayloft of Barrack 5, a particularly inhospitable stable that he said "reeked with a pungent aroma" and had "fresh manure still clinging to the walls". The dark hayloft, he said, was "cold as ice" and "as black and forbidding as a coal hole", and was home to a "seething, misshapen mass of humanity, tumbling and jostling restlessly for elbow room in which to settle down".

It was no wonder that he and his colleagues sought outdoor activities. "Determined to enjoy a little diversion we hunted up a few rags and some odd lengths of string, and from these contrived a primitive rag-ball," he explained. "This was the first diversion introduced into the camp, and it proved a great success."

More rag-ball matches followed, with many prisoners

keen to play, and many more keen to watch. Football broke the monotony and took the minds of the players and spectators away from the worries of the situation in which they had found themselves. It was the first of several entertainments and distractions that would begin to occupy the prisoners. Musical instruments were retrieved from cases, and impromptu concerts were held. A chess board appeared, and prisoners crowded shoulder-to-shoulder to watch every move.

Then it began to rain, turning the compound into a muddy quagmire, and the prisoners retreated to the dreaded barracks. (They were told it was forbidden to call them stables.) Many of them had no winter or waterproof clothing, and a soaking only worsened the miserable chill.

"As we were then in the midst of a very hard winter, and as a number of the men were past the prime of life, the hardships and the sufferings of a lot of the prisoners will be readily understood," said Bloomer. "Complaints were heard on every hand. Then on top of this, the food that was served out to us was not fit for dogs. There was no nourishment in the stuff at all, and when complaints were made, we were told that the 'swine of Englanders' would go to the swill tub for their food. It very soon dawned on me that these conditions would be the death of a lot of the men unless something was done quickly."

Many of the prisoners would have recognised Bloomer, but he was not the only celebrity in the camp. During his first days in Ruhleben, Bloomer met William Drummond, the Earl of Perth, a popular figure (and a champion chess player) who would be nicknamed the "Pearl of Earth". Bloomer also met Sir John Irving, a commercial fishing magnate, and John Balfour, a diplomat who was the nephew of former British Prime Minister Arthur Balfour, and cyclist John Halpin, known to the prisoners as "Bicycle Billy", who was arrested in Germany while undertaking an epic ride from London to Moscow.

And, of course, there were other footballers. Along with Bloomer and Dutton, one of the first to arrive was England international Sam Wolstenholme, who played alongside Bloomer for England and played against Bloomer's Derby for Everton. Born in Little Lever, near Bolton, in 1878, Wolstenholme was a blond-haired and moustachioed half-back who was regarded as "possibly one of the cleverest exponents in the position in the country". Described as "an intelligent right-half and thinker" and "as agile as a squirrel", he made more than 150 appearances for Everton, and also played for Blackburn and Norwich in a roaming career.

Wolstenholme and Bloomer played together three times for England, the first in April 1904, when Bloomer scored the only goal of the game in a 1-0 win over Scotland. Wolstenholme, now aged 37, was working as a coach for the North German Football Association when the war broke out. He was arrested in Hamburg on 6 November and immediately transferred to Ruhleben, where he was placed in Barrack 9.

Also introduced to Bloomer during the first couple of days of captivity were a couple of amateur footballers, Alf Mills and Tommy Miller. Mills, like Edwin Dutton, was born in Germany to British parents. He had played for Dutton's old club, BFC Preussen in Berlin. At the outbreak of the war, he was working as a club trainer alongside his younger brother John, who was also arrested and sent to Ruhleben.

Tommy Miller was from Dreghorn in Ayrshire, but he'd played football in Düsseldorf for more than a decade, as a half-back or full-back with Düsseldorfer SC and Viktoria Ratingen. Both Mills and Miller were 32 years old when they arrived in Ruhleben.

On the second full day in the camp, Sunday 8 November, the prisoners were instructed to nominate translators for each barrack. Initially, this was intended to help facilitate communication between the Germans and the prisoners, but the role of the translators would evolve. They were referred to as "captains", and became important players in the administration of the camp. Bloomer's Barrack 1 nominated EM Trinks, who was subsequently appointed as overall captain of the camp. Joseph Powell, captain of Barrack 10, was appointed as his deputy.

Trinks, who was a lodging-house keeper from Hamburg, became almost immediately unpopular, revelling in the authority of his role, and aligning himself with the German captors rather than the English prisoners. The prisoners regarded him as a "German at heart". It was reported that he had written to a friend in England stating that he hoped the British armed forces would get a "thundering good licking". He boasted that he would soon be released – and he was, along with several other "PGs" or Pro-Germans, in January 1915. After that, Joseph Powell would step up as camp captain.

In the meantime, the prisoners continued to occupy themselves as best as they could with their makeshift entertainments – chiefly football. One rag-ball match, played on the Monday afternoon between the barracks, was between "Tilly's" and "the Jockeys". The Tilly's team was made up of men from Tilly's Academy, or Institut Tilly, a Berlin "cramming" school for intensive study of German as a foreign language. A dozen British Tilly's students were arrested and sent to Ruhleben, where they ended up in Barrack 10 with Joseph Powell.

The Jockeys, meanwhile, were professional horsemen who were arrested while working at German courses including Hoppegarten, the "German Newmarket", which was around 20 miles east of Berlin. Harry Blades, Frank Lowe and Charles Moore were all Hoppegarten jockeys. Former champion apprentice Freddy Winter, from Feltham, was employed as a rider by the Kaiser himself. Some of the jockeys were in Barrack 1 with Steve Bloomer, and the others were in Barrack 2.

Tilly's won the match 4-0, in pouring rain on "frightfully muddy" ground. The Tilly's team captain was Thomas Wyndham Richards, a 23-year-old schoolmaster from Cardiff. Richards, known to his pals as Wyndham, was a keen and highly-rated amateur footballer who played for Cardiff St Albans and had previously played for Newtown North End. He would become an influential footballing figure at Ruhleben – arguably the most influential amateur.

Richards had travelled to Berlin in July, leaving behind his sweetheart Jessie James, who was also a teacher. He expected to be there for only a few weeks, but, following the outbreak of war, he was advised that he could not leave the country, and must remain at Tilly's. The school continued to charge fees to the stranded students, and Richards ran out of money. A request for assistance to the Cardiff Teachers' Association went unheeded. It was expected that Richards would be handed over by the school to the authorities. In the end, he was arrested along with the other British Tilly's students, and the other Brits in Berlin, on 6 November and taken to Ruhleben with Bloomer and the others.

Richards kept a diary during his stay would record the growth of football in the camp. He also recorded, in sparse prose, some of the difficulties and discomforts experienced by the prisoners. Most prominently, during the first few days, he noted the difficulty that he and the others had sleeping. "Did not sleep well," he wrote after the first night. "Bad night, very stiff," he wrote after the second. Then it was, "Slept spasmodically, only one blanket," and then, "Had poor night, very cold." The food was another conspicuous subject, with Richards noting that he bought bread rolls, ham and coffee from the canteen almost every day to supplement the meagre rations. The pouring rain and "frightful" mud were also repeatedly noted.

Richards' diary entries were necessarily brief because it was difficult to write in the dark, cramped conditions of the barracks, and too cold to write more than a few words at a time with chilled fingers. Free time between work and football was spent writing home to his mother and Jessie, and chatting to other prisoners. Richards noted meeting several sailors, who arrived on the Monday from Hamburg where they had spent months confined in "stinking hulks". "My heart bleeds for them," wrote Richards.

One of these sailors was a former professional footballer. Walter "Wattie" Campbell began his career at Moffat FC in Scotland, then won the English league championship with Everton in 1891, but suffered a career-ending knee injury in the following season and quit the game to become a marine engineer. Aged 47, he was regarded as being in poor health, whether due to his injury or his confinement in the hulks, and he would not kick a ball during this time in Ruhleben – although he would become a keen spectator and was involved in the management of the camp teams.

For the men of Ruhleben, aside from impromptu music concerts, the muddy, rag-ball football matches were a rare distraction. Steve Bloomer was extremely interested in the makeshift matches and became convinced that football could improve the prisoners' plight. "During these exhibitions, one truth made a deep impression on me," he said, "and that was that if only the game could be played on properly organised lines an interest would be created that would go a long way towards relieving the monotony of the life we were leading. Even these 'back-entry kickabouts' drew their 'gates'."

Bloomer became convinced that if something wasn't done to break the monotony and take the prisoners' minds off their hardships, then "serious trouble would ensue". "My experience of football told me that if that did not provide sufficient interest, nothing else would," he said. So Bloomer, Dutton, Wolstenholme and several others got together. "We held a confab, and came to the unanimous decision that King Football would have to do his best to keep us from moping."

"When we came to that decision, we had no idea of the big task that lay before us," said Bloomer. For starters, the men had no pitch, no goal posts, and – most crucially – no football, nor any boots, kits or other equipment. "Our guards were unsympathetic," said Bloomer, "and all our appeals met with refusal. All that we were permitted to do in the way of football was to kick a bundle of rags about in any little bit of space we could find among the barrack buildings. But we were not discouraged."

The rag-ball kickabouts continued through the first few days at Ruhleben, as the rain fell and the temperature dropped. The men trudged to and from the Tea House for their rationed slops, queued at the standpipes and latrines, and huddled around the barracks, smoking and speculating on just how long this whole ordeal was going to last. Conditions in the camp were so poor that it was assumed there must have been some kind of mistake, or it was all a "German bluff", and things would surely be rectified within a few days. Jokes were shared, and brave faces were shown, but for even the most spirited of the Ruhlebenites, it was a miserable, morale-draining experience. "Then the great day dawned," recalled Bloomer. "A German football found its way into the camp."

According to Henry Mahoney, the ball was sent by a "kindly sympathiser". Back in Britain, a laced leather football would have cost around 15 shillings. But in Ruhleben, the ball was priceless. And the effect this little brown ball had on the camp's thousands of prisoners was pronounced. "The camp went wild with delight and life assumed a brighter guise," recalled Mahoney. "That ball revived our drooping spirits as speedily and completely as the sight of gold affects a prospector, and the fun we extracted from the football would pass all comprehension."

4

The Ruhleben Cup

"The first few days of my captivity in Ruhleben Camp will always remain with me as the most remarkable experience of my life," recalled Steve Bloomer. There were now around 4,000 men crammed into the barrack compound, and all of them were miserable, cold and hungry. They shuffled around in the mud, amid a hubbub of mixed accents, as the guards yelled, *"Ruhig sein!"* "Be quiet!"

The main subjects of conversation were the inadequacies of the facilities and the incompetence of the administration. New arrivals were seen to go white with shock as they gazed around at the chaos into which they had been thrown. Other prisoners described the disorienting experience as "surreal" and "dream-like". Although it seemed obvious that the ordeal could not last much longer, the prospect of spending even a few extra days in this place felt like a distressing, suffocating, living nightmare. Something had to be done right away to improve the prisoners' lot, and that something would have to be done by the prisoners themselves.

Led by the barrack captains, the unshaven and dishevelled Ruhlebenites began to organise themselves into a community. Among the masses were individuals with a multitude of useful skills, from doctors to carpenters to tailors. Gradually, these men would use their skills to turn the hell that was Ruhleben into a habitable home for the remainder of their stay, however long that might be.

For Bloomer, the arrival of the leather football represented a great opportunity. "As a professional footballer I felt that there was some useful work in the camp which I could accomplish," he said. The barracks needed fixing, the latrines needed cleaning, the food needed improving, but also the men needed a distraction from their ordeal. "Others more capable than myself took upon themselves the duty of apportioning the work, etc.," said Bloomer, "but I devoted myself to the organisation of sport, a matter on which I knew something." The result, after a conflab with Edwin Dutton, Sam Wolstenholme and the other footballers, was the creation of the first Ruhleben Cup competition.

Sixteen teams entered the knockout tournament, each drawn from individual barracks or hometowns, or ships' crews or shared professions, and each named after a popular English First Division club. Each team had a squad of 12 or more players, meaning around 200 prisoners participated. A group of men from Manchester took the name Manchester United. The jockeys from Barrack 2 were Everton. The public school boys, led by Wyndham Richards, played as Oldham Athletic. And there were two "scratch XIs", Bradford City and Tottenham Hotspur.

The Tottenham team was captained by Bloomer and included his fellow pros Dutton and Wolstenholme, plus German league players Alf Mills and Tommy Miller. Perhaps unsurprisingly, Bloomer's Tottenham were regarded as favourites to win the competition, followed by Bradford City, and then Oldham.

For Bloomer, these were in effect the first organised

football matches he had played since leaving Derby County, and the differences could not have been more pronounced. Rather than playing in front of the packed terraces of the Baseball Ground for Derby or Ayresome Park for Middlesbrough, or at the Crystal Palace or Hampden Park for England, he was playing within the barbed-wire confines of a wretched prison camp for a makeshift team of bedraggled prisoners. There were no touchlines, no corner flags, no goal nets, nor even any goal posts. This was football in very reduced circumstances.

"Our 'ground' was the largest open space in the camp – a division between two barracks, which measured about 32 yards by 15 yards," said Bloomer. This was around a third of the size of a full football pitch. Nevertheless, the games played in this cramped space were 11-a-side. At each end of the ground, stones and coats were laid down as improvised goal posts, as they might be in a park game between kids. The prisoners had no football boots or any kit, so they played in street clothes and the shoes they had walked in with. The ground was still muddy, although the rain had eased, perhaps because the temperature was so low. This small and soggy makeshift pitch became the centre of attention for the next few days.

The entire competition was scheduled to be played over three days. Time was of the essence because the prisoners expected to be released very shortly. News had reached the camp that the US government was officially protesting the men's internment. Rumours suggested that a prisoner exchange had been agreed. The men would be leaving on the following Monday, or Wednesday at the latest. All the talk was of their release, with bets placed on the precise day they would walk out of the gates. When one prisoner bet they would spend Christmas in Ruhleben, the suggestion was met with howls of laughter. For the first time, the stable compound was filled with "jokes and chaff", as the promise of freedom created a "buoyant atmosphere". It was amid this cheer that the Ruhleben Cup competition kicked off.

The first round of matches was played on Wednesday 11 November, which was the fifth day in Ruhleben for the majority of the prisoners. Wyndham Richards hadn't slept well, and he woke up with toothache, but he captained Oldham against West Bromwich Albion and scored twice from centre-half in a 7-0 rout. Bloomer's Tottenham had a tougher game against Manchester City but won 4-2. The Everton jockeys were knocked out by Manchester United, while Bradford City, Sunderland, Sheffield Wednesday, Blackburn Rovers and Chelsea all made it through to the next round.

That evening there was a concert in the grandstand, which helped raise spirits before bedtime, and made up a little for the fact that there was no supper to be had. Then it was back to the barracks, and the now-familiar yells of "*Schlafen gehen!*" Richards reported that he had a better night. But in the morning the weather had worsened. On the march to breakfast, the men were lashed by driving sleet that was whipped along by the freezing east wind. The weather was so bad that there was no football, with the men huddling in the barracks for shelter, and stamping their feet and waving their arms to keep warm. The second round of the Ruhleben Cup would have to wait.

During the morning, the prisoners were summoned by the ringing of the roll-call bell out into the freezing cold and instructed to line up in front of their barracks. Baron von Taube, wrapped in his greatcoat and chewing on his cigar, addressed the men and ordered the *Israeliten* to step forward. There were an estimated 300 to 400 Jewish prisoners in Ruhleben, but only around 70 identified themselves – the others being understandably wary of what might transpire. Among those who stepped forward was Israel Cohen, the journalist who was arrested in Berlin at the same time as Steve Bloomer. The Baron informed the 70 men that they would be provided with kosher food supplied by a Jewish soup kitchen in Berlin. To facilitate this, they would be segregated from the other prisoners. They were made to gather their belongings, then marched four-deep under armed escort out of the camp.

As they left, Cohen later recalled, they were jeered by some of the remaining prisoners. Anti-Semitism was a simmering issue in Europe prior to the war, with negative Jewish stereotyping prevalent in Britain and Germany. But it had not been an issue during the first few days in Ruhleben, with prisoners from all walks of life mixing and bonding in shared circumstances. The segregation made it an issue. It marked the Jews as different from the other prisoners and gave the impression that they were receiving superior treatment – an impression that was entirely false. Cohen and the others were marched to the Emigrants' Station, where they were ordered to bed down on straw in the station's waiting room. Over the next few hours, around 200 more Jewish prisoners were brought to the station after the Baron threatened to punish those who did not identify themselves.

There were now more than 250 men packed into the dirty waiting room. When their kosher food arrived, it was rotten, causing a dreadful outbreak of diarrhoea, and many of the men, including Cohen, had to relieve themselves in the station's small yard, which soon became a reeking morass. The men would remain in this horrendous place for two days, after which they were marched back into the camp and placed in Barrack 6, described by Cohen as "the oldest and dirtiest stable in the compound". The Jews now became a distinct group viewed with suspicion by other prisoners. It was the first sign of inequality in Ruhleben. One of the few areas of camp life in which the inhabitants of Barrack 6 would be treated as equals was at football – although their stay at the Emigrants' Station meant they would miss the next round of the Ruhleben Cup.

In the meantime, the other prisoners continued to work on the barracks in an effort to improve their living conditions for however many days remained. Horseboxes were swept, boards were laid on muddy floors, and beds were moved to accommodate as many men as comfortably as possible, as the population of Ruhleben gradually increased. The work was organised by the barrack captains, who could be recognised by the cloth armbands they wore.

Between themselves, the captains had already undertaken other important work. They had made contact with the US embassy in Berlin, requesting assistance, medical treatment, clothing and money for those in need. They had petitioned for the release of men, mostly sailors, who were under 17 or over 55 and therefore not of fighting age. And now they began to appoint officials to undertake essential tasks such as handling mail, guarding against fire, and maintaining order – in effect raising a small civilian police force to limit the intervention of the camp guards.

Elsewhere, entrepreneurs began to offer their services

and skills in return for cash or barter. The first Ruhleben entrepreneurs were shoeblacks, who were in huge demand. During the early part of the 20th century, shoeblacks provided an indispensable service, and in civilian life operated on almost every busy street corner. It was regarded as a menial task, and few gentlemen would lower themselves to polish their own shoes. Even in a muddy prison camp, clean and shiny shoes were requisite. A cobbler and shoemaker also appeared, setting up shop in Barrack 4, and providing a vital service to those who had damaged shoes unsuitable for the wintry conditions.

Other entrepreneurs with Berlin connections arranged to have supplies delivered to the prison gate. Over the next few days, cocoa, tea and Oxo arrived and were sold for 10pf a cup. One man startled his fellow prisoners by offering cups of what his sign called "mother's milk".

Another service that appeared in the camp during its second week was a lending library, opened in Barrack 1 by chartered accountant John Platford with 83 books supplied via the US embassy. Reading was an essential pastime, although the lack of light made it difficult to do in the dark barracks. In the evenings, men would gather in the dimly-lit corridors, perched on stools or suitcases, poring over books. Requests for more books were made among the prisoners and in letters home. By the beginning of December, Platford's library would hold 370 books.

The Ruhleben Cup resumed on Friday, 13 November – another typically cold day. The second round, the quarter-finals, saw Bloomer's Tottenham overcome Manchester United in a high-scoring 8-4 win. And there were plenty of goals when Richards' Oldham beat Bradford City 5-4.

Richards scored two in what he described as a "hard game". Overall, the gathered crowd of spectators saw 33 goals in the four quarter-finals, with Sunderland and Chelsea also progressing.

Alongside Richards in the Oldham team were a pair of former Eton footballers, Richard Frampton "RF" Kindersley and AS Belmont. Both had played the public school's idiosyncratic wall game and field game – variations of football that were unique to Eton. RF Kindersley was the son of all-round sportsman RS Kindersley, an England rugby international and Oxford University boat race champion. AS Belmont, who was born in Australia, was just 18 years old. Like Richards, he was studying German at Tilly's school when the war broke out. It was noted with surprise that, while he had played rugby and the Eton games, Belmont had never played the association version of football before arriving in Ruhleben.

Also in the Oldham team was another of Ruhleben's sporting celebrities, the champion rower Tom Sullivan. New Zealand-born Sullivan had spent a lot of time in Britain and had won the English Sculling Championship. He was coaching the Berlin Rowing Club when the war broke out. The internment of New Zealander Sullivan and Australian Belmont reminded that Ruhleben's prisoners came from across the British Empire.

The cup semi-finals were played on the following day. Bloomer's Tottenham beat Chelsea 4-2, and Richards' Oldham beat Sunderland 3-1 to progress to the final. Meanwhile, back at home on that Saturday afternoon, the real Oldham Athletic beat the real Tottenham Hotspur 4-1. Despite the outbreak of war, the Football League season continued as usual and would be played to a conclusion.

There was much opposition to football, vocalised by Sherlock Holmes author Arthur Conan Doyle, who said, "There was a time for games... There was a time for everything, but there is only time for one thing now, and that thing is war." It was argued that football was preventing fit men from signing up for the armed forces. "If a footballer has strength of limb, let them serve and march in the field of battle," said Conan Doyle. But footballers were under contract with their clubs and were prevented from signing up, while fit and able supporters were signing up at football matches, which acted as useful recruiting events. So the suggestion that football was damaging the war effort was not necessarily true.

In Ruhleben, after the semi-finals, the prisoners enjoyed a "ripping" concert in Barrack 10, with musicians and music hall performers entertaining a cheering crowd, despite repeated warnings from the guards to *"Ruhig sein!"* Music, reading, chess, card games and of course football brought enjoyment to this desolate place. Although there had been no further movement concerning their release, and at least some of them must have begun to fear the worst, the men remained relatively upbeat. There existed a kind of "exaggerated cheerfulness" that masked the unhappiness and depression. It was encapsulated in a call-and-response cheer that became the Ruhleben prisoners' stock greeting: *"Are we downhearted? No!"*

The first Ruhleben Cup final, between Tottenham Hotspur and Oldham Athletic, was played on Monday, 16 November 1914. It was a wet and miserable day – the tenth day of captivity for most in Ruhleben. There was much excitement ahead of the game, and almost 2,000 prisoners gathered to watch around the cramped, muddy pitch. A hand-drawn poster, written in pencil, advertised the 1.45pm kick-off, listed the Oldham and Tottenham line-ups, and advised spectators, "Please (in your own interest) keep fairly quiet." This was a reminder that the match was being played under the strict gaze of the camp guards and officers.

Sam Wolstenholme refereed the final, and the game provided plenty of entertainment for those around the touchlines. Bloomer controlled things from the back for the Tottenham "Scratch XI", with Dutton at outside-left, and Mills in goal. "The Tottenham forwards kept well up on the Oldham backs, who had little chance of clearing the ball," it was reported.

Richards captained the Oldham public school boys, alongside Kindersley and Belmont, with fellow Tilly's student DH Lee in goal. "All played badly," noted Richards, who griped that his opponents included "six professionals". That may have been a slight exaggeration, but Bloomer's team was perhaps unfairly loaded with talent. The result was an "easy win", 9-2 to Tottenham.

Bloomer was impressed with his winning teammates, who were each presented with a box of cigarettes. "Although under those conditions it was impossible to form a correct judgment of individual play, I know that I had some promising players in my team," he recalled. "I liked the way they shaped. It was apparent that some of them had a pretty thorough knowledge of the game. Of course, as the skipper of the winning side, I came in for more than my fair share, of the congratulations."

He recalled being congratulated by Edwin Dutton, who told him, "You did well, Steve."

"Yes," Bloomer admitted. "But it makes me feel a bit ambitious. That 'back entry' business is very unsatisfactory. Now, if we only had a decent ground."

"Aye," said Dutton, as his eyes followed Bloomer's over the stable compound and through the fence towards the large open field inside the racetrack. "Then we should see some games."

But the idea of playing football on an actual field was much further away than it appeared. "Far from that hope being realised," Bloomer recalled, "our efforts to establish the game on any footing at all were dashed to the ground."

Bloomer and Dutton got a closer view of the overgrown playing field later that week when the prisoners were ordered to march around the racetrack for 90 minutes. It was the first march of a new exercise regime. The prisoners marched slowly four or five times around the mile-long track almost every day. The track was at least well-drained, and it was less of a muddy trudge than in the stable compound. To the north, clouds of smoke belched out of the chimneys at the Spandau munitions works. To the south, a seemingly endless convoy of troop trains rattled along the railway embankment.

The prisoners' main discomfort remained the cold. It was something the camp administration could not ignore, and later that week a makeshift heating system was installed in the barracks. A coal-powered boiler pumped steam through a network of pipes, but it could only be run for a few hours a day to conserve fuel. Often the coal would run out, and the prisoners would have to wait several days without heating for a new delivery. So it was an improvement, but not a solution, and the prisoners remained damp and cold as the outside temperature dropped and snow began to fall. The snow was a particular problem for those in the lofts as it drifted in through the gaps in the stable eaves. On some nights, prisoners stuck in the lofts would wake to find themselves covered with a layer of snow.

Another discomfort was the latrines, known to all and sundry as the "bogs". A trip to the bogs was an unpleasant ordeal, more so in snow or darkness. In the dark, the men had to find their way using their sense of smell. The putrid stench hung like a cloud over the compound. The filthy, overused toilets were described as "a danger not only to the camp but to Berlin". Something needed to be done, so the barrack captains raised a fund intended to pay for the cleaning of the latrines. Essentially, those who had money would pay those who did not to clean the bogs.

And then there was the wretched food. The rations in Ruhleben were catered by a contractor named Griese, who was expected to provide breakfast, dinner or tea, and supper on a budget of 66pf (approximately 30p) per prisoner per day. The fare that was served was accordingly meagre, typically consisting of watery soup or "skilly", weak coffee apparently made from acorns, and occasional pieces of blood sausage and black "war bread". It was reported that Griese was redirecting cuts of beef or mutton intended for the prisoners and reselling them outside of the camp to make a profit. Those who were able to afford to could supplement their diet with items bought from the canteen, but the majority of the prisoners, including almost all of the seamen, had little or no money and were forced to exist on the paltry rations. They were in danger of starving.

The rations were not only insufficient; they were often inedible. Things came to a head one afternoon in what was, for most prisoners, the third week of captivity. "It was a particularly cold day," noted Bloomer, "and on drawing our tea rations, we found that the skilly was not in a fit state for human consumption. Besides the ordinary ingredients, there appeared to be small insects floating about in it." For many of the Ruhlebenites, having tolerated the freezing, filthy, badly-organised conditions for almost three weeks, this was the final straw. They began to revolt. "The complaints were loud and continuous," said Bloomer. One group of prisoners, on their way back from the tea-room, took the unprecedented step of entering the officers' quarters and confronting Baron von Taube.

"Well? What is it?" the Baron demanded.

"This skilly, sir, is verminous," replied one of the prisoners, placing his bowl under the Baron's nose. "Look. You can see the things kicking about."

The Baron gazed at the crawling slop for what seemed like an age, before reluctantly agreeing. "It is bad," he said. "Go back to the barracks, and I will see that something else is prepared for you."

Believing the matter to be resolved, the prisoners returned to their barracks and spread the word among the other prisoners, who gladly poured away their rotten skilly and hungrily awaited something better. But, after an hour, nothing better arrived. "A lot of the men became restive," said Bloomer. "Always hungry, an extra hour between meals added pain to the ordinary discomfort of hunger."

More time passed, and, in Bloomer's words, "restiveness developed into rowdiness". "Anger was written on every face," he said. The prisoners began to gather around the camp in groups, cursing and yelling threats at the guards and officers. Violence simmered, and it seemed that the prisoners were on the verge of attempting to overthrow their captors. Then, suddenly, the fire bell was sounded, the camp gates opened and a platoon of armed soldiers from the neighbouring Spandau garrison hurried inside.

The trained and drilled soldiers – over 50 in number, with more waiting at the gates – were a completely different proposition from the often ineffectual camp guards. Brandishing their rifles and bayonets, the soldiers quickly forced the prisoners back into the barracks, using the butts of their rifles for encouragement where necessary. The swift quashing of the revolt provided a valuable reminder of exactly who was in charge at Ruhleben. The prisoners were confined to their barracks – angry and hungry – for the rest of the night.

The incident became known as the "skilly riot" and, according to Bloomer, it "marked the breaking point of our endurance". Herr Griese would eventually lose the catering contract and rations would gradually improve. But the episode infuriated the Baron and caused him to take a harder line with the prisoners. And it confirmed to the prisoners that the Baron and his men could not be trusted or relied upon, whether due to incompetence or malice, to protect their welfare. Unless something was done, men would die. Or, rather, more men would die.

The first death in the camp occurred on 21 or 22 November, and it could be directly attributed to the terrible conditions. Robert Bowditch was a donkeyman who worked in the engine room of the merchant ship SS *Sappho*, which had been impounded in Hamburg at the outbreak of the war. He died of pneumonia aged 57, after just two weeks in the freezing, filthy hell that was Ruhleben.

Meanwhile, the men continued to play football on their makeshift pitch in between the barracks. On 25 November, Wyndham Richards captained his team and scored in a 4-2 win against unrecorded opposition. It was the last game of football anyone would play in Ruhleben for a long while. After the game, the prisoners were lined up in front of the barracks to be addressed by von Taube. Bloomer was standing beside Dutton as the cigar-chewing Baron approached.

"I don't fancy the look of that man," Bloomer told his chum. "I'll bet he turns out to be a bad 'un."

"I could forgive him a lot if he would only smile," replied Dutton. "I've not seen his face crack since we've been in the camp. When it does, he'll never get it right again."

The men were silenced, and the Baron began to speak in his clipped accent. Those prisoners who did not speak German had to wait a few seconds for a muttered translation from their barrack captain. But the tone was clear – the Baron was furious. The translation didn't quite make sense. A considerable number of windows had been broken, he said – although none of the prisoners were aware of a single breakage. Football was the cause, he insisted, and he would not have any more damage done. "*Diese fussballspiele müssen aufhören!*" he yelled. "These football games must stop!"

And with that, almost as soon as it had started, football was banned. The men – including 200 keen players and more than 2,000 ardent spectators – were devastated. Mumbles of dissent could be heard around the courtyard, but there were no angry outbursts from the men, who, Bloomer recalled, were "fearful of the consequences".

Their precious ball was confiscated and carried away

under the arm of one of the guards. It was easy to imagine it being cruelly punctured with a bayonet. There would be no rag-ball, either, and no football at all.

"This was indeed a blow, and the real grief which it created was reflected on every face," said Bloomer. "My own disappointment can be better imagined than described. Life was just becoming bearable, and to have the cause of this new joy suddenly snatched away was, to say the least, very annoying."

Were the men being punished for the skilly riot? Or was this just an act of cruelty on behalf of their captors? "In discussing the ban we came to the conclusion that the stoppage of these harmless games was but part of their policy to break our spirits," said Bloomer. "But they had set themselves a hard task. We were not so easily beaten as all that."

5

A Long Winter

Fred Pentland arrived in Ruhleben on 30 November, and barely had time to drop his bags before he was taken to Barrack 1 to see his old pal Steve Bloomer. "He was at the time giving the same earnestness to a game of Ludo with a crowd of racing men as the old warrior would have done to an international match with Scotland," Pentland later recalled. The two men had last played together four years earlier, and their careers had taken similarly unusual paths, with their pioneering coaching careers rudely cut short in Germany. The reunion must have rekindled in both men memories of happier times – of games, grounds and goals, of skilful teammates, difficult opponents and excited fans. But, if Pentland was hoping to play football with his friend once again, Bloomer had bad news for him.

Pentland and Bloomer were at Middlesbrough together between 1908 and 1910, during Bloomer's period away from Derby County. Pentland was almost a decade younger than Bloomer, and he greatly admired his veteran teammate. He was eager to learn everything he could from him – just as Bloomer had learned from Johnny Goodall. "I found everything he said was right," wrote Pentland. "He has always been, in my view, the greatest inside-forward the game has ever known or is ever likely to know. He knows the playing of football from A to Z. In fact, one could truthfully say he knows absolutely everything there is to know about football."

Throughout his playing career, Pentland retained a smart, clean-cut appearance, with a whiskerless face and neatly side-parted hair. Behind the sharp look, he was a shrewd and single-minded character. Born in Wolverhampton in 1883, Pentland began his career with Small Heath (later renamed Birmingham City) Reserves, then played a few games for Blackpool, before making his name in the First Division during three seasons at Blackburn Rovers. A nippy winger who could also play through the centre, he was described as "a very smart and alert forward [who] possesses an abundance of speed".

After Blackburn, Pentland played for a season each at Brentford and Queens Park Rangers in what was becoming an itinerant career. But it was at Middlesbrough alongside Bloomer that he really found his feet and established himself as an England international.

Boro were known to be the richest club in the country, although they were struggling in the First Division. This was despite the presence up front, alongside Bloomer and Pentland, of Alf Common – the first £1,000 footballer following his record-breaking transfer from Sunderland. It was Bloomer, reaching the age of 36 during the 1909-10 season, who kept the club out of the relegation zone with a double-figure goal tally. But Pentland, creating opportunities for his teammates with penetrating runs and dangerous crosses, impressed enough during this period to get the call for England. "You have got the biggest honour in the world," Bloomer – no longer an international – told him. "I only wish I was playing with you."

Like Bloomer, Pentland could be a difficult character. He had previously fallen out with the board at Blackburn Rovers, with one director stating, after the transfer to Brentford, that he "would not pay him in washers". The supporters loved him, though. According to the *Lancashire Evening Post*, he was "immensely popular with the Blackburn people" and had a "remarkable send-off" at the railway station when he left Rovers, with the Palace Theatre Band leading the gathered crowd in renditions of *For He's A Jolly Good Fellow* and *Auld Lang Syne*. But he soon fell out with the Middlesbrough board. He lost his place in the Boro team following a suspension, reportedly for "neglecting his training" – echoing a similar dispute Bloomer had with Derby County. Newspapers suggested this was "not likely to improve his popularity" with the directors. He was transferred, in the summer of 1912, to Halifax Town.

Halifax were in the Midland League, which represented a substantial demotion for Pentland, who was still only 29 years old and not yet ready to step out of the football spotlight. He was offered the role of player-manager, which must have appealed. But financial problems at Halifax meant he was soon transferred to Stoke, in the Southern League, for a "substantial amount". Whether he fell out with anyone at Stoke isn't recorded, but he did suffer a knee injury, which restricted his appearances, and he was back at Halifax within a few months, again as player-manager.

Pentland showed an interest in coaching through the latter stages of his career. He coached young players while at Middlesbrough, and described those times as "some of my happiest days". It was Middlesbrough chairman Philip

Bach who first suggested Pentland might enjoy the opportunity of coaching abroad. And it was a meeting with pioneering former German international Walther Bensemann that sent Pentland to Germany in May 1914.

Bensemann was a co-founder of the German football association, the Deutscher Fussball-Bund (DFB). He was also involved in the formation of two clubs – Karlsruher FV and Frankfurter Kickers (which later became Eintracht Frankfurt) – and would go on to set up the influential German football magazine *Kicker*. By 1914, Bensemann was living in England, working as a teacher of modern languages at Birkenhead School on Merseyside. He maintained close links with the DFB and was tasked with enlisting a high-profile British footballer to coach German players ahead of the 1916 Olympic Games.

Bensemann interviewed Pentland at the Adelphi Hotel in Liverpool. The 32-year-old Pentland was coming to the end of his playing career and, as a famous England international with a flair for coaching, he seemed the perfect candidate. When Bensemann offered him the job, Pentland was eager to accept. It seemed a great opportunity – one that he probably shared with Bloomer, and perhaps with several other of his contemporaries who found themselves in Germany in 1914.

Pentland was sent to southwest Germany, and ended up in Karlsruhe, on the Rhine. France was just across the river, but Pentland remained stuck in Germany after the declaration of war. Like Bloomer and the other British men, Pentland was arrested on the morning of 6 November. "A detective awakened me from sleep with the order to dress at once," he recalled in his written account. "He was a decent chap. He waited while I breakfasted and got ready.

Together we went to the local police office."

Unlike Bloomer and the others, Pentland was not taken immediately to Ruhleben. "Someone mentioned prison," he wrote, "but no one thought it was serious. However, our doubts were soon removed." Pentland and his fellow captives were taken to Karlsruhe Prison, where they were advised by the warden in no uncertain terms that they were prisoners and would be treated as such. The prison guards, Pentland wrote, "had faces of iron and spoke like lions".

Pentland was one of ten Brits held in Karlsruhe. He described the others as a man of leisure and his chauffeur, a factory manager, a student, a foreign correspondent, a language teacher, a baker, a businessman and a tea dealer. "A pretty comprehensive crowd, eh?" he wrote. The prisoners had their bags taken from them and were ordered to turn out their pockets, before being marched individually to small, lonely cells.

Within five minutes of being locked inside, Pentland said, the monotonous, solitary experience became "intolerable". "Fancy a footballer and a man used to an open-air life, with his ears and eyes tuned to the enthusiasm of the spectators, attempting to amuse himself by walking up and down in a cage after the fashion of a captive animal," he wrote. "I began to do something else than bless the day that brought me to Germany."

After three nights in Karlsruhe Prison, existing on war bread and water, Pentland and the others were taken from their cells, provided with their belongings, and marched to the railway station, "much to the interest of onlookers". There they met with another party of almost 100 prisoners from Baden-Baden and boarded a train, which they were told would take them to Ruhleben. But this would not be the case.

Due to the overcrowding at Ruhleben, it was decided to delay the arrival of new prisoners until additional accommodation was arranged. Instead, the train took them to Berlin's Beusselstrasse station, around four miles east of Ruhleben, from where they were marched across the Beusselstrasse Bridge over the Spree to the Charlottenburg-Wilmersdorf district and the imposing red-brick Plötzensee Prison. It was two o'clock in the morning by the time they arrived, and the tired men were searched, separated, and placed into filthy cells that Pentland said were "for all the world like animal cages".

Pentland spent three weeks in Plötzensee, sleeping on vermin-infested beds and eating meagre rations. Permission was given to buy extra food, but not everyone had money with them. The man of leisure, "who was supposed to be a millionaire", had neglected to bring his wallet, and was reduced to asking Pentland if he could spare some bread. Pentland spent his time reading "terrible" reports of the war in newspapers and learning German from his fellow prisoners. The men heard conflicting rumours about conditions at Ruhleben but Plötzensee was so bleak that there was great excitement when they were finally transferred to the camp.

Pentland was billeted in Barrack 10 at Ruhleben, with Wyndham Richards and Joseph Powell, along with other men from Plötzensee. Workers from Berlin were busy in the compound constructing two new barracks, numbers 12 and 13, but they were not yet ready. Pentland was allocated a berth, and given a towel, a bowl and empty sacks, which he filled with straw to make bedding and pillows, before sampling the camp coffee and skilly. He quickly realised that the accommodation and canteen arrangements were "ridiculously inadequate". But the biggest disappointment came when he heard about the football ban. The only "mild form of exercise" permitted was the regular trudge around the racecourse.

On one occasion, the marching prisoners startled a hare, which darted across the track in front of them. "The sporting spirit was too strong in us," wrote Pentland. "We broke away from the march and gave chase. The hare was captured, but it was put over the rails of the racecourse and given its freedom." The prisoners could only dream of being so lucky.

During another march, someone began to play a harmonica, and the prisoners sang *Onward, Christian Soldiers*. After that, a series of bespoke marching songs were composed and sung, featuring topical verses and gallows humour that chronicled and lampooned the men's shared experiences. The most popular of these songs was the *Ruhleben Alphabet*, an A to Z catalogue of camp life that began, "*A is for all of us locked up in here, B for the bastards who won't give us beer...*" then went on to, "*F for the football they won't let us play.*" The song's chorus was recorded in his writings by Joseph Powell:

"Merry, oh merry, oh merry are we,
And Ruhleben Camp is the one place for me.
There's soup and there's skilly, and coffee and bread,
And a nice German coffin as soon as you're dead."

In the absence of football, the men sought an alternative pastime in the form of a "new sort of game", which Steve Bloomer described as "a cross between baseball and the rounders that are played usually at Sunday school picnics". "For this game, we used a chair leg and a tennis ball," said Bloomer, "and although the game fell far short of football or cricket, we managed to keep ourselves interested, which, of course, was the main thing."

Bloomer was an excellent baseball player and had won the British baseball championship three times during the 1890s with the Derby County Baseball Club. Baseball was introduced to Britain in 1890 by Francis Ley, the Derby industrialist and the owner of the iron foundry where Bloomer worked with his father. Ley built a baseball stadium, Ley's Baseball Ground, and formed the National Baseball League of Great Britain and Ireland. His Derby team, with Bloomer at second base, won the championship in 1895, 1897 and 1899.

In 1895, Derby County Football Club moved to the Baseball Ground, meaning Bloomer played both football and baseball there. But baseball never quite took off in Britain, and the Derby baseball team folded after the 1899 championship. (The football team would remain at the Baseball Ground until 1997.) Bloomer kept his hand in and was still playing baseball a decade later at Middlesbrough. "As a baseball player, he is among the best on this side of the Atlantic," noted *Pearson's Weekly*, "and he has frequently expressed his astonishment at the comparative unpopularity of the game here."

Bloomer found a fellow baseball fan in Ruhleben in the shape of a Canadian named Dr Brawnbach. One morning, Brawnbach approached him and asked, "Say, Steve, you play 'ball?" – meaning baseball.

"A bit," Bloomer replied.

Brawnbach was "a lovely pitcher and very proud of the

fact". But, at their first face-off, Bloomer smashed Brawnbach's pitch over the fence and out of the camp.

"Say, Steve," remarked Brawnbach. "You know a lot more about this game than you pretend. I've never been knocked out of a ground before."

Bloomer laughed and said, "I wish I had a pound for every match I played in at Derby."

Gradually, the baseball-rounders-softball hybrid became more popular, and the prisoners raised five teams. "It was equally popular with young and old, and the compound was crowded to overflowing each time a match was in progress," recalled Israel Cohen. "The cheers that went up as a rounder was hit were often quite deafening and quite upset the guards, who on more than one occasion threatened to put a stop to the game if the onlookers and players persisted in what they called our 'stupid habit of yelling' whenever a small ball was hit in the air."

Fred Pentland appreciated baseball – in the absence of football, at least. He recalled an incident during one game when the ball smashed a window in front of a guard. Given Baron von Taube's reaction to alleged window breakages caused by football, the prisoners must have feared similar repercussions. However, the Baron never got to hear about it. "Fortunately, the guard was a decent fellow," said Pentland, "and beyond making us pay for the damage, he said nothing."

Wyndham Richards also played baseball, and noted it in his diary. Richards also described playing "bumberino", a boisterous playground game (also known as "high cockalorum" or "Johnny on the pony") played without a ball in which one team must maintain a rugby-type scrum while their opponents attempt to leap-frog onto their backs.

Richards also noted in his diary at the end of November that he obtained a two-week-old copy of the *London Standard*, probably smuggled into the camp by one of Pentland's new arrivals.

English newspapers were banned, and anyone found in possession could be punished with 72 hours in solitary. As a result, real news about the war was scarce. But here, beneath a list of men killed in action, Richards and the others could read about: the doubling of income tax to fund the war effort; the dilemma posed by German mining of the North Sea; the court-martial of a 21-year-old German in London found guilty of possessing an illegal wireless set; and an official notice stating "Your King & Country need another 100,000 men". In the sporting news column, the *Standard* reported that the Scottish Football Association had called a meeting between all four British associations "to consider the playing of football during the continuance of the war".

Fred Pentland was not the only professional footballer who arrived in Ruhleben at the end of November. Another high-profile new arrival, billeted in Barrack 10 with Pentland, Richards and Powell, was John "Jack" Cameron, the former Scotland international and player-manager of Tottenham Hotspur. Cameron had been coaching Dresdner SC in Dresden. He was arrested after asking for directions on the evening of the declaration of war and was locked in a prison cell before being transferred to Ruhleben.

Born in Ayr in 1872, Cameron was 42 when he arrived at the camp. He began his career as a teenager at Ayr Parkhouse before making his name as a centre-forward at then-amateur Queen's Park FC, where he won his only international cap. He was described as "an exquisite exponent of the dribbling code [with] a deadly shot".

"He is just the right build for a forward: square-framed, lean and muscular, carrying not an ounce of superfluous weight." wrote a reporter for the *Lancashire Evening Post*. "Quick to settle on the ball, he can drive along with it at a merry gait, and, using either foot with equal facility, whether for dribbling, dodging or shooting, he is a decidedly dangerous man to have against you."

In 1896, Cameron moved to Merseyside "owing to business" and joined Everton as an amateur. "His doing so caused friction with the other players," noted the *Sporting Life* newspaper, "and the result was, though much against his will, he became a bona fide pro." As a professional, he became involved in attempts to unionise footballers.

He was the first secretary of the National Union of Association Players, and he campaigned to abolish the maximum wage. This was unsuccessful, and in 1898 he quit Everton and the Football League to join Tottenham in the Southern League, where there was no cap on earnings.

In the following year, he became player-manager at Spurs and began to instil a distinctive passing style which had been pioneered by Queen's Park in Scotland but remained relatively foreign to teams in England.

Under his leadership, Spurs won the Southern League in 1900 then won the FA Cup in 1901, with Cameron scoring in the victorious final replay against Sheffield United. He retired from playing in 1905, but remained in charge of Spurs for another couple of years as secretary-manager, meaning he had control of the entire operation, including transfers. He proved to be an effective administrator, but he resigned in 1907, "owing to the various differences with the directorate".

Like Bloomer and Pentland, Cameron had strong views about the game, and little appetite to change them. After leaving Spurs, he qualified as a referee and wrote a pioneering coaching manual, *Association Football and How to Play it*, published in 1908, before moving to Germany. He lived in Dresden with his young wife, who was understandably dismayed by his arrest and incarceration.

Another new arrival was Jack Brearley, a Liverpudlian who played under Jack Cameron at Tottenham and, before that, played alongside Cameron and Sam Wolstenholme at Everton. With the addition of Brearley, alongside Cameron, Wolstenholme and Wattie Campbell, there were now four former Evertonians in Ruhleben.

Brearley, described as a "contemplative" inside-forward, also played for a couple of seasons at Crystal Palace, before moving to Millwall Athletic as player-manager, Brearley was an England reserve but never got the chance to play for his country – although he would become an international of sorts at Ruhleben. Like Bloomer, Brearley was coaching in Berlin, at Viktoria 89, when the war broke out. He was in hospital recovering from illness, when, on 19 November 1914, he was arrested. When he got to Ruhleben, Brearley was 39 years old.

Percy Hartley was another pro footballer known to Bloomer and the others. An "auburn-haired" left-half, Hartley, from Bolton, signed for Preston North End in 1906, with both Manchester United and Blackburn Rovers said to be keen on his signature. "Of splendid physique, he is a clever tackler, capable feeder, and a better shot than many forwards," said the *Manchester Courier*. After a couple of years, he moved to Huddersfield Town, and then to Exeter

City, but knee trouble stunted his career. A coaching opportunity took him to Belgium, with CS Verviers, where, while still only 29 years of age, he was caught up in the maelstrom of war and sent to Ruhleben.

The arrivals of Fred Pentland, Jack Cameron, Jack Brearley and Percy Hartley to join Steve Bloomer, Edwin Dutton, Sam Wolstenholme and Wattie Campbell meant there were now eight professional footballers in Ruhleben, alongside numerous amateurs such as Wyndham Richards, Alf Mills and Tommy Miller, although – for now – there was no football.

Music provided an alternative distraction, and on 5 December an "extraordinary" concert was given to a large audience in the alleyway next to Barrack 6 by half a dozen string instrument players, including the famous cellist Carl Fuchs, a professor at the Royal Manchester College of Music. The players, in old sweaters and muddy clogs, were a bedraggled lot who looked like "ragged street performers", but they made a beautiful sound that brought tears to many eyes. Baron von Taube was in the audience, and he was moved enough to give permission for further concerts to be held in the restaurant hall under one of the grandstands. Such was the appetite for more music, the hall was quickly prepared, and a concert featuring the string sextet and a choir was held there on the following evening. This time Count Schwerin attended and, afterwards, he gave a speech of thanks in which he said "he loved music more than he hated his enemies".

If the prisoners went to bed that night with raised spirits, they were brought back down on the following morning by the worsening winter weather. Rain had poured all night, turning the already-muddy camp into a soggy swamp. Wyndham Richards wrote that it was "frightful underfoot" and that he waded through three or four inches of mud to get his morning coffee. Some prisoners, including Fred Pentland, decided to give the coffee a miss. "It became so bad that we preferred to go without our rations than wallow through the mud for them," he said.

It rained almost every day during December, and temperatures often fell below freezing. "In consequence, the health of the prisoners became affected, and colds were prevalent," said Pentland. Wyndham Richards was one of those who fell ill. One night, he fainted in the barrack corridor, banged his head, and ended up with two black eyes and broken teeth. Games of baseball or bumberino became less appealing, and even impossible, in the wretched conditions. Large ponds appeared all over the camp. "In the absence of anything better to do, our men made toy boats, rigged them up with sails, and floated them about the pools," said Pentland.

Indoor pursuits such as chess tournaments thrived. Many prisoners spent much of the day in bed, as it was the only place they could find warmth. Concerts continued, lectures were delivered, and a debating society was formed. One early debate pondered the question: "Is life worth living?" Pentland attended, and commented, "The result, in the circumstances, was obvious." Another debate – of particular interest to Pentland and the others – asked, "Is professionalism beneficial to sport?" Such diversions were welcomed, but they couldn't disguise the worsening reality of the situation in Ruhleben.

"Life in the first winter was brightened by high spirits, patriotism and deceptive hopes, but it was a hard life, and concerts and lectures could not hide its crude and graceless character," wrote prisoner J Davidson Ketchum in his book *Ruhleben: A Prison Camp Society*. "The prisoners' world was made up of barbed wire and sentries, stables and kitchens, rain and mud, food, sleep and excretion. Existence was on a primitive level, and clothes, conduct and speech were rough and uncompromising. Garments were as warm and durable as possible; these were the only standards, and no one tried any longer to dress fashionably or eccentrically. Wooden-soled clogs, procured from the canteen, were universally worn, and the prisoners' movements were heavy, flat-footed, and marked by incessant clumping and scraping. Heads were wrapped in knitted helmets, and full beards added a further pioneer touch."

As Christmas approached, life got particularly difficult for those prisoners with family still in Germany. Many British women and their children did not yet have permission to leave, and others had decided to stay to await their husbands' release or the end of the war. Some of the women who lived in Berlin or the surrounding area came to Ruhleben to attempt to deliver parcels or just to exchange waves with their loved ones through the fences. But parcel delivery was banned, and the vantage points that allowed husbands to see out and wives to see in were soon blocked out with wooden beams.

On 17 December, 86 black prisoners arrived from Hamburg. Mostly sailors from West Africa and the West Indies, they were placed in the newly-built Barrack 13. Like the Jewish prisoners, they had been segregated. There was undoubtedly some casual racism. Wyndham Richards referred to the men using the N-word in his diary, although he did not necessarily intend offence. But there were also signs of integration. Fred Pentland wrote that he enjoyed a "gala day" organised by the black prisoners, surely intended to build rapport. Pentland was subsequently asked to give a lecture on football to the new arrivals, most of whom were entirely unfamiliar with the association game.

"I was asked if a player might charge with his feet!" recalled Pentland. "Others wanted to know what happened when the ball burst and another inquired what would become of him if he took the game up as a professional and had his leg broken. When I told him that he would be entitled to £1 a week as compensation he was quite appeased. I made up my mind that if we played football again that I would organise a team of coloured men, a proposal which my audience hailed with delight."

The prospect of playing football again seemed remote, but the men could at least look forward to Christmas. They hung sprigs of evergreen in the barracks and began to sing Christmas carols. Snow fell on Christmas Eve, and the camp was covered in a pristine white layer. Snowball fights were organised and a "raid on the Tea House" resulted in some broken windows. The guards were in a lenient mood and, as with the baseball breakage, issued no punishment. That night was quiet except for carol singing in some of the lofts and the occasional disturbance caused by drinkers of smuggled liquor.

On Christmas morning, the men woke to find that rain had turned the ground into a "quagmire" of mud and slush. There were a few Christmas treats. Each prisoner received a Christmas card from the barrack captains and a sugared bun with their morning coffee. But rumours of a sumptuous Christmas lunch were exaggerated. "We got some potatoes and gravy, a slice of pork and a gherkin," said Pentland.

After lunch, the men were presented with a cigar, a small packet of toffee and a bottle of beer. They used the latter to toast each other's health.

In the evening, a performance of Handel's *Messiah* was given in the restaurant hall by an ensemble including a 25-piece orchestra and a 100-man choir. According to Pentland, it was "a great success". Afterwards, Count Schwerin made an emotional speech, in a trembling voice and with tears running down his cheeks, in which he thanked the men for the music and their good behaviour and said was touched by the way they were bearing the sadness of being far away from home "without a Christmas tree". He hoped, he said, that by next Christmas they would all be home again. The prisoners applauded and gave the commandant three cheers.

Later, a crowd gathered as a Scotsman in a kilt with an empty beer bottle as a sporran marched around the barracks playing bagpipes. German guards were ordered to seize the piper and take his "infernal machine" from him. But when the guards grabbed the bagpipes they emitted a loud shriek, and as they carried the pipes away – much to the amusement of the gathered prisoners – they continued to produce their peculiar skirl. As Wattie Campbell observed, "They seem to be as much afraid of the pipes as they are of the lad in the kilt."

Then Pentland, Cameron, Richards and Powell retreated to Barrack 10 for a Christmas feast. They had procured tinned sardines, ox tongue, sausages, figs, dates, oranges, biscuits and nuts. They raised two toasts – to the King and to those at home. "We followed with songs, stories and *Auld Lang Syne*," said Pentland, "and altogether, while the most peculiar Christmas of our lives, it was a happy affair."

Pentland and several of the other pros sent Christmas greetings to their supporters back in England via a postcard sent to the *Football Evening News*. "It is far from being the Hotel Cecil here," said the card. (The Hotel Cecil was a grand establishment on the Strand in London.) "But we are making the best of it and are also far from downhearted. The only game we are allowed to play is rounders, and we are cock of the walk... 'Tis the simple life here: up at 6.30, bed at 8.30. We are allowed to receive letters (no war news)... We are not allowed to receive papers, so you would be giving great pleasure to many if you would get one of your henchmen to type the positions of the League clubs, including Scottish." The card was signed by Pentland, Bloomer, Cameron, Brearley and Wolstenholme.

There was no football played in Ruhleben on Christmas Day, but there were several kickabouts 500 miles away along the Western Front. The 1914 "Christmas Truce" saw around 100,000 troops pause hostilities to exchange gifts, sing carols and play football. A letter written by Staff Sergeant Clement Barker of the 1st Battalion Grenadier Guards explained how the truce and the kickabouts started. "A German looked over the trench – no shots," he wrote. "Our men did the same, and then a few of our men went out and brought the dead in and buried them. The next thing, a football [was] kicked out of our trenches and Germans and English played football."

By the end of 1914, the British forces had suffered around 90,000 casualties. The Germans had more than 140,000 casualties, the Russians more than 300,000, and the French more than 400,000. Staff Sergeant Barker would survive the war, but millions of others would not.

6

The Field

The arrival of 1915 was greeted with muted celebrations in Ruhleben. On New Year's Eve, a warning notice was posted in the camp: "Anyone found making a demonstration outside the barracks at midnight will be fired upon by the sentries." Nevertheless, outside at midnight, Wyndham Richards and around 60 other men began to exchange handshakes and sing *Auld Lang Syne.* A guard arrived with a loaded rifle and yelled, *"Los, los."* "Off you go, off you go." More armed guards approached, so the men said goodnight and swiftly dispersed. Not all went quietly. One prisoner, a camp fireman, was badly beaten by the guards, and it was reported he would probably lose an eye.

Despite the relentlessly brutal winter conditions, Richards described a "great wave of optimism" that swept through the camp. "Cannot explain it," he wrote. The wave might have been driven by rumours of impending release. 450 men would be released on Wednesday, and 800 in the following week, predicted Richards. The camp would be closed by the end of the month.

Expectations of release created a craze for souvenirs. Prisoners hurried around the camp with autograph books, collecting the signatures of their fellow detainees – including the famous footballers. Henry Mahoney, the footballing engraver, carved the word "Ruhleben" onto pipes and spoons and made £150 from the venture.

Several rumours focused on the monthly train to the Netherlands, which was due to leave Berlin on 6 January, and would surely be used to disperse the released prisoners. The train did leave on that date, carrying many British women and children out of Germany. But the men of Ruhleben could only watch and wave from their fenced compound as it passed them by on its way to freedom. The departure of the train, one prisoner said, exploded all rumours of release. In reality, the population of Ruhleben was growing – to 4,500 in early 1915. Richards, feverish and shivering from cold and toothache, lost his optimism. "Hating Germany more each day," he wrote.

Football was becoming a fading memory. In mid-January, Richards found the FA Cup first-round results in a smuggled-in copy of *The Times* and posted them at the Tea House, creating great interest. Steve Bloomer and Fred Pentland's former club Middlesbrough had beaten Goole Town 9-3. Bloomer's beloved Derby County had lost 2-1 to Leeds City. Jack Cameron's Tottenham beat Sunderland 2-1. Everton, the former club of Cameron, Sam Wolstenholme, Jack Brearley and Wattie Campbell, beat Barnsley 3-0. And Sheffield United – who would go on to win the cup – beat Blackpool 2-1. The realisation that football was continuing at home was both comforting and frustrating. These scorelines torn from a newspaper provided a glimpse of normality and a reminder for the Ruhlebenites of what they were missing.

It was Bloomer's 41st birthday on 20 January. He was invited by Pentland into the loft at Barrack 10 for tea and a smoke. A week later, there was another birthday celebration in Ruhleben, this time for the Kaiser. A German flag was raised in the compound, and the Pro-German prisoners – the "PGs" – cheered. That night, someone cut the flag's rope, bringing the black, white and red striped *Nationalflagge* of the German Empire down onto the muddy ground. The prisoners were confined to their barracks all day as punishment. The guilty party was never caught.

Bloomer and the others continued to play chair-leg baseball, but Richards was often too ill to play. He stayed in his barrack, trying to keep warm, and reading in his trafficked newspapers about German advances. "Oh to be in Belgium or France to get one blow at these cursed Huns, and die," he wrote. On top of his cold and cough and toothache, Richards also developed diarrhoea. Regular trips to the latrines were no fun in the freezing winter conditions. "Must brush snow off seat," he reminded himself.

Richards – like many of the Ruhlebenites – was treated for his ailments by Dr Jephson, a prisoner with enthusiastic medical knowledge who may or may not have been an actual doctor. Jephson was called upon to treat everything from boils and broken limbs to dysentery and measles. The camp had official medical officers, but they were unreliable at best. The camp's first official medic, Dr Lachman, was well-regarded, but he died of appendicitis within a few weeks of arriving at Ruhleben. His replacement was Dr Reiche, a lazy and heartless military man who was transferred elsewhere during the winter. Then came Dr Geiger, a cold and "cadaverous" man who peered through thick round glasses, and withheld treatment and anaesthetic out of cruelty. Patients were treated at the doctor's office or at the *lazarett* – a filthy makeshift hospital set up at the Emigrants' Station.

Geiger was described as having "a venomous hatred of

Englishmen". He could not speak English, and any patient who could not speak German had to bring an interpreter. It was reported that Geiger at least once operated on the interpreter instead of the patient. Geiger resented the competition provided by Jephson and called him to his office for a dressing down. The small number of medical supplies Jephson had managed to obtain were confiscated, and he was put into solitary confinement for 72 hours over the New Year period with no bed and no food. He described the experience as "worse than hell". From then on, Jephson was prohibited from helping his fellow prisoners.

Ruhleben's lack of medical provision was illustrated in February 1915 when one of the jockeys, named by Bloomer as Billy Lister, became seriously ill. Lister went to Geiger and told him he had heart problems and needed to go to the hospital. Geiger refused. Lister "broke down and cried like a child" in Geiger's office, which was full of waiting patients. When other patients pleaded the jockey's case, Geiger told them he was "not half as bad" as they thought. Lister died a few days later. Geiger was shaken by his mistake, and seemed to attempt to reform his ways, but from then on "nobody consulted the doctor who could possibly avoid it". Many in the camp referred to Lister's death as murder.

Life for the remaining prisoners did begin to improve. The establishment of a parcel service, and the decision of the camp authorities to allow the receipt of parcels from Britain, provided a real lifeline. Prisoners immediately wrote home asking for food. According to Joseph Powell, the parcel service "saved the camp from hunger, if not from actual starvation". Many prisoners asked for bread, which was mouldy by the time it arrived. The mouldy portion had to be cut away before the rest could be eaten. Hundreds of parcels arrived in carts each day. Wyndham Richards and several of his Barrack 10 bunk mates worked in the parcel office. He called it "hard but interesting work".

Then, at the end of February, relief payments of 4 marks per week began to be made by the British government via the American embassy to any prisoner who requested them. More than half of the Ruhleben population applied. The payments were intended to be loans, although they would never be recalled. Now every prisoner had funds and could begin to pay to improve their conditions, with better food, clothes, accommodations and even entertainments. The relief payments would eventually allow the prisoners to create their own civil administration and effectively run the prison for their own betterment.

Further improvements followed the departure of the prisoners' deeply unpopular camp captain, EM Trinks, and the promotion of his deputy, Joseph Powell. Trinks had been preparing a report on conditions in the camp for the British government, but he was known to be a Pro-German, and it was suspected that his report would not properly reflect the extent of the prisoners' suffering. A petition of 3,000 signatures was raised to demand the report be approved by a committee of barrack representatives. But before the report could be completed, Trinks was released into Germany – a perk of being a "PG".

There were several hundred PGs in Ruhleben, and their existence was just about tolerated by the other prisoners. But on a gloomy night in mid-January, the fragile peace was broken by a noisy commotion. Some of the PGs were holding a prayer service in German. It was interrupted by the booming voice of an unidentified sailor, who yelled: "These bloody Germans want knocking a hundred miles the other side of hell, and that's where they'll find themselves before we've done with them!" The PGs complained to Baron von Taube, who rang the fire bell to call a meeting and furiously addressed his captives.

"It stands to reason that, in a camp like this, there must be both Englishmen and Germans," said the Baron. "The English, being in the majority here, have attempted to oppress the Germans. It has even come to this – that certain Englishmen have permitted themselves to speak of the Germans as 'the bloody Germans'. On their behalf, I throw that insult back in your teeth. It is you who are 'the bloody English'! It was you who began this war, but it is we Germans – thank God! – who are the victors at all events up till now, and there is every reason to hope that we shall remain the victors. Now, therefore, I call upon those of you who are good friends of Germany to step forward."

Around 300 to 400 men stepped forward. Some were born in Germany, some had German accents, some had German names, and some had German wives. Some who were about to step forward were held back by friends. Some who did step forward seemed to reconsider and step back when they realised what the consequences of their actions might be. (Edwin Dutton, the German international footballer, did not step forward.) Those men who did identify themselves as PGs were "instantly cut dead" by the other prisoners. "I've finished with them," said Richards, of the 30 or so men who stepped forward from his barrack. They would never again be trusted.

Von Taube's overreaction to an overheard insult had ripped the camp apart. "It was the worst error of tact that Baron von Taube ever committed," noted Joseph Powell. When Trinks was released, it only confirmed suspicions that he had been colluding with the German authorities. Trinks may have been unfairly maligned by the Ruhlebenites, as he had made some efforts to improve the prisoners' lot. But things improved much faster following his departure when Powell became the new camp captain, with Lewis Beaumont named vice-captain.

Joseph Powell would be referred to by the Ruhlebenites for the remainder of their stay as Captain Powell, although he was not a military man. He had previously been the European sales manager for the French film production and distribution company Eclair in Berlin. His cinema experience would subsequently prove useful, but it was his skill as an administrator and his command of politics that allowed him to succeed as camp captain and improve the lives of the other men. He wasn't universally popular, but it was difficult to please 4,500 prisoners, and impossible to make demands of their intractable captors. He realised that he had to defer to – and perhaps massage the egos of – Schwerin and von Taube in order to gain incremental improvements. There would be many such improvements, but one of the most significant involved football.

The game was still banned but, as Steve Bloomer recalled, "We had not allowed the prohibition on football to remain without our making an effort to remove it." Captain Powell, acting on behalf of Bloomer and the other football enthusiasts, continually appealed for permission to resume playing. "It was put to Baron von Taube that we must have something to occupy our attention," said Bloomer. "Sport was one of the best methods of keeping everyone out of mischief, and, as we caused damage inside the camp by our games, why not permit us to go out on to the racecourse and do the thing properly?"

Powell's initial appeals were rejected, but they were perhaps being made to the wrong men. Both Schwerin and von Taube had only limited autonomy, with the real responsibility for controlling the camp held by the Prisoner of War *Kommandantur* (Headquarters) in Berlin and its commander-in-chief General Gustav von Kessel, the War Governor of the Mark of Brandenburg. "He was the Kaiser's right-hand man," wrote Powell, "and had only to breathe a word to override any other man's decision."

Von Kessel inspected the camp on 20 March, with snow thick on the ground, and he met with Powell and Beaumont as the heads of the prison's civil administration. "Count Schwerin, in introducing us, commended the work which we had done in that capacity," wrote Powell. "Von Kessel then inquired, in the brusque tone of a jail governor doing his rounds, whether we had any complaints to make or any requests to prefer. We were standing, at the time, quite close to the wire barrier which separated us from the racing track. I pointed to it, and said that our crying need was for the use of that space as a playing field."

"Very well, you shall have it," said von Kessel.

It was not quite that simple. The field was still owned by the proprietors of the racetrack, and the prisoners needed to obtain their permission. Powell would be allowed to go into Berlin to negotiate with them, and would eventually agree to a rental payment of £40 out of the camp fund for six months of use. (There was little point in agreeing to a longer term when release seemed imminent.) But before that, Powell hurried off to find Steve Bloomer.

Bloomer and Pentland were walking up and down the grandstand with a couple of other prisoners when they spotted Powell approaching "at express speed".

"Hullo," one of them remarked, "Powell looks mighty excited."

Powell, out of breath, grabbed Bloomer's hand, shook it, and said, "Steve my lad, we've got it."

Bloomer had no idea what Powell was talking about, and his companions were equally baffled. "Got what?" Bloomer replied "The 'flu?"

"No, my lad," said Powell. "The ground. *This.*" He waved his arm at the overgrown patch of grass in the middle of the track, and jubilation ensued.

"We all shook hands and danced," wrote Bloomer. "Then we shouted the good news to all those who were sitting on the stand, and a cheer such as had never been heard before in Ruhleben went up from thousands of throats. Afterwards, one could hardly hear oneself talk because of the din of chattering tongues. Songs were started and sung with great enthusiasm, and when the time for our departure for barracks came one voice shouted out above all others: 'Are we downhearted?' '*No!*' came the response, with sufficient volume to shake the roof."

"No one who was there will forget the magnificent cheer which greeted the news," recalled Pentland. "Visions of league matches and cup ties with all the friendly inter-barrack rivalry which characterised all phases of sport in the camp rose before us. Small wonder that the prospect of football with a full-sized ground and goal posts and all the necessary correct paraphernalia filled out thoughts and circumstances for the following days."

Jack Swift, the captain of Barrack 2, was given the task of preparing the field for football. It was not an easy task for the former racehorse trainer from Aintree. "He was confronted with all sorts of difficulties which might have upset the equilibrium of a less-balanced man," said Pentland. "On the day he inspected the ground, the rain came down like some fiend resenting the appearance of a stranger."

According to Pentland, the grass was in some places "at least a yard high." This had to be dealt with manually, in an era before petrol-powered lawnmowers. A good portion of the western half of the field had become a rather large pond. But, as Pentland explained, "Captain Jack's spirit of sport was superior to small matters of that sort." Swift marched into the field with a measuring tape and a bucket of lime whitewash, and within a day or so Ruhleben had two full-size football pitches.

On 22 March, representatives of each barrack met on the grandstand to discuss the way forward. It would be possible, they agreed, to form a league with teams drawn from each barrack. Football captains were elected for each barrack – to be distinct from the camp captains. Bloomer was captain of Barrack 1, Jack Brearley of Barrack 4, Sam Wolstenhome of Barrack 9, and Pentland of Barrack 10. Wyndham Richards was elected to Barrack 10's football committee under Pentland.

The men still lacked equipment, including footballs. Powell obtained permission for Edwin Dutton to have all necessary kit supplied to the camp from his parents' sports outfitter's in Berlin. The camp authorities benefited from this arrangement – they deducted a percentage from every purchase. Each player was able to buy football boots and socks, and each barrack raised a fund to buy a set of shirts and shorts. Balls and flags were also procured. Goal posts were made by one of the prisoners, a carpenter named Osborn. Goal nets were omitted for the time being, as they were too expensive.

Four days later, on 26 March 1915, the prisoners formed the Ruhleben Football Association. Fred Pentland was named chairman and Jack Cameron was secretary. Joseph Powell was honorary president and Lewis Beaumont and Jack Swift were vice-presidents. It was decided that the league would have first and second divisions, and there would also be a cup competition. Each barrack would be represented by two teams – a first team and a reserve team – and each individual could only play for their own barrack. Team colours were to be sanctioned by the association, and no clogs would be allowed. Betting on matches by players and officials would be strictly forbidden.

The football field was opened with a grand exhibition match on Sunday 28 March, arranged with less than a week of preparation. Boots and kit had arrived on the previous day and were distributed by Pentland and Cameron. Wyndham Richards had his boots altered by a cobbler, then enjoyed a "little shooting practice". Changing into proper football kit inside a prison camp was an unusual experience. "What a funny feeling!" he wrote. The men were allowed to use the field from 9 to 12 in the morning and from 2 to 5 in the afternoon. The game was played at 10.15 on Sunday morning.

The match was billed as "Ruhleben v The Rest", although all involved were inextricably Ruhleben men. The Ruhleben XI was the pros' team, captained by Bloomer, who played up front alongside Pentland, Cameron and Dutton, with Brearley and Wolstenholme backing them up. Also in the team were talented amateurs Tommy Miller and Alf Mills, and goalkeeper Joseph Powell – making his only notable appearance in a football match at Ruhleben.

The "Rest" were captained by Richards, who said he considered it a privilege to lead out the team. Alongside him were former Old Carthusians forward Hugo Dixon, from Southport, Lionel Warner, from Mansfield, who played for Hanau in Germany before the war, and Alf Maw, an outside-left who was originally from London and whose name would become well known to his fellow prisoners in subsequent months. In goal was Harry Palin, a seaman from Grimsby, who would make a name for himself as one of the best players in the camp. Jack Swift, who had worked so hard to prepare the pitch, acted as referee.

"The game created a great deal of interest and enthusiasm," noted Steve Bloomer. "Practically everyone, including the Hun guards, was in attendance." This included Baron von Taube, who attended the match with his wife – and performed the ceremonial kick-off. "A roar of cheering applauded his effort," said Bloomer, "but it really signified the pleasure of the spectators that football had actually started." Von Taube bowed and smiled as he threaded his way past the players to the touchline, where he stood with his fellow officers and the Baroness.

Richards called it a "proper professional opening" with a "terrific crowd". He was at centre-half for The Rest and said he played a fair game. But Richards' all-amateurs could not defeat Bloomer and the other professionals. Ruhleben beat The Rest 4-2. For all of the players, half-starved and beaten-down after four months of captivity, it was quite an exertion. Richards was "absolutely exhausted" and "awfully, awfully hurt all over" after the match – so much so that he had to miss his evening prayer meeting.

But, as Pentland explained, it was worth it. "To those whose previous games in the camp had taken place by the Tea House on a ground including a few trees as bunkers," he wrote, "the experience of playing football on a real full-sized ground with everything else in correct comparison was a 'rare and refreshing fruit'."

"Something was certainly needed to distract our minds from the sordid pessimism which had slowly but none the less surely crept into our lives during those long, dark, dreary days of winter," he said. "That something was sport. Everyone knew that. It would pass the time not only for those actually playing but would find a pleasant recreation for the spectators. So, from the moment the sports ground was given us, the general spirits of the camp rose."

Jack Cameron called the opening of the football field "the first gleam of sunshine" in the men's bleak outlook. Steve Bloomer said that after the field was opened "life in Ruhleben began to get easier". Bloomer admitted that the improvement wasn't just down to football. The prisoners' relief payments – raised from 4 to 5 marks a week in April 1915 – were invaluable in allowing the men to purchase the essentials that made life bearable. And the decision to allow the prisoners to receive private parcels from home was another lifeline. "But to me," said Bloomer, "the greatest concession was the throwing open of the sports ground."

The playing field offered hope, but Ruhleben remained a place of misery. It was still cold, dirty and overcrowded. The rations were still atrocious, and the captors were still unkind. On one occasion, according to Wyndham Richards, Count Schwerin saw a prisoner throw away his disgusting soup and sneered, "His wife and children in England will soon be glad to have such to eat."

Some prisoners became desperate, and at least one attempted to take his own life – cutting his throat and stabbing himself in the chest. He survived, and Richards called it a "poor attempt".

Captain Powell worked diligently to try to improve conditions. Extra relief payments were obtained to pay for improvements. Officers were appointed to oversee the canteen, the latrines and the cleaning of the barracks. Work teams were employed using camp funds to carry out cooking, cleaning, maintenance and other essential tasks. The civilian "police" force began to patrol the barracks and keep order – and reduced confrontations with guards.

Two new barracks were built in the grandstand compound to reduce overcrowding. After the construction of Barracks 12 and 13, these were Barracks 14 and 15. Unlike the permanent brick stable blocks, the new barracks were temporary wooden constructions.

Another new building was the Convalescent Barrack, or Invalids Barrack, which went some way to replacing the dreadful lazarett. The Convalescent Barrack contained a surgery, a waiting room, and a ward with 12 beds. One of the prisoners, Stanley Lambert, was appointed as the captain and translator for the barrack. An export agent for a London coal company, Lambert had no medical knowledge. However, he selflessly devoted himself to the well-being of his fellow prisoners, obtaining equipment, medicines and dressings, and acting as an intermediary between patients and Dr Geiger to ensure they got the treatment they needed.

After Geiger was transferred away from Ruhleben in the summer of 1915, Lambert continued to run the barrack, alongside the German Dr Kapp, who had previously worked in London as a "beauty specialist". Thanks to Lambert's "cheerful devotion", the Convalescent Barrack was much preferred to the lazarett – and to Dr Weiler's Sanatorium in Charlottenberg, where prisoners who could not be treated in the camp were sent, at a cost to them of up to 12 marks per day.

The construction of new barracks and buildings was welcomed, but it also served to crush any hopes of release. As Henry Mahoney noted, "It was not until we observed one building after another going up that the awful truth dawned upon us. Then we realised we were condemned to stay in this prison for an indefinite period."

Such loss of hope placed a great strain on the men's well-being. Powell attempted to address the failing mental health of some of the prisoners, and the sinking depression referred to in the camp as "barbed-wire disease". The condition, as described by Swiss physician Adolf Lukas Vischer during the war, is a form of post-traumatic stress disorder related to long-term incarceration and involving confusion, clouding of consciousness and amnesia. "Some men are made nervous, others quarrelsome," noted Powell. "Loss of memory is another frequent symptom, while, in extreme cases, speech wanders, and becomes incoherent. A complete nervous breakdown follows."

Barbed-wire disease would affect a large proportion of

the prisoners and was perhaps the greatest danger faced by the men in Ruhleben. "Sport was the antidote to that danger," said Powell, "or, at all events, one of the antidotes, and one of the most widely helpful."

Back in England, Everton finished top of the First Division and Tottenham finished bottom and were relegated in the last season played before the suspension of the Football League due to the war. Football in England was over, but football at Ruhleben was just getting started.

7

The First Season

The Ruhleben Football League kicked off on 6 April 1915. It was a major undertaking, played by almost 500 footballers and watched by several thousand spectators. For several weeks that spring, the two lime-marked football pitches on the muddy playing field in the middle of the racetrack became the centre of attention for the majority of the prisoners in the camp. Crowds of between 2,000 and 4,000 men were pushed up against the touchlines and scattered across the grandstands for almost every game. And there were a lot of games, requiring careful organisation from Fred Pentland, Jack Cameron and the Ruhleben FA.

Fixtures were drawn up, duplicated and posted around the camp. The football captains of each barracks were tasked with recruiting their teams. Subscriptions were set at 20 marks per barrack for the league and five marks for the cup. Wyndham Richards went around the barracks collecting the subs and got an "awfully good response". All games would be played according to the rules of the English FA, except that matches would only last one hour. The opening exhibition match had lasted 90 minutes, but it had been too strenuous for some of the men – including Richards – who were weakened by malnutrition, illness and idleness. Also, the reduced running time meant more games could be played.

There were 14 teams in each division – 12 teams representing Barracks 1 to 12, plus a combined Barrack 14 and 15 team and a Tea House team. (Pentland's promise to form a team from the black prisoners in Barrack 13 was not fulfilled.) Circumstances meant there could be no home and away ties, so every team played each other only once. That meant each team played 13 matches. First Division matches were played in the morning, between 9 and 12, and Second Division matches were played in the afternoon, between 2 and 5. There were 182 league matches, plus four rounds of cup matches and a couple of representative matches, all to be squeezed into six weeks.

There were lots of prospective footballers to be squeezed in, too. Sixty-six men took part in the Barrack 10 trial matches, under the watchful eyes of Pentland, Cameron and Richards. According to Richards, they discovered "some really good talent". Thirty-nine players were selected for the combined first and second team squad. Pentland, Cameron and Richards were, of course, in the first team. Also in the first team were goalkeeper FB Bennison and half-back Wallace Allen, both seamen from Sunderland, plus inside-forward Ernest Perry, from Wandsworth, and the highly-rated goalscorer Bobby Slade, from Surbiton. Rower Tom Sullivan, and Richards' fellow Tilly's students AW Hill and Charles Roupell were in the second team. While Pentland captained the first team, Australian-born Tilly's student AS Belmont captained the second team.

Several referees were appointed, and they were assisted by linesmen drawn from the competing clubs. One ref was a Mr Willis, who had refereed several "important games" in Germany. Another was Clifford Lewis of the

Surrey FA, who was a statistical accountant and was in Barrack 10 with Pentland, Cameron and Richards. Pro footballer Jack Brearley, captain of Barrack 4, and Lionel Warner, captain of Barrack 8, also took turns refereeing matches.

Each team played in a distinct kit – or at least in distinct jerseys. Steve Bloomer's Barrack 1 wore white and green, Jack Brearley's Barrack 4 wore blue and red, Sam Wolstenhome's Barrack 9 wore red and white, and Pentland's Barrack 10 wore white and blue. Each team had a coloured crest, which appeared on notices and banners, and some had mascots. One team's mascot, carried onto the pitch before every match, was a curious carved wooden animal that appeared to be a winged rabbit. As the season progressed, each team was bestowed with a nickname, such as the "Canaries" and the "Cock-a-Doodle-Doos" – the latter named due to its players' constant bragging.

Barrack 10 were favourites to win the First Division, and their odds with the camp bookies – who defied the Ruhleben FA's rule against betting – must have shortened after Pentland's men won their first match against the Barracks 14 and 15 team 8-0. "Excellent game, but too easy," remarked Richards, who played at centre-half. "Our forwards were wonderful." But two days later, in driving wind and rain, Barrack 10 lost 3-0 to Barrack 11. "Astonishing," wrote Richards. "Our forwards were disgustingly slow in shooting, and no power."

Barrack 11 was captained by Alex Bodin, who had played as an amateur for the Rangers "A" reserve team in Glasgow, and was good enough to be selected for a representative Scottish Reserve League side. In 1912, he was presented with a gold watch and chain in appreciation for his services to Rangers and to mark his appointment as assistant professor of Logic at Glasgow University. Deeply religious, Bodin chose not to participate in any match played on a Sunday – which would be problematic given Ruhleben's extremely crowded fixture list.

Steve Bloomer's Barrack 1 won their opening game against Barrack 4. They were helped by the fire bell, which brought the match to an end five minutes before time with Bloomer's men winning 1-0 and their opponents pushing for an equaliser. Bloomer said the task of picking his team was "no easy task", but he ended up with "some really rattling players". His 26-man squad included four jockeys, three music hall artists, a foreign correspondent, a hotel waiter, a tailor and several seamen and engineers. In addition to Edwin Dutton, Bloomer singled out his half-back trio of George Treseder, Jimmy Quinn and Frank Heath for particular praise.

Treseder was a nurseryman or horticulturalist from Cardiff who played at left-half. "One would have to tramp a long way before coming up against an exponent quite so clever in that position," said Bloomer. Quinn was a civil engineer from Bootle, and Heath was a language teacher from Macclesfield. "All of these men are exceptionally fine amateur players," said Bloomer. "They improved even under the conditions imposed upon them at Ruhleben, and I have no hesitation in saying that if they were trained with First League players they would blossom out into fine, class men. If I were the manager of a club I would not have the smallest doubt of signing them up."

The challenge of working with and improving promising players particularly excited Bloomer, and he threw himself into the task, training, cajoling and admonishing his charges with inventive routines, inspirational guidance and coarse language. Pentland, Brearley and Wolstenholme also dedicated themselves to improving their respective teams, and their coaching efforts were appreciated in the camp as much as their playing abilities.

Bloomer's Barrack 1 won their second match, then played Pentland's Barrack 10. Despite having lost their previous game, Pentland insisted on playing the same team. It looked to be a good decision. Playing against the wind, Barrack 10 were "all over them" in the first half, although they failed to score. But Barrack 1 improved in the second half – perhaps due to a barracking from Bloomer – and Barrack 10 fell apart. "Forwards were disgusting, backs and goal even worse," noted Richards. "Bennison very poor." Barrack 1 won 3-0.

That afternoon, the Barrack 10 second team beat the Barrack 1 second team 6-0, with Richards' Tilly's pal AW Hill scoring all six goals from centre-forward. Afterwards, following a "long debate", Pentland agreed to promote Hill to the first team. And they began to win again – 5-0 against Barrack 12 and 5-2 against the Tea House. During the Tea House match, Richards received a "hell of a kick" on his shin. He played on but afterwards found it to be badly cut and swollen. "Thank God I had a shin guard on," he said.

The injury meant Richards had to pull out of an "International Match" arranged for Saturday 18 April between Steve Bloomer's "England" team and Jack Cameron's "The Rest". Fred Pentland and Sam Wolstenholme were due to play for England, and Welshman Richards had been selected by Scot Cameron to play for The Rest. All of those names were included on a written programme that was distributed ahead of the match. But the match would not take place as advertised.

That morning at roll call, von Taube once again asked the Pro-Germans to step forward. The Baron was more subdued than he had been on the first occasion back in January. He seemed apologetic, and it was assumed he had realised how damaging his previous outburst had been, but he was now acting on orders from above. "He no longer foamed and boiled," said Joseph Powell. "He no longer thumped his fine protuberant chest. He seemed to be thoroughly ashamed of himself, compelled to discharge an unpleasant duty."

Fewer PGs stepped forward this time, perhaps 200 or 300, with the others having no doubt reflected on the previous reaction. Von Taube announced that the PGs would be segregated. They would be moved into the Tea House and parts of Barracks 1, 14 and 15. The prisoners who already occupied those barracks would be dispersed elsewhere. "You will all collect your baggage and clear out of here at once," von Taube told them. The rest of the day was spent moving the Pro-British out and the Pro-Germans in. "Funny sight, seeing all the luggage in squared carts," noted Wyndham Richards.

The dispersed prisoners included Bloomer and Dutton, who were moved from Barrack 1 to Barrack 11. "We were hustled inside to gather our possessions together, and then scattered to the four winds of the camp," said Bloomer. "Of course, the team on which I was building such great hopes for the next season was broken up altogether and distributed all over the camp."

In an apparent effort to relieve tension, it was declared

that PGs should be released in certain circumstances, for example, if they agreed to enlist in the German army, or if they had a son serving in the German army, or if they had business interests that were of benefit to Germany. Over the next few months, many PGs were released, and the segregation had an immediate effect on the previously mixed barracks. “No more Pro-German trouble,” wrote Richards in his diary – although that would not quite be the case.

The International Match was postponed until the following morning, and Bloomer, Pentland and Wolstenholme didn’t play – probably due to the upheaval in the camp. Richards was injured and Dutton, who could have qualified for either side, also missed the match. It was left to Jack Brearley, the only remaining English pro, to captain his country against Cameron’s The Rest. And it was England who had the better of the majority of the match. With just ten minutes left to play, Brearley’s side led 3-1. But then Cameron’s team, in his own words, “veritably pulled the match out of the fire”. The Rest, “playing up gallantly”, scored three good goals in quick succession and won 4-3 in front of a large and appreciative crowd.

Pentland watched the match as a spectator, and he was very impressed. “In a fairly long experience of the game,” he said, “I have never seen a better, more interesting exhibition of football as it should be played than in this match.”

The segregation of the PGs threw the football league into disarray. It was decided that players would continue to play for the barrack they had resided in at the beginning of the season – so Bloomer and Dutton would continue to play for Barrack 1, even though they had been moved to Barrack 11. The Tea House, which had the biggest number of dispersals, found it could no longer raise enough players to form two teams. So the Tea House second team resigned from the Second Division, and all of its results were expunged. Then, within a couple of days, matches resumed.

Wyndham Richards bound up his injured shin in cotton wool and returned to action. As well as football, he also played a game of rugby, which was squeezed in on a free afternoon on a third pitch to the east of the football pitches. Rugby had initially been regarded as "too rough and not at all a nice game", but was beginning to find favour among enthusiasts. It did Richards' injury no good. He played football for Barrack 10 against Barrack 9 in a "very fast and hard" game in front of a big and excited crowd. Barrack 10 won 2-1, with Pentland scoring both of his team's goals. "Pentland played brilliantly," said Richards. "He was angry with McGill and me for playing rugger yesterday. I was off form. McGill was very poor."

Pentland's anger reflected something of a rift that was opening up between the footballer and his barrack mates, who seemed to resent his demanding coaching style. Away from football, Pentland seemed to have little in common with the young men of Barrack 10, who were known as the "public school crowd". There was nothing snobbish or aloof about Richards and his barrack mates, and they were generally admired by the rest of the camp – and not only because they ran the essential Parcel Service. Much of the admiration was down to their sporting prowess. As the author and prisoner Douglas Sladen wrote: "There is no surer passport to being influential and respected in the Ruhleben camp than proficiency in sports."

By the beginning of May, spring had arrived at Ruhleben, and Richards described "glorious" weather interrupted by seasonal showers. On 2 May, a second "international match" was played. This time, captain Bloomer, Pentland and Wolstenholme did play, alongside Brearley, in a very strong England team against a "The Rest" team captained by Englishman Bob Stewart and featuring several of the stars of the league campaign but no professionals.

In a downpour of rain, a large crowd were "amply rewarded for their wetting" with, according to Jack Cameron, "an exhibition of football from the English side which was reminiscent of first-class football at home and which will live long in the memories". England won 4-0, but Cameron said The Rest were "in no way disgraced by succumbing to such a great combination".

In the league, Barrack 10 recovered from their early defeats, but they lagged behind Jack Brearley's Barrack 4, who won their first six games before eventually falling away, Bob Stewart's Barrack 5, a team without any professionals who just couldn't stop winning, and Steve Bloomer's Barrack 1, who put together a seemingly invincible run of wins without conceding a goal. When Barrack 1 finally conceded, in their 11th match, it was a wonderful goal. The opponents were Barrack 6, the home of Ruhleben's Jewish prisoners. "Jolly fine players they were," said Bloomer. "They were a keen, hard-playing, sporting side, and in this particular game they were all out to win."

According to Bloomer, the goal was a fine individual effort from Barrack 6's "small, tricky and very speedy" inside-left, who went "like the wind" past his opponents' half-backs and full-backs, steadied himself, then fired the ball "like lightning" past the helpless goalkeeper and into the net. "I am not very clear about what happened afterwards," said Bloomer. "I remember that the full Barrack 6 team surged past me and, making for the little scorer, instead of shaking him by the hand, hoisted him on their shoulders, and carried him right round the playing field."

The final whistle blew before the match could restart. Barrack 6's momentous goal was nothing more than a consolation. Barrack 1 won 5-1. In their next match, Barrack 1 conceded again, but it was an even smaller consolation. Bloomer's team won 8-1.

A little over a month after it began, the Ruhleben Football League reached its climax. Pentland's Barrack 10 and Stewart's Barrack 5 both still had a chance of winning, but they needed Barrack 1 to slip up, and that seemed unlikely to happen – despite their defence having eventually been breached. Barrack 1's final opponents were Alex Bodin's Barrack 11.

The match was played on 8 May, a day that began under a black cloud of bad news. Wyndham Richards was emerging from his usual 6.30 am cold wash when he was told about the sinking of the *Lusitania*. The British ocean liner had been torpedoed by a German U-boat off the coast of Ireland on the previous day. A "startled and shocked" Richards heard there had been 900 passengers on board. In fact, there had been 1,266 passengers and 696 crew, a total of 1,962 people. 1,198 of them lost their lives. "I feel I could torture to death any German who should ever fall into my hands," wrote Richards. "Feel very depressed."

Steve Bloomer recalled the attitude of a particular Pro-German following the tragedy. This unnamed PG, a successful businessman in Germany, was known for "toadying" to the officers and the guards, who he called the "heaven-sent saviours of the world". On the morning the news of the sinking reached the camp, Bloomer saw the PG approach Baron von Taube and tell him, "It was a glorious act. War is war, and Germany must show England that she will stand no fooling." The comments created a huge disturbance, particularly among the large number of seamen in the camp.

"The seafaring men went hunting round the camp for the fellow, openly declaring their intention of taking his life," recalled Bloomer, "and I feel sure that, had he been delivered into their hands, they would have torn him limb from limb." Fortunately for him, the Baron heard of their intentions and hurried the PG out of the camp. The sinking of the *Lusitania* caused anger and outrage far beyond the confines of Ruhleben, and played a crucial part in shaping the direction of the war.

Football, as always, provided a much-needed distraction, and the match between Barracks 1 and 11 that morning was thoroughly engaging. "Right from the moment of the first whistle the game was carried through with a bustle that left an old player like myself a little breathless," said Bloomer. "It was evident, in view of the successes achieved during the two previous matches, that Barrack 11 did not consider us to be invincible, and they laid themselves out to beat us. On our part, we were determined that another goal would not be registered against us that season."

But Bloomer's team were dealt a blow after 20 minutes when Edwin Dutton broke his arm after an accidental collision and had to leave the field. Then, just after half-time, Steve Sams, who Bloomer called "Speedy", suffered a cut to his ear and also left the game. There were no substitutes – in Ruhleben or in football in general at this time. So Barrack 1 had to play out the remaining half an hour with just nine men. "But we were not downhearted and still continued to hold Barrack 11 to check," said Bloomer. "Then I got the ball and, beating the backs, banged it into the net, scoring the only goal of the game. When the match was finished our supporters rushed the ropes and carried me shoulder-high back to our barracks."

Barrack 1 won the First Division without a single defeat or draw and with only two goals conceded. Barrack 5 pipped Barrack 10 for the runners up position on goal difference. Barrack 12 finished bottom, a point behind the Barracks 14 and 15 team, although it was noted that those barracks had the smallest pools of players and often struggled to raise a full team. The Barrack 10 second team, captained by AS Belmont, won the Second Division. But it was Bloomer's First Division champions that took the main plaudits. "I can assure you that I felt very proud of my team at the end of the season," said Bloomer. "Our record was a really fine one, and I felt that I could look forward and with hope to the next season."

Over the course of the season, a swell of "local patriotism" had built up in the barracks. According to Henry Mahoney, the engraver, the intensifying league competition had "put greater vim into the matches, both among the players and spectators". "The supporters of each side rolled up in overwhelming strength," he said, "and they vied with one another in cheering and spurring their representatives quite as keenly as the teams battled between themselves."

The inter-barrack rivalry was, according to Israel Cohen, "exceedingly keen". "The notice-board of the Ruhleben Football Association, with the punctiliously recorded results, was studied as closely as the tables of first league matches in England," said Cohen. "And the shouts that went up from a thousand throats whenever a goal was scored must have alarmed the garrison in the neighbouring town of Spandau."

Before the season ended, there was the Ruhleben Cup, a four-round competition contested between all 14 first teams. It kicked off 24 hours after the league ended and was completed within just nine days. Pentland and Richards' Barrack 10 beat Barracks 3, 5 and 11 on the way to the final. The other finalists were Brearley's Barrack 4, who got a bye through the first round then beat Bloomer's Barrack 1 and Barrack 9.

The final was played at 9.30 am on Monday 17 May in front of a huge crowd that Richards said included almost everyone in the camp. Barrack 10 were "slight favourites" and there was "tremendous excitement". With Richards at half-back and Pentland on the wing, Barrack 10 struggled to break down their opponents. Richards wrote that the forwards – including Pentland – were "BR", meaning "Bloody Rubbish". With 15 minutes left to play, the score was 0-0, and Richards said Barrack 4 had "practically given up". But then Barrack 10 keeper Crossland, a student from Huddersfield, made an error, and Barrack 4 scored. "I nearly wept," said Richards, "and so did Pentland."

The game finished 1-0 and Barrack 4 won the cup – to the delight of the spectators, and the bemusement of the guards. "Our wardens were bewildered by the strenuous manner in which we let ourselves go," recalled Henry

Mahoney. "One would have thought, from the deafening final cheer which went up from 4,000-odd throats, that the British Army was crossing the Rhine, instead of its being a paean of praise to the crack barrack football team of an internment camp."

Pentland said the cup win was a fitting reward for Jack Brearley, who he called "a quiet, unassuming, thorough sportsman". And he was full of praise for Steve Bloomer, the captain of the league champions and "my old comrade and friend". "Such generalship, such unselfishness, such keenness for the success of his side need no words of mine to praise," he wrote. "A toast to Steve, 'Good luck, old sportsman'."

Engraved medals were presented to the winning teams at a concert, held on 3 June and directed by Roger Day, who had played alongside Pentland for Barrack 10 and alongside Bloomer for "Tottenham". Pentland presented the medals to Bloomer's league winners, and Powell made the presentation to Brearley's cup winners. The First Division runners-up and Second Division champions also received medals. Pentland and Cameron were presented with inscribed medals for services to camp football, and Pentland received a football autographed by his Barrack 10 teammates – indicating that the "public school crowd" had not entirely fallen out with their captain.

Finally, Cameron announced he had a surprise presentation to make – a medal for Sam Wolstenholme, "provided by a few of his friends as a mark of esteem". One further presentation could not be made. Mr Rosenberger of Barrack 6 had generously promised to provide, free of charge, silk ties and badges in barrack colours to every footballer in the league – a total of 480 ties and badges. Unfortunately, it was announced that, due to the apparently unforeseen difficulty of getting them woven in England, he would not be able to fulfil the promise.

The presentations were followed by a variety show featuring songs and music, including the specially-written and rather torturously-named violin solo *A Bloomer (B)rearley Nice*, and a performance of the music hall comedy *Stiffy the Goalkeeper*. The football comedy, about a lazy and drunk but seemingly invincible keeper, had been popularised back in England by a touring production with the Liverpool-born comedian Harry Weldon in the lead role. (Early performances also featured a pre-fame Charlie Chaplin and guest appearances from real footballers including Fred Spiksley, the England international who avoided Ruhleben by escaping Germany with his dodgy knee.) In Ruhleben, Stiffy was played by another Liverpudlian comedian, Harry Stafford, who "kept the audience in a roar of laughter from beginning to end". There were footballers in the cast – Steve Bloomer's Barrack 1 teammates Percy Maurice and Alf Jackson, and Barrack 10's footballing rower Tom Sullivan.

Three days after the football concert, on 6 June, the prisoners published a camp magazine, *In Ruhleben Camp*. The first issue contained jokes, sketches and small ads for services ranging from tailoring and shoemaking to pedicures and elocution lessons. The camp printer, LJ Spicer, had an ad, as did the camp's sports outfitter Edwin Dutton, although Dutton was named as "Button" – perhaps a mistake or perhaps a joke. Many jokes within the pages of the magazine are cryptic to non-Ruhlebenites.

The magazine also included a review of the football

season, written by Fred Pentland, and interviews with Bloomer and Dutton. In his interview, Bloomer said it was difficult to compare football played in Ruhleben with that played at home, but the standard had been high considering the circumstances. "The feature of the play here which struck me most forcibly was the splendid sporting spirit shown," he said. "A tremendous improvement has been shown since the beginning of the season, individually and collectively." Bloomer also praised the crowds of supporters who watched each game. "Every sport depends to a far greater extent than people imagine on its spectators," he said, "and I must say that our spectators here in Ruhleben have watched us and judged us like real Britishers."

Bloomer reckoned a team selected from the best players at Ruhleben could give an English Football League reserve side a very good game. That team, he said, could include any of 28 players: John Collinson, Oates Lithgow and Jimmy Quinn of Barrack 1; George Rogans and David Gillespie of Barrack 3; Robert Still of Barrack 4; Bob Stewart, John Dugdale, Alf Maw and Harold Owen of Barrack 5; Arthur Hanson of Barrack 6; Hugo Dixon and Charles Ellis of Barrack 7; Lionel Warner of Barrack 8; Clem Burnill and Harry Palin of Barrack 9; E Crossland, Ernest Perry, Wyndham Richards, Charles Roupell and Tom Sullivan of Barrack 10; Alex Bodin, Arthur Facer and Alf Mills of Barrack 11; Tommy Miller of Barrack 12; JA Falck and David Owen of Barracks 14 and 15; and Alexander Garden of the Tea House.

In a subsequent interview, Bloomer also named Billy Dixon of Barrack 2 and Bobby Slade of Barrack 10 alongside the previously mentioned Owen and Burnill as the camp's most promising players.

Wyndham Richards was particularly pleased to be named on the first list. He wrote to his parents: "Yes! The Richards referred to by Bloomer as being among Ruhleben's best footballers is your humble, who is some rotten centre-half in my opinion."

In his interview with the camp magazine, Edwin Dutton spoke of something most of the camp did not want to hear about – a second season. The prisoners still hoped to be released before the summer was over, although it was now hope and not expectation. "Next season – well you needn't grin because there is going to be one – I think we shall see some really hot football," said Dutton, "and the struggle for the trophies will be a harder one, and I am sure a better one."

During the summer, the Ruhleben Football Association produced a handbook, compiled by Pentland and Cameron. The handsome little yellow-covered booklet was published by the Ruhleben Printing and Publishing Department and printed in Berlin. It contained an introduction by Pentland and a secretary's report by Cameron, with a list of the association rules, a map of the playing field, a summary of the first season, some notes on coaching, and a register of players with pen portraits of the barrack captains. The register, containing name, address, date and place of birth, profession and date and place of arrest, was a particularly valuable record.

The handbook also included a balance sheet. Over the course of the season, in addition to raising 350 marks from league and cup subscriptions, the Ruhleben FA made collections from supporters during matches and sold programmes, raising a total of 715.95 marks. Expenditure, including the costs of balls, pumps, goal posts, flags, whistles, medals, printing and the services of a "messenger boy" also totalled 715.95 marks, meaning the FA had broken exactly even. "Really," noted Cameron, "I cannot see from the figures how we can be accused in any way of extravagance."

In his introduction, Pentland described how the Ruhleben Football Association had been formed and the value football held for the prisoners. "Only those who have been incarcerated in a concentration camp can appreciate what happiness is derived from the playing of games," he wrote. "Although the conditions here were cramped and artificial, nevertheless we enjoyed to the full the small mercies which fell our way." But Pentland took no credit for the success of the first season, and instead praised the captains and their teams. "The delegates from the barracks were excellently chosen and the entered into their duties with a zest and wholeheartedness which assured the success of the Ruhleben FA from its inception."

For his part, Cameron thanked the captains, the referees, the linesmen, and "the whole camp, individually and collectively". "Our hurricane season came at a most opportune moment and did the whole camp an enormous amount of good, both physically and morally," he wrote. "We were all heartily sick of ourselves and everything, and speaking without favour I can honestly state that no other game or amusement could have created such great interest and so enabled us for a few hours to forget our enviable lot."

That "enviable lot" was represented by one artistic prisoner in a heraldic sketch depicting the "Ruhleben Coat of Arms", which appeared in various camp publications.

The sketch showed two rats supporting a quartered plate bearing a tin mug, a German sausage, a piece of war bread and a boot. Above the plate was a flat cap, and below it was a motto: *"Dum spiro spero"* "While I breathe, I hope".

8

A Lust for Freedom

Geoffrey Pyke arrived at Ruhleben in February 1915, in the frozen pits of winter. Pyke was a 20-year-old journalist who had been working as a special correspondent for the *Daily Chronicle*. He had travelled to Berlin to cover the war in the previous September ("it is hardly necessary to add 'unknown to the German authorities'") using an American passport he had purchased from a sailor. He was arrested in a hotel room while writing his first article, and spent four months being transferred between various prisons before eventually landing at the former racetrack on a bitter evening as dusk's gloom was enveloping the camp.

There were six inches of snow on the ground, and the soles of his boots had worn away during his captivity. So Pyke trudged through the snow in stockinged feet through the gates and into the square, under the flickering arc light, where he saw hundreds of unshaven men, wrapped up in blankets, overcoats and hats, stomping between the barracks to keep warm. Pyke was taken to his barrack and – being a late arrival – was directed up the staircase to the hayloft, where he sat on a straw sack and watched snowflakes drift gently through gaps in the roof. It was dark, damp and "intensely cold". There were 200 men packed into the loft in four rows. "The atmosphere was as thick as cheese," Pyke recalled in his memoir. "Humanity, when compressed, stinks abominably."

It was the cold that nearly killed him. "Prison, though it had its drawbacks, was warm," he wrote. "Ruhleben was never so." Ten days after arriving, Pyke became very ill, overcome with fever and struggling to breathe. His new friends in the loft called Dr Jephson, who diagnosed double pneumonia. The official camp doctor, then Dr Reiche, refused to visit Pyke until ordered by the commandant, then lazily gave him two aspirins. It was left to the prisoners to nurse Pyke back to health. "The long and short of the matter was that for days I lingered at death's door in the atmosphere of that loft," he said.

It was during those long weeks of recuperation, lying on his back in the cold loft, that Pyke began to dream. He had seen relatively little of the camp, but the stories he heard from other prisoners made him determined to avoid "the misery and the futility" of life in Ruhleben. He dreamed of England and imagined "the fortunate citizen at home who can play football without an armed sentry on the touchline". He became overcome by "the determination to escape".

By his own admission, Pyke did not have a plan or any real idea how he might achieve this, but he knew he would face several difficulties: "First you have to get out of the camp. Second, it is almost essential that your absence should not be missed for at least one night. Then you have that great stretch of Germany to get across before you reach the frontier. And, finally – a thing by no means to be despised – the frontier itself."

It was after he had hauled himself from his sickbed that he began to formulate the plan, with the assistance of a new friend, Edward "Teddy" Falk. The pair met when

Pyke went to one of the prisoners' stores to buy a shaving mirror. An "extremely handsome boy with merry blue eyes" approached him and asked, "Oh, excuse me, but aren't you the fool... er, I mean aren't you the fellow who was in England for the first two months of the war, and who came over here?" Pyke admitted that he was. "Well," said Falk, "come along and have some tea."

Falk was a former military man and the commissioner for the British government in colonial Nigeria. He was arrested while on holiday in Germany. He had three attributes that particularly appealed to Pyke. First, he spoke perfect German, which Pyke did not. Second, he had a great knowledge of geography. Falk had given lectures on geography to the prisoners and, for that purpose, had been allowed to bring maps of Europe into the camp. Third, Falk was thoroughly sick of life in Ruhleben and desperate to get out of its barbed-wire confines.

It took a month for Pyke to mention his idea to Falk. "It is difficult to propose such a thing as escape," wrote Pyke. "We were both very careful and approached the matter delicately." While wandering around the camp, Pyke pointed to part of the fence. "That's not very carefully guarded, is it?" he said to Falk. "Look how slack the sentry is. One ought to be able to get out there if one was fairly sharp about it."

"Yes," replied Falk, "but what would one do when one had got out?"

Over the next few months, as winter turned to spring and spring became summer, Pyke and Falk formed their plan. They prepared food and clothes and planned a route across Germany using Falk's maps. They studied the movements of the guards and noted sentry positions and blind spots, pinpointing weak points in the fences. Still, though, the teeming confines of Ruhleben seemed to offer few opportunities for an unnoticed departure. They considered bribing a guard but decided they could not trust any of their captors. To get out of the camp, they would need a distraction.

Sport continued in Ruhleben after the end of the football season. The brutal winter had acquiesced into a fine spring. Such was the change in the temperature that prisoners began to complain about the heat rather than the cold. The camp's numerous puddles and pools disappeared, and the muddy playing field hardened into a dusty, rutted plain that began to show green sprouts of grass. Winter coats and hats were abandoned, and shirt-sleeves were rolled up. The prisoners began to enjoy the sunshine. Some cultivated small gardens outside their barracks and others were seen "lolling" in deck chairs.

"The fine weather has made everybody sunburnt, and we must look a very healthy lot of people," wrote one prisoner, named Graham. The weather became so agreeable that a group of prisoners began to sunbathe in shorts on the field. However, this display of male flesh offended Baroness von Taube, who complained to her husband. The Baron immediately closed the field and refused to reopen it until the camp captains assured him there would be no further incidents of such indecency. The camp police were ordered to look out for offending sunbathers, and the field was reopened.

The improved weather did not entirely improve morale. Rumours and expectations – of Britain and Germany meeting in The Hague, and Austria petitioning for peace –

came to nothing. Resignation and frustration plagued the camp. "Sick of heat," wrote Wyndham Richards. "Had terrible attack of homesickness. So, so sick of life. Sat in deck chair and nearly wept. But awfully sick. Oh why am I not fighting?"

One prisoner, a keen cricketer named Ewing who had a brother in the trenches, wrote home saying, "One doesn't have much heart for games, but they are good exercise, and we must keep fit, I suppose."

Another prisoner who wrote home around this time was the well-known jockey Sam Heapy, who was from Derby and was an old friend of Steve Bloomer. A "great football enthusiast", Heapy had travelled with Bloomer to Derby County's away matches during his winter breaks from his racing job on the continent. He was riding in Belgium for the racehorse owner Baron Bruggman de Walzin at the outbreak of the war. Heapy was arrested while trying to prevent the Baron's horses being requisitioned for the German army. He was accused of shooting at a soldier, and he recalled having six pistols pointed at his head by a German patrol. But, rather than meeting what he called "an untimely end", he was sent to Ruhleben, where he met up with Bloomer.

Heapy described in his letter how the racecourse had been opened for the prisoners to use, although there would be no horse racing taking place. "Football clubs have been formed," wrote Heapy, who played for Barrack 2. "Of course, Steve Bloomer has made his team the best." Heapy asked his friends and family to send bread and plain biscuits, as delicacies, "particularly chocolate cakes and all confectionary", were forbidden. "I do hope all of us will come out of this terrible affair all right," he wrote. "I am pleased to say that so far my health is good, but I am very much afraid of what might happen during the summer unless some change is made in the camp."

At the end of May, the prisoners organised a grand sports day, featuring various athletic events plus a football dribbling race and a tug-of-war, and involving all the preparation and ceremony of a proper athletic meet. According to Steve Bloomer, it was "absolutely the red-letter sporting event of the whole of my internment".

It was the rower Tom Sullivan who first approached Captain Powell with the suggestion of a sports day. Sullivan had become a popular character in Ruhleben for his cheerful breeziness and his many colourful stories of life in his native New Zealand.

"Our idea is to hold a meeting that will be a credit to the sporting reputation of Great Britain," Sullivan told Powell. "We don't want a race round the barrack buildings for a box of fags, but a properly-constituted gathering that will thoroughly test all the men in the camp."

"That's a bit of a tall order, isn't it?" said Powell.

"Perhaps," replied Sullivan. "But it's possible. Will you put the matter before the Baron?"

Powell went to see von Taube, and messages were passed between the camp officials and the authorities in Berlin. After a few days, von Taube called Powell back to his office and showed him a memo from Berlin. "This gathering of runners is permitted," said the Baron. "Berlin has agreed, and the camp can do exactly as it likes."

"Thanks very much, sir," said Powell.

"If you can guarantee the meeting to be orderly," the Baron added, "I have no doubt that the Baroness will distribute the prizes."

Excitement grew in the week that preceded the sports day, with preparations made and heats run ahead of the final event. Distances were carefully measured, and competitors were kitted out in athletic vests with numbers on the front and back. Races were started with a miraculously-sourced starting pistol, and results were announced via a megaphone by Tom Sullivan. Baron von Taube and his wife watched the event from the "royal box" in the grandstand, while thousands of prisoners crowded along the railing that ran around the racetrack.

One race was a "75-yard old-age handicap" for the over-40s. Bloomer breezed through the heats, starting from scratch, then won the final. He received an inscribed silver cup, presented by the Baroness from a small table set up in front of the grandstand. It was another reminder of Bloomer's sporting prowess. According to Sam Heapy, Bloomer "except in age, never was better". But Bloomer was beaten into second place by Fred Pentland in the football dribbling race. Bloomer's baseball friend, the Canadian Dr Brawnbach, won the cricket ball throwing contest. Jack Brearley's Barrack 4 beat Pentland's and Richards' Barrack 10 in the tug-of-war, and became known as "John Bull Barrack".

But the real star of the sports day was a recent arrival named Harry Edward. Just 17 years old, Edward was the son of a German mother and a West Indian father. His father was a former cabin boy from Dominica in the Windward Islands. Although Edward was born in Berlin and had apparently never visited the West Indies, he was interned in Ruhleben because Dominica was a British colony. Before the war, Edward had excelled at athletics. During Olympic trials in Berlin in 1914, he ran 200 metres in 21.7 seconds, which was just a tenth of a second short of the Olympic record. (The Olympic Games were due to be held in Berlin in 1916, but were cancelled due to the war.)

In Ruhleben, Edward – representing Barrack 11 – won all of the open sprint contests, over 75 yards, 100 yards and 220 yards. "Edward showed himself, in style, to be the perfect runner," noted *In Ruhleben Camp* magazine. "Edward's running was characterised by its extreme suppleness and looseness in all his motions, his free swing of the arm and long stride." His time for 220 yards – 24 seconds – was regarded as particularly fast. "A top-hole performance under the circumstances," said the magazine, which reminded readers that the competitors were malnourished prisoners, running on sand and in "all sorts of conditions of shoes".

By the middle of June, the cricket season was underway, with exhibition games and an inter-barrack league. Matting wickets were used at each end to compensate for the poor state of the field. A canvas tent was erected for the batting side, and a folding table was set up for the official scorers. The score was shown on a blackboard.

"Cricket naturally had its numerous devotees in the summer," wrote Israel Cohen, "but it did not arouse as much enthusiasm as football, and only when an exceptionally interesting match was played did the onlookers, mostly seated in deck-chairs or on folding-stools, extend right around the field."

Several footballers excelled at cricket. Jack Brearley was a "very deadly" bowler, and Steve Bloomer was as handy with a cricket bat as was with a baseball bat. In one early match, Brearley took seven wickets for 51 runs with the ball and scored 85 runs with the bat, and in another Bloomer took six for 15 and scored 76. "Let me tell you something," wrote one prisoner in a letter home. "Bloomer has developed into a first-class cricketer." In a subsequent match, Bloomer hit a double century with 204 not out.

The cricket league was won by Barrack 10, led by star batsman John Masterman, who would excel at several summer sports. A final exhibition game, billed as "the Match of the Season", saw Barrack 10 beat a combined Camp team by 164 runs, despite a "brilliantly hit" 52 and 66 from Bloomer. "The contest, which was fought to a finish, lasted four days," said Cohen, "and was followed throughout by a large, applauding crowd."

Edwin Dutton sourced bats and flannels from his family's shop for the cricket season. And he added further equipment to his stock as other sports emerged over the summer – including tennis racquets, hockey sticks and golf clubs. Preparations were also made for a new football season, and there would be improved fixtures and fittings – including corner flags and goal nets. "Dutton can get you anything you want in the sports line," said an ad in *In Ruhleben Camp*. Not everything, though, was easy to source.

That summer, Jack Cameron wrote a letter to Frederick Wall, the secretary of the English FA, asking him to send a dozen footballs as quickly as possible as they were difficult and expensive to get hold of in Germany. "Just now we are having a cricket season," he said, "but it is falling flat and, as there seems to be little hope of an early release, we have been asked to make arrangements for another football season." Cameron added that Pentland, Brearley, Wolstenholme and Bloomer all sent their kindest regards: "We all hope that our brother professionals are alive and doing

Stephen Bloomer.

Ruhleben FA Handbook; In Ruhleben Camp magazine;
Ruhleben FA crests, first season, 1914-15; Steve Bloomer

Steve Bloomer and Fred Pentland in England kits, 1895 & 1909;
Bloomer (seated, second left) and Sam Wolstenholme (seated, right)
in England team line-up, 1904-05

Opposite page: Bloomer scores for England v Ireland, 1897; Pentland and Wolstenholme (8th & 9th) in Blackburn Rovers team, 1904-05; Edwin Dutton (back row, 8th) in Germany international team, 1909

Ruhleben camp sketch, from Ruhleben Camp Magazine, June 1917;
Football match at Ruhleben, with Spandau munitions works in background, from Illustrated Sporting and Dramatic News, April 1917

Views of the playing field at Ruhleben prison camp in summer (top) and winter, postcards, 1917

Overleaf: Map of Ruhleben Camp, 1916, with Ruhleben coat-of-arms

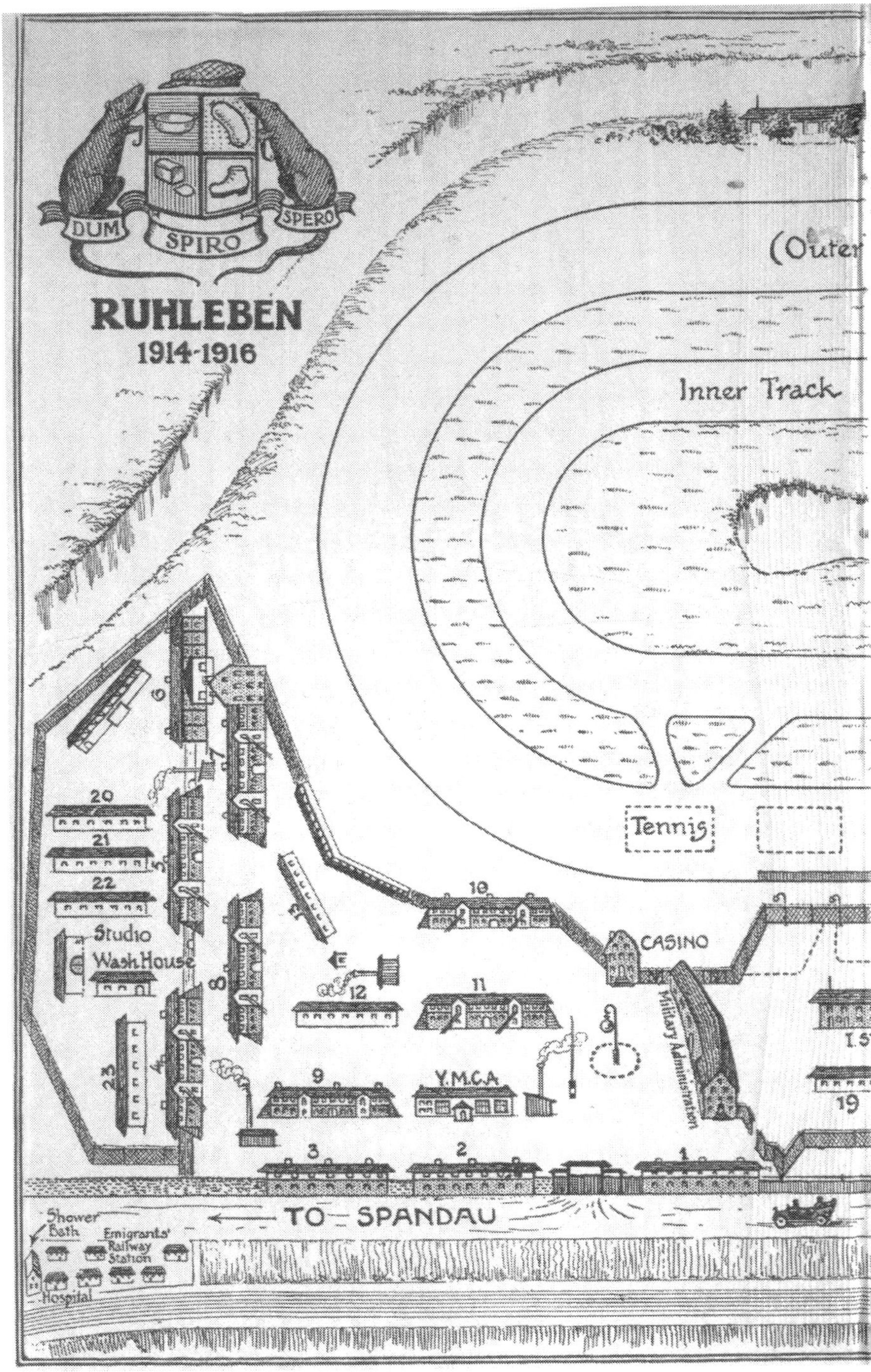
DUM SPIRO SPERO
RUHLEBEN
1914-1916
(Outer
Inner Track
Tennis
CASINO
Military Administration
20
21
22
Studio
Wash House
12
11
10
9
Y.M.C.A
3
2
1
19
TO SPANDAU
Shower Bath
Emigrants' Railway Station
Hospital

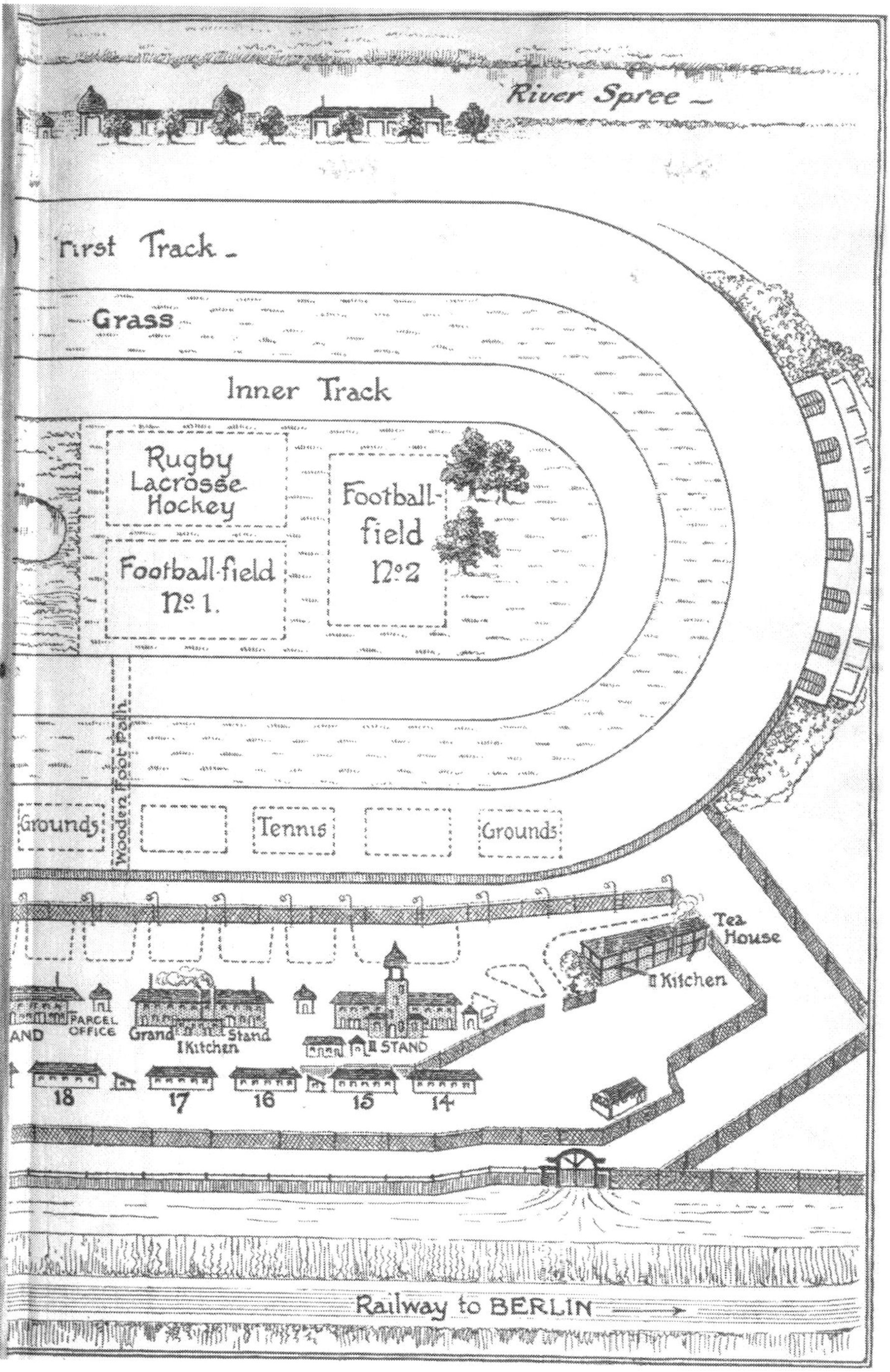
River Spree
First Track
Grass
Inner Track
Rugby
Lacrosse
Hockey
Football-field
No. 2
Football-field
No. 1.
Wooden Foot Path
Grounds
Tennis
Grounds
Tea House
II Kitchen
AND
PARCEL OFFICE
Grand Stand
I Kitchen
II STAND
18
17
16
15
14
Railway to BERLIN

Camp administration: (from left) Captain Joseph Powell, Count Schwerin, Baron von Mutzenbecher, Baron von Taube, Rittmeister von Brocken, Count von Hochberg; Parcel Post with Wyndham Richards (middle row, 5th), Gordon Nicoll, AS Belmont, RF Kindersley

Ruhleben camp barracks; Boxing match at Ruhleben

Overleaf, top: Ruhleben Sportsmen: (back row) J Richardson, golfer; Oswald Groening, British hurdles champion; John Masterman, tennis player and cricketer; Fred Pentland, footballer; (front row) Steve Bloomer, footballer; Tom Sullivan, rower; Freddy Winter, jockey

Overleaf, middle: Ruhleben Footballers: Bloomer in centre; Pentland, Jack Cameron, Sam Wolstenholme, Jack Brearley and Percy Hartley also shown

Steve Bloomer's Farewell Match, Ruhleben 20 March 1918

Bloomer's team: Fred Pentland; Bloomer; Jack Brearley; David Owen; Sam Wolstenholme; Gordon Nicoll; Oates Lithgow; Edwin Dutton; Bob Stewart; Bobby Slade

Opposite, bottom: Bloomer Family: Steve with wife Sarah, Hetty and Doris

Steve Bloomer sketched by Charles Mendelssohn Horsfall in Ruhleben, from Ruhleben Camp Magazine, March 1917

their duty for king and country."

The growing abundance of sports equipment needed to be stored somewhere, so the prisoners commandeered a small wooden shed, about six feet wide, on the racetrack. The shed, which was bolted at night, had a single small window and was piled high with bats, balls and nets. Guards regularly checked the shed, peering through the window and looking inside. But it captured the attention of Pyke and Falk. Sport would be their distraction, and the sports equipment shed would be their stepping stone to freedom.

It was just after 6 pm on 9 July 1915 when Pyke and Falk made their move. The day's summer sports were finished, and the two men stood by the grandstand watching their fellow prisoners clearing the playing field and heading back to the barracks. They were not the first men to attempt to escape from Ruhleben. There had been five previous attempts. All had failed. "I knew that I was risking prison and solitary for the rest of the war," wrote Pyke, "but I was driven forward, in spite of myself, by a lust for the fresh clean air of freedom."

In order to escape, Pyke and Falk needed to get past two fences – the inner fence around the barrack compound and the outer fence around the racetrack. Both fences were patrolled by armed guards and watched over by sentries with searchlights. But the pair realised that at night, after the prisoners were confined to their barracks, the guards concentrated on the inner fence. The prisoners were allowed out beyond the inner fence onto the racetrack each day. In the evening, when the prisoners were returning to the inner compound, Pyke and Falk would hide in the "no man's land" of the racetrack, wait for nightfall, then climb the outer fence under cover of darkness. They would not be missed until roll call on the following morning, by which time they hoped to be well clear of Ruhleben.

There was one obvious hiding place on the racetrack – the sports equipment shed. Pyke had noticed that, in the evening, the glare of the low sun made it impossible to see in through the shed's window. If he and Falk covered themselves with football and tennis nets, they would be almost invisible to any guard who peered through the window. Pyke also realised that the shed's bolt could be opened from the inside with a stiff piece of wire, allowing them to get out after dark. They could then crawl across the racetrack, evading the sentries, and climb over the outer fence without being seen.

"You are quite certain of the whole thing?" whispered Falk, as the pair gathered their nerves.

"Perfectly," answered Pyke. And off they went.

They loitered over to the shed, slipped inside, and climbed under the nets. The camp bell sounded, and the remaining prisoners were removed to the barrack compound. The shed was bolted shut, and Pyke and Falk waited in silence for more than three hours. Then, once it was dark, they unlatched the bolt, crept out of the shed and – with their boots hanging from their mouths – inched on their bellies along the dusty ground towards the outer fence. It took them almost two hours to crawl 200 yards. When they reached the fence, they lay still for five minutes so they could be sure there were no guards nearby. Then Pyke boosted Falk up onto the fence, and the two men climbed up and over the barbed wire, which rattled agonisingly as they jumped to the ground.

But they were not quite free yet. As they hurried down

towards the Spree, they found their way blocked by two further eight-foot fences that had not been accounted for. Pyke was still weak from his illness, and he struggled with these extra obstacles. It took several attempts but, eventually, they were both sitting, breathless, on the bank of the Spree. "We were safe," wrote Pyke. "We had 'done' von Taube and his sentries this time all right." "What a wigging he will get!" said Falk. They crept down to the river and hurried along the dark towpath.

By one o'clock in the morning, they were around three miles from Ruhleben and had reached the pine-filled Charlottenburg Forest, where they rested in a small hollow on the top of a rise. The stars were shining brightly in the sky, and the only noises that could be heard were far in the distance. "We tried to sleep and could not," said Pyke. "We were both excited at what had been accomplished. The great scheme for getting out of the camp had worked without a hitch."

In the morning, Pyke and Falk walked into Charlottenburg and casually boarded a tram to Berlin. To their horror, they saw two soldiers from Ruhleben on the tram. But they had been careful to wear clothes that they had not been seen in at the camp, and – as two out of more than 4,000 faces – they were not recognised.

In the city, the pair had breakfast and bought supplies, then walked across Potsdamer Platz, where they spotted a familiar figure coming out of a cafe. It was Baron von Taube. Miraculously, he walked right past them. "What a colossal joke!" Pyke told Falk. "He doesn't know either of us from Adam." Von Taube turned into a side street, and they never saw him again.

Pyke and Falk took a train from Potsdamer, and spent

several days travelling east, past Magdeburg and through Goslar, until they reached Bielefeld, around 60 miles from the Dutch border. Then they trudged through dense forests and crept past villages, being soaked by heavy rain as they neared their goal. Eventually, on Friday 23 June, two weeks after their escape, they reached a position that they determined to be a mile from the Dutch border. The last step, they decided, would be a rush through the German sentry lines.

But, as they prepared to leave their hiding place, they were disturbed by an armed soldier. Exhausted and with no means of escape, they admitted to being escaped prisoners. The soldier looked at them and asked if they realised they were in Holland. "No!" yelled Pyke. Falk grabbed the soldier by the lapels and begged him to tell them the truth. The truth was that the two men had miscalculated their progress and had crossed the border into the Netherlands by accident. "We had crossed the German sentry line without seeing a single man," wrote Pyke.

The Dutch army and local villagers treated the escapees with great kindness. After spending a "delicious" night in a proper bed for the first time in ten months, Pyke and Falk travelled to Amsterdam. From there, they travelled by boat back to England. They were free.

Back at the camp, Pyke and Falk's disappearance was discovered early on the morning after their escape, when the pair failed to show at roll call, and the shapes in their beds were found to be bundles of clothes. According to Wyndham Richards, the "alarm bell went to count us because of our dear old friends Pyke and Falk". None of the prisoners knew how they had escaped and, although Pyke wrote about his adventure on his return home, he didn't reveal his method or mention the sports equipment shed until after the war for fear he might thwart other attempts.

Baron von Taube reacted with fury. His first instinct was to take away sports. Captain Powell recalled: "Baron von Taube, with that uncertain temper of his, held over our heads the threat that, if any more men escaped, or if this, that or the other thing which he did not like ever happened again, the recreation ground would be closed." However, this did not entirely deter would-be escapees.

Before they left, Pyke and Falk had considered involving a third man, Wallace Ellison, but when they mentioned the idea he "roared with laughter". He must have regretted that reaction, but he recognised that their escape might not have been successful if he had gone with them. "When I look back on their success," Ellison later said, "I do not regret my decision, for, after all, it was infinitely better that two out of three should escape rather than three should be captured."

Ellison was an important character in Ruhleben. An economics lecturer who had been working at Frankfurt University at the outbreak of the war, he was the captain of Barrack 13, where the black prisoners were segregated (and unfortunately known as the "N—s' Barrack"). In March 1915, Ellison presented to Captain Powell a memorandum suggesting a means of civil administration in the camp. "We have, in this camp of 4,000, a town in embryo," wrote Ellison. "The suggestions which I am bringing forward are in essence an appeal to the captains to perfect the organisation of the camp by copying those features of English municipal government which would be of advantage to the camp at large."

Many of Ellison's suggestions were acted upon, and by the summer the camp administration was handled by eight committees: finance; kitchens; canteens; watch and works (police and labour); sanitation; education; entertainment; and sports. Fred Pentland headed the sports committee, and he absolutely understood the importance of sport in the camp. "For those interested in sport, the days fly past remarkably quickly," he noted, "so much so that, before we know where we are, we shall be amid the excitement of our second football campaign." Ellison was put in charge of education. By the summer, the Ruhleben school had 100 different classes and upward of 1,000 students.

Unfortunately, Ellison's involvement in the running of the camp was short-lived. In April, he was reported by a Pro-German for making "remarks offensive to the authorities" and was sent to the Stadtvogtei prison in Berlin, where he suffered terribly. On his return, he became determined to escape. He bribed a guard during a work duty, and successfully got out of the camp and across Germany. But Ellison was arrested before he could cross the border into the Netherlands, and was sent back to the Stadtvogtei.

Ellison made several more attempts to escape from Ruhleben. After the third attempt, when he returned from several weeks in solitary confinement, he was approached by Steve Bloomer, who was appalled by his beaten-down appearance. "Never in all my life have I seen a breathing man with a stronger atmosphere of death wrapped round him," recalled Bloomer. "His whole frame sagged for want of the necessary strength to hold his bones in position. There was not an ounce of flesh on him, and his eyes peered out feverishly from deep sockets."

"My advice to you is to drop this escape stunt and make the best you can of the camp," Bloomer told Ellison, "just as we old dodgers are doing."

But Ellison could not be dissuaded. "They've not broken me yet, Steve," he said. "I'll be all right when I've had a decent meal or two, and my luck may hold next try."

Summer in Ruhleben was immeasurably better than winter, partly due to the weather but also because of several improvements to the camp pushed by the new administration. New barracks were erected – numbers 16 to 19 in the grandstand compound and numbers 20 to 22 in the original barrack compound – and the lofts were cleared. In July, a new pair of latrines, nicknamed "Spandau" and "Charlottenburg", were installed at either end of the camp. They stunk, but were still much better than the previous "bogs". Also, from the summer of 1915 each prisoner was guaranteed a shower once a week.

Sports expanded. A boxing ring was erected between Barracks 2 and 3 at a cost of 176 marks. Hundreds of men crowded against the ropes to watch fights, while others stood on the barrack stairs to get a good view. The German guards were particularly keen spectators. During one bout, on 21 July, violence spilled out of the ring. "At boxing ring, man gets DTs, attacks soldiers and goes properly mad," wrote Richards in his diary. Delirium tremens (DTs) is usually associated with withdrawal from alcohol, but in Ruhleben, with alcohol relatively scarce, it was more likely an episode of mental confusion related to the illness they called barbed-wire disease. According to Richards, it took six guards to subdue the suffering man.

Richards also acted as an umpire for tennis matches on new courts that were marked out on the sandy track in front of the grandstands. Eventually, there would be eight tennis courts, separated by nets. Because the courts had to be laid out along the racetrack in an east-west bearing, the players sometimes had to play into the sun, which drew many complaints. Despite this, around 200 men joined the Ruhleben Tennis Association, paying a subscription of 20 marks each. Unlike football, tennis at Ruhleben was hardly inclusive. "The main drawback to the tennis sport was that men without means were excluded from it," wrote Israel Cohen, "owing to the high subscription fee and the cost of racket, ball, and shoes."

Cohen noted that many of the Tennis Association members came from Richards' Barrack 10, which housed a "big contingent of university men". Barrack 10's sporting hero John Masterman particularly excelled at tennis – he would reach the fourth round at Wimbledon in 1923. So he was a popular draw on the Ruhleben courts, but he wasn't infallible. During one doubles match, in which he and his partner were defeated, Masterman lost his temper and, according to Richards, provided the crowd with great amusement. The future Wimbledon star's tennis tantrum predated those of another famous John by more than 60 years.

Other star tennis players in Ruhleben included James O'Hara Murray, a Barbados-born mechanical engineer who had played in numerous international tournaments, in the Netherlands, Sweden, France and Germany, and GK Logie, who had reached the final of the German Open in 1908 and had represented Germany at the World Hardcourt Championships in Paris in 1913.

Another popular summer sport was golf, which was played at the far end of the racecourse. Five holes were marked out, and there was also a driving range. Like the Tennis Association, the Golf Club had around 200 members. Many of them were professionals who had been working in Germany at the outbreak of the war. There were more than ten professional golfers in Ruhleben, including Robert Murray, who had been working at a golf club in Dresden and played football in Ruhleben for Barrack 5, and Arthur Andrews and John Brown, who had been working as golf pros in Hamburg and played football for Barracks 3 and 10 respectively. Other Ruhlebenites were completely new to golf. “A large number received their first lesson in the game in captivity,” wrote Cohen, “and diligently smacked their captive balls against a net.”

Other sports that could be seen on the playing field included baseball, hockey and lacrosse. And in the spaces between the barracks, prisoners played quoits, croquet, chair-leg skittles and the Basque ball game pelota. There were also exercise activities, with dumbbells, Indian clubs and parallel bars available in Ruhleben’s outdoor gymnasium. More than a hundred men could be seen doing “physical jerks” every morning

Among the new non-sporting entertainments was a cinema, set up in the main grandstand, and administered by movie distributor Captain Powell. The cinema opened on Saturday 21 July, and all of the camp officers and the Baroness attended. For an entrance fee of 11pf, prisoners got to see three German-language films, including *Bilder aus dem Engländer Lager Ruhleben* (*Pictures from the English Camp at Ruhleben*).

The Ruhleben film delighted the audience with footage

of the barracks, with washing lines strung between the buildings, and of camp celebrity Andries Ventner, a 6'7" Transvaal Boer circus performer who dressed as a Native American and had to be accommodated in Ruhleben in a specially-elongated bed. There was footage of the parcel office distributing packages from a cart with a slide attached to it. Several of the camp's favourite theatre performers were shown in costume, most of them in drag, and Ruhleben's many talented artists were pictured at their easels. The film also offered a short glimpse of the playing fields, showing prisoners strolling along the promenade in front of the grandstands, playing tennis on the sandy courts and, surrounded by spectators who lined the pitches, playing football.

Powell arranged for the film programme to change each week. Many of the newer movies were German war propaganda films, but there were some more popular programmes, including Charlie Chaplin pictures. Each film was vetted by camp officials during a private performance before being shown to the masses.

By the end of August, scores of merchants and tradesmen had set up shop along the grandstands and between the barracks. Alongside Dutton's athletic goods store were barbers, carpenters, tailors, engravers, greengrocers, shoemakers, tobacconists, watchmakers and more. The bustling alley between Barracks 10 and 11 became known as "Bond Street". The row that housed the camp's printers and magazine office was known as "Fleet Street". More Ruhleben landmarks were bestowed with London names. The courtyard inside the main entrance became "Trafalgar Square" and the gate leading from the barrack compound to the grandstands became "Marble Arch".

One of the camp's tradesmen was a strapping fellow, with long bushy beard and hair, named Mortimore Howard, of Barrack 5. Prior to the war, Howard had been a lion and bear tamer in a circus, and he wore around his neck a lion's claw that he said belonged to an exceptionally dangerous animal that he managed to tame, after which it followed him around "like a dog" until its death. Howard was always ready with a song and a joke, and was very popular in the camp. But his main contribution to camp life was his formation and management of the Ruhleben Exchange and Mart, which allowed the prisoners to barter and swap everything from books and canned goods to boots and overcoats, and proved useful – and sometimes vital – to many in the camp, particularly those who could not afford to buy the things they needed.

The camp's civil administration was growing under the leadership of the captains, and the prisoners were taking over the running of many aspects of life in Ruhleben. Work teams and committees were busy with construction and organisation of accommodations and services across the camp. "You English seem to work as if you were founding a new colony," remarked a German guard. The captains approached the camp officers to request further improvements and concessions, although not every request was granted. One of the officers told them, "You are forgetting that you are prisoners."

Ruhleben was becoming an increasingly autonomous society within the confines of the camp's fences. And it was about to come even more autonomous. On 15 September 1915, Captain Powell was summoned to see Count Schwerin. "He told me that his 150 German soldiers were more trouble to him than his 4,000 prisoners, and that we were most orderly when left alone," Powell recalled. "He proposed therefore, if I would take full responsibility for order in the camp and would undertake to report daily the number of men in each barrack, to withdraw the soldiers then living in the barracks, and place the civil administration in full control." Powell agreed, and the guards were withdrawn.

On the following day, von Taube, who, Powell suggested, did not agree with Schwerin's decision, officially announced that the camp would now be under civil rule.

"All soldiers withdrawn from barracks without notice," wrote Wyndham Richards in his diary. "What is going to happen?"

9

The Second Season

"Who are the Best Footballers in the Camp?" That was the interesting and – it would turn out – contentious question posed in *In Ruhleben Camp* magazine in September 1915. Ruhleben's second football season would open with an England v The Rest exhibition match, and the magazine was inviting readers to vote for their choice of players. "We are glad to see that so many of our readers are football enthusiasts," remarked the magazine after more than 1,600 votes were received.

The return of football was a great boost now that summer had faded into autumn, even if it did serve as a reminder that, with no end to the war on the horizon, there was no imminent prospect of release. "What is the use of wasting time over vain regrets that we are here for another season?" wrote Fred Pentland. "We are here and likely to remain for some time, so let us make the best of the present circumstances and look forward to what the Gods have in store for us with as much optimism as we can command."

The Ruhleben FA re-formed for the new season and set up an office next door to Edwin Dutton's athletic store at the end of the first grandstand. Pentland and Jack Cameron were re-appointed as chairman and secretary. "Our experience in connection with football is absolutely at the service of anyone caring to ask for advice," said Pentland, "and we shall only be too glad to answer any inquiry or help in any possible manner."

There would be some changes for Ruhleben's second season. Due to the improved condition of the prisoners, thanks to food parcels and the restorative summer, it was decided that match duration would be increased from 60 minutes to 70 minutes – 35 minutes each way. New goal nets were hung, and ropes and posts were placed around the pitches to keep spectators from encroaching on the playing surfaces. A refreshment stall selling coffee, biscuits and sausages would be set up during matches. The camp magazine put up a trophy – "an ordinary Ruhleben coffee mug, suitably engraved" – for the best individual or team performance of each fortnight. But the main change was caused by what Pentland called "the exchange" – the transfer of prisoners between barracks to accommodate the segregation of the Pro-Germans.

Although there were now 24 barracks, including the Tea House, there would only be 11 teams in the First Division and 13 in the Second. Barracks 2, 3, 4, 5, 7, 9, 10, 11, 17 and 20 each fielded two teams, one in each division. Barracks 15 and 20 each fielded a team in the Second Division. The Tea House and the remaining barracks were unable to put up teams. The Barrack 20 team was "the Boys" – ship's boys aged 18 or under. The Barrack 15 team was made up of Pro-Germans from around the camp, and Steve Bloomer recalled that their matches were "very funny to watch". "I am afraid that very often they were made the medium for working off a lot of old scores," he said.

Bloomer's championship-winning Barrack 1 team had been broken up to make way for the PGs. Bloomer and Dutton were now in Barrack 11. Bobby Slade, George

Treseder and Jimmy Quinn had all moved to Sam Wolstenholme's Barrack 9. John Collinson went to Barrack 2, and Frank Heath went to Barrack 7. Oates Lithgow and Steve Sams had moved to join Wyndham Richards in Barrack 10.

Meanwhile, Fred Pentland had moved from Barrack 10 to Barrack 11 to join Bloomer – or perhaps to get away from Richards and the other public school boys, with whom he was never a comfortable fit. Richards replaced him as Barrack 10 football captain. Jack Cameron, the oldest of the pros at 43, stepped back from barrack football, although he continued to play in exhibition matches, and remained, in Pentland's words, "the guiding spirit" of the Ruhleben FA.

For this season, there would be "home" and "away" fixtures, and it was expected that each team would play a game approximately every four days. League matches would be restricted to one of Ruhleben's two football pitches, and men who were not selected to play for their barracks would have the opportunity to play in friendly games on the free pitch.

"Taking it for granted that the ground is open from 9 to 11.30 am and from 2 to 5 pm, we have five and a half playing hours per day," wrote Pentland. "This gives 39 hours a week for non-league players, or three hours for each barrack. It will be seen, therefore, that non-league players will really have more football than those who are playing for their barracks."

"Well boys," declared the camp magazine ahead of the first match, "football has begun, and here's to a jolly and final season in Ruhleben!" Unfortunately, the season began with controversy. The vote to select the England and The Rest teams had been rigged. According to the Ruhleben FA, "a few enthusiasts" had selected two teams and then "jellygraphed" or duplicated their forms, which helped explain the huge number of responses. "In reference to the teams nominated by the readers of your paper," said a statement from the FA, "we regret that we cannot accept their choice, as in our opinion the selection does not represent the real views of the camp on this matter."

The magazine's editor responded that the FA had "no justification whatsoever for not keeping its word, for we were given a guarantee that the teams chosen by our readers should be played." It was all a bit of a mess, but the result was that "England v The Rest" became "Bloomer's XI v Cameron's XI", with the teams chosen by the old internationals. After two days spent preparing the pitches, the exhibition match was played on 3 October.

In the event, the selected teams did not differ too much from those chosen in the vote. Bloomer's XI had Harry Palin in goal, Jimmy Quinn at centre-half, and a formidable front five consisting of Bloomer, Pentland, Clem Burnill, Ernest Perry and Bobby Slade. Cameron's XI had Dundee-born student Gordon Nicoll in goal, Bob Stewart at the back, Jack Brearley and George Rogans at half-back, and John Collinson alongside Cameron up front. Sam Wolstenholme missed out with a cold, while Edwin Dutton – who had missed the entire summer of sport – was still recovering from his broken arm. Wyndham Richards watched the match but didn't play.

Another spectator was "Young Bird", a new football columnist for *In Ruhleben Camp*. "Cricket may be the 'noble old English pastime' and all that sort of thing, but without doubt this is the football age," he wrote. "Something short and strenuous, a buzz of excitement, and a chance to exercise the lungs is the demand made by the English crowd of today, and the Ruhleben crowd is no exception. There was something in the faces of the men and the air and the whole place that was reminiscent of an English bank holiday, a fresh, snug Sunlight-soap sort of feeling with everybody looking quite satisfied with the world and himself, but careful not to let his feelings get the better of his decorum. The weather was ideal, the ground good and the crowd big, what more could the football enthusiast ask?"

Baron von Taube once again agreed to kick the match off and "things commenced with a bustle". As might have been expected, the professionals were the standout performers. Bloomer and Pentland "took the brunt of the work" and Brearley and Cameron "showed a mastery of the game". Pentland's crossing and Brearley's "wonderful vigour" drew particular praise. There was praise, too, for Stewart and goalkeeper Nicoll and their efforts to suppress Bloomer and his fellow forwards. Cameron was so impressed with Stewart that he promised to arrange a trial when they got home. Nicoll, who had never kept goal before coming to Ruhleben, also fully justified his inclusion. "He brought off several remarkable saves," wrote Young Bird, "and who can blame the lad if he lets a couple through off that terrible old head of Bloomer's."

In the end, Bloomer's XI won 5-2. Stewart's man-of-the-match efforts against Bloomer and Pentland saw him awarded "the palm of the game". "Altogether it was a good match," said Young Bird, " much better than the opening games of last season, and given decent weather we ought to see some really fine football on the course this year."

Despite its largely enthusiastic tone, Young Bird's match report caused controversy due to its criticism of two players – Collinson and Rogans. According to the pseudonymous critic, Bootle-born hotel waiter Collinson was "woefully inefficient and spent most of his time offside", while fellow Merseysider Rogans, formerly of Garston Gasworks in the Liverpool County Football Combination amateur league, was "an absolute passenger throughout".

Fred Pentland wrote a letter of complaint to *In Ruhleben Camp*, which published a four-page debate on the issue. "While granting that he has every right to express his opinion of the game and the players, I consider some of the remarks in reference to some of the players to be outside the bounds of criticism," wrote Pentland. "To slate a man as Young Bird did Rogans and Collinson is rather hitting below the belt." According to Pentland, both were young players who had proved their ability in camp football and did not deserve such "condemnation". It was the aim of the Ruhleben FA to teach and improve such young players, said Pentland, "but all efforts will be in vain if Young Bird or anyone else knocks the stuffing out of them by passing such caustic and hurtful comments when they have a day off".

Young Bird was given the right to reply. "I am exceedingly surprised that a player of Mr Pentland's standing should take up an attitude with regard to criticism which I can only define by the phrase 'namby-pamby'," he wrote. The suggestion that he was "hitting below the belt" was, according to Young Bird, "absurd", as it was his duty to give an honest opinion on what he had seen. "For shame, Mr Pentland, you too have lost your mental perspective in Ruhleben," he wrote. "If Mr Pentland plays a rotten game in Ruhleben – and all things are possible in this most wonderful of worlds – I shall have to say so. Will Mr Pentland's spirit be broken and the stuffing taken out of him for subsequent games? If so, it is time he gave up football and took to croquet."

Instead, it was Young Bird who gave up football – or at least football writing. His pseudonym never appeared in the camp magazine again, and his identity remained unknown to most – perhaps all – of the camp. Pentland seemed to have no idea who the columnist was, although he had an increasing number of critics, particularly among his former barrack-mates, for his demanding captaincy style. But, if Young Bird was one of the boys from Barrack 10, Wyndham Richards never mentioned it in his diary. Whoever he was, Young Bird flew away, and football in Ruhleben continued without his critical eye.

For the next week, the pitches were given over to practice, with each team getting four hours to train and select their best sides. The second league season kicked off on 11 October 1915 and, according to Bloomer, it was a "tip-topper". The opening match was between Hugo Dixon's Barrack 7 and Bloomer and Pentland's Barrack 11. Barrack 11 won 4-1 but, according to Wyndham Richards, the crowd's negative reaction "demonstrated Pentland's unpopularity". A few days later, Barrack 11 lost 3-1 to Lionel Warner's Barrack 8. "Crowd delighted to see Pentland and Bloomer combination lose," wrote Richards.

Meanwhile, Richards' Barrack 10 were winning. They won 6-1 against Barrack 2, with Ernest Perry scoring five goals, then won 3-1 against Barrack 7 in a "very fast, hard game". They "won easily", 4-0, against Barrack 17, then came back from a goal down to win 2-1 against Barrack 3.

"Whole team not quite so good," wrote Richards, "but Barrack 3 played spoiling game." On 27 October, Richards scored the winning goal in a 2-1 victory over Barrack 20. But, on the following day, football came to a halt after the prisoners woke to find the camp covered in three inches of snow. Winter had returned with a vengeance.

Although the camp had changed substantially since the previous winter, with the steam heating system installed in the barracks, and the lofts cleared, it was still bitterly cold. "Temperature of barracks cruel to live in," wrote one prisoner. The return of winter reminded many in Ruhleben that they had now been incarcerated for a full year. 6 November, the first anniversary of the date the majority had first arrived in the camp, was marked with the release of around 150 prisoners who, it was determined, were not really British. Some of them were PGs, and many of them did not speak English. As they left the camp, the guards shouted, *"Auf wiedersehen!"*

One of those released was John Crerar, who was born in Glasgow but had moved to Germany as a child with his parents. He was very much not a PG. He had lived in Flensburg for 25 years and had a German wife and two children, but his time in Germany had "in no degree diminished his British sympathies and feelings". Crerar was released on health grounds and repatriated to Scotland. When he arrived in Glasgow, a doctor told him "if I had been four weeks longer in the camp it would have finished me." His wife, children and parents remained in Germany, and he had no idea when he would see them again.

Back in the camp, it was impossible to play football due to the bad weather, so the men stuck to indoor pursuits, playing card and board games, attending lectures and participating in debates ("votes for women" was one topic) and listening to concerts and watching plays (including a French production, *L'Anglais tel qu'on parle* – "not very good," according to Richards).

Fred Pentland encouraged the men to take advantage of the many available learning opportunities rather than wander aimlessly around the closed playing field. "Fortunately, for a great number of those here it is in their nature to take advantage of our present compulsory inactivity by studying," he wrote. "The events which have placed some of the most brilliant scholars in Europe in this camp and their generous willingness to give those desiring it the benefit of their knowledge creates a unique opening for those who wish to broaden their education."

When football resumed, during a temporary improvement in the weather, Barrack 10 got another 2-1 win, in a "very, very hard and enjoyable game" against Barrack 5. Then came their clash with Pentland and Bloomer's Barrack 11. Richards played centre-half in a "tense and exciting" match played in front of a "tremendous" crowd. In his diary, Richards didn't mention Pentland, but he could not hide his admiration for Bloomer.

"Bloomer, playing marvellously, was instrumental in defeating us 2-1," wrote Richards. "His generalship was superb, and his play." But one familiar aspect of Bloomer's character was not so admirable. "His language was appalling," wrote Richards. "He cursed us right and left. Quite frightened Perry and Lithgow, who were quite off the game." Ernest Perry was so frightened that he missed a penalty.

Bloomer, now approaching his 42nd birthday, had

modified his game during his year in Ruhleben. "Bloomer does not run about much nowadays," wrote a prisoner named JR Cottell in a letter home, "but for all that, he scored some pretty head goals and he has been a very good coach for his team. He coaches his men more than anything else. He does not do much actual work himself in midfield. But if there is a goal to be headed he is there."

Wyndham Richards' Barrack 10 lost again in the following week in a bad-tempered clash with Sam Wolstenholme's Barrack 9, the league leaders. Barrack 10 were winning 1-0 with five minutes left to play, but a mistake by Tom Sullivan allowed Barrack 9 to equalise, then another goal from a free-kick gave them the win. "Excitement was intense," wrote Richards, "and Barrack 9, who had not lost or drawn, lost their tempers completely. Sam Wolstenholme and myself were at loggerheads and I flatter myself I gave him as good as he gave."

Bad behaviour was not always ignored by Ruhleben's football authorities. During November, Bradley Heath, who had previously been the captain of Barrack 6 but now played for Barrack 20, was suspended indefinitely from all matches and practices by his Barrack's selection committee due to a "most unsportsmanlike display" in a game against the Boys' team. He was also banned from using barrack property for rugby or any other sport.

Not that there was much sport being played. During December, the temperature stayed below freezing, and the football calendar was regularly interrupted due to snow. A coal shortage meant heating and hot water were cut off three times that month.

As Christmas approached, the number of parcels arriving in the camp increased. For the parcel workers, there were only occasional opportunities for recreation. They were now able to listen to music while they worked. McGill had obtained a gramophone and some records. And, when weather allowed, there was football. Wyndham Richards played for a Parcel Post team against Letter Post team and scored twice on a 4-3 win. During the week before Christmas, Richards and his colleagues worked day and night to distribute 15,000 parcels. Christmas puddings and tins of custard and stewed pairs were popular festive treats, along with regular staples such as butter, condensed milk and Veda long-life bread ("stands transport and keeps fresh").

Richards' own "wants" list, sent to friends and family at home, included bacon, tea and candles, plus reprints of covers from *Nash's Magazine*, which featured colour images of glamourous women painted by artist Harrison Fisher. Richards particularly wanted a picture called "A Fair Breeze" but was happy to receive others – "the prettiest, of course".

The prisoners' second Christmas Day in Ruhleben was more comfortable than the first. Their accommodations were a little warmer and less crowded, there were no guards in the barracks to dampen the celebrations, and they had plenty of food and drink, courtesy of parcels from home. Richards' Christmas dinner was a "big feed" starting with soup, then chicken, peas and potatoes, followed by pudding and custard, then mince pies. The men in Richards' box also had alcohol – Madeira and white wine. In the evening, Richards was allowed to spend an hour in the Casino where he drank vermouth and beer. Several of his friends, he said, were "very, very boozed".

Alcohol was still prohibited, but there was an active

trade in smuggled wine, spirits and beer. Much of the smuggled drink came via the Casino, which selected prisoners could access with a temporary pass, usually issued as a reward for work done in connection with the administration of the camp. The main smugglers were the guards, who diverted supplies away from the Casino or brought contraband from Berlin to supplement their meagre pay. One of the smugglers, a guard named Pyrro, had already been sentenced to 72 hours' solitary confinement for "treating prisoners as if they were his personal friends" when he was caught smuggling and dismissed from the camp. On the night he left, Pyrro went around the barracks handing boiled sweets to the prisoners.

Count Schwerin, while lenient on many matters, was particularly strict when it came to alcohol – although he was not teetotal. On one occasion, he rode into the camp in his carriage and began to lecture a group of men on the evils of alcohol before announcing that any guard found smuggling alcohol would be court-martialled. He had no idea that hidden under his seat were a dozen bottles of brandy, smuggled into the camp by the guard who was driving his carriage.

On New Year's Eve, the extent to which alcohol was being smuggled into Ruhleben became evident. Wyndham Richards worked in the parcel office until 5 pm, then went to the Casino, where he drank four bottles of beer in half an hour. Then he went back to the parcel office, where he drank more beer and listened to gramophone records. At around 9 pm, a sing-song began, and the men began to down whisky and sodas. By 11.15, Richards felt "unaccountably bad". In his own words, he "spewed heart and soul up, and teeth, down bog".

"Feeling awful, awful, awful," wrote Richards in his diary. "Nearly whole camp drunk." There was singing and yelling, and a big crowd in Trafalgar Square. A makeshift band played tunes on empty tin cans, and drunken prisoners made bawdy speeches. Prisoners and guards were seen to embrace. One prisoner staggered around in a German uniform, and another relieved a sentry and took his place on watch. The excitement and "general hell" continued until four or five in the morning. By that time, Richards had staggered to his bed. "God," he wrote, "some end."

Over Christmas and New Year, the prisoners enjoyed a pantomime, *Cinderella*, starring the camp's favourite comedian Harry Stafford, from *Stiffy the Goalkeeper*. The show's songs included *It's a Long Way to Walk to Spandau*, *Ruhleben Girl* and *Stewed Prunes and Prisms*. Another song, *I'm Shy, Cinderella, I'm Shy*, sung by Stafford, was "a great hit" – as later recalled by Steve Bloomer, who was a big fan of Stafford's comedy. The pantomime was such a success that it ran for three weeks.

Other Christmas attractions included a performance of *A Christmas Carol* by the Debating Society, and a packed carol service in the grandstand. A new YMCA hall – a large wooden hut that could hold 500 people – was erected between Barracks 2 and 11 by 100 volunteers and opened on Christmas Eve. The former Rangers footballer Alex Bodin headed a committee that provided a programme of lectures, bible classes and prayer meetings, plus various informal entertainments.

The best Christmas treat, however, was given to 90 seafarers aged over 55 or under 17 – including several of "the Boys" – who were sent home.

At the end of 1915, the halfway point of the second football season, Sam Wolstenholme's Barrack 9 were top of the league ahead of Wyndham Richards' Barrack 10. The invincible Barrack 9, with Wolstenholme backed by the likes of Slade, Treseder and Quinn, had won all ten of their matches, scoring 33 goals while conceding just 4.

Wolstenholme reckoned several of his players were good enough to deserve trials for English league clubs. "It would hardly do for me to mention names," he said, "but there are men here who I shall certainly recommend to first-class clubs when the proper time arrives." Interviewed by Pentland for the camp magazine, Wolstenholme acknowledged the support given by the camp to the game and to his team, and remarked that he didn't know what we would have done without football.

Steve Bloomer also praised his fellow footballers in an interview for the magazine. "Why, the lads all play grand," he said. "Some of them would, of course, do better if they'd play with their heads a little more and if the forwards would shoot oftener and not mess about so much in front of goal. But, the football they play is marvellous considering everything, and it would be grossly unfair to criticise them very minutely. Give them the opportunity and a bit of the right coaching and one or two of the lads here would be class enough for any team."

The first half of the season had not been without casualties. The camp magazine listed 15 football injuries that had occurred during the first three months of the season, involving ankles, knees, elbows, shoulders, ribs, eyes, ears and a spine. There would be more injuries to come.

The camp magazine also printed a complaint made by walkers about footballs that were being kicked onto the running track and ruining their strolls. "It is no fun to receive a football to the face, no matter how great the hilarity which follows," wrote the complainant. With recreation so restricted, it was "a real injustice to pedestrians" to rob them of the enjoyment of walking. "Will those persons whose somewhat thoughtless enthusiasm is the cause of this annoyance take a friendly hint, and give others fair play?"

Football resumed, despite hangovers, on New Year's Day morning with an England v Scotland amateurs match. The only professional permitted to play was Cameron. "This was a necessary rule," explained Steve Bloomer, "as the English side, besides having the greater number of men from whom to choose a team, had five professionals on whom they could have called." Cameron was allowed to play because, according to Bloomer, "it was generally conceded that his real playing days were behind him". Bloomer was the referee, and Pentland and Brearley were the linesmen.

With kick-off time approaching there was no sign of the Scotland team. Then, with a wail of bagpipes, the Scots appeared, led by a piper in a kilt. Scotland won the match 3-2 with a late goal in what Bloomer called "one of the closest games I have witnessed during the whole of my football career".

The start of the second half of the league season was delayed by a combination of snow, frost and heavy rain. Jack Cameron suggested suspending the league until March when interruptions would be less likely and the pitches might be more playable. But football was too important to be delayed for long and, despite the weather, the league resumed in the second week of January.

Pentland said Barrack 9's big lead had "robbed the competition of a certain amount of interest". "No other team has got a ghost of a chance of preventing them from winning the league comfortably," he said. According to Pentland, the only barrack capable of giving them a run for their money was his former home, Barrack 10. "But 10 always remind me of an epitaph I once heard suggested for a man at home: 'he lived a life of going-to-do, and died with nothing done'. They have a side on paper and on the field equal to any in the camp; and yet for some reason they never quite 'get there'."

Pentland's criticism of Barrack 10 seemed fair after they were well-beaten on a muddy pitch 6-2, to the great amusement of the spectators, by Jack Swift's Barrack 2, who were bottom of the league before the break. But the most remarkable of the January league games was between Barrack 11 and Barrack 8. Bloomer and Pentland's Barrack 11 raced to a seemingly-unassailable 5-0 lead within 20 minutes, before Lionel Warner's Barrack 8 managed to pull back a couple of goals to make the score 5-2 at half-time. Then Barrack 8, with none of the camp's recognised star players, staged an incredible second-half comeback, and eventually won 6-5.

Letters and particularly parcels remained lifelines for the Ruhlebenites, providing emotional and physical sustenance. There were 39,994 parcels received in the camp in January 1916. That month, Pentland wrote a postcard to his brother, Malcolm, in Birmingham requesting tea, sugar, jam, currant bread, condensed milk and cigarettes. "Dear Old Generous Brother," he wrote. "All your splendid messages and all your nice parcels have reached me and are more appreciated than I have words to express... All my fondest love to mother and all."

A few weeks later, the Birmingham *Sports Argus* printed a request from a friend of Pentland asking local clubs to send parcels for the Ruhleben footballers. "We have plenty of proof of how cheerful they try to be in their concentration camp, football being their chief pleasure," wrote the friend, "but I also know they require something to keep the body and soul together."

The *Argus* added its support. "I should like to point out that Fred is helpless," wrote the paper's football columnist. "He is there through no fault of his own. He is not allowed to do anything to better his life. Now it is all very well to sympathise with Fred, but sympathy in words will not relieve his wants." The *Argus* donated "a sum of money" for the purpose of sending some parcels to Pentland, and asked local clubs and any "old Birmingham friends" to send "a few comforts". The paper gave his address as: *Fred Pentland, Prisoner of War, Barrack 11, Kriegs-Gefangennenlager, Ruhleben, via Spandau, Germany.*

All of the prisoners' correspondence was censored, and the officer responsible for that task was Baron von Mutzenbecher. Rather than being maligned for his work, von Mutzenbecher was the most popular officer in the camp. This was because, in addition to redacting war talk and other sensitive information, he went out of his way to ensure messages reached family and friends. On occasion, von Mutzenbecher would write to the mothers of prisoners to assure them of their sons' well-being. According to Captain Powell, von Mutzenbecher was "both a gentleman and a sportsman" who "always took a sympathetic interest in the camp sports". And, said Powell, one of his remarks, made at the end of a "hotly-contested" football match, "endeared him to all who heard it". "When I see how you play football," said von Mutzenbecher, "I quite understand how it is that we have failed to beat your 'contemptible little army'."

At the end of January 1916, Ruhleben's footballers were shocked by a snippet of news that reached the camp from the Western Front. It concerned the famous Chelsea forward Vivian Woodward, who had played alongside Bloomer, Pentland and Wolstenholme for England (scoring 29 goals in just 23 appearances), and had played under Cameron during a spell at Tottenham Hotspur.

Woodward played as an amateur, so wasn't tied to a club contract. At the outbreak of the war, while professional football continued, Woodward joined the 17th Battalion of the Middlesex Regiment, known as the Football Battalion. After the Football League was suspended, Woodward and his fellow amateurs were joined by many professional players. Frank Buckley, Jack Cock and Walter Tull were among the other notable footballers who joined the battalion.

Woodward attained the rank of captain and travelled with the Football Battalion to France in October 1915. By January, they were on the front line, living and fighting in the trenches. During a two-week period, the battalion suffered four fatalities and 33 injuries. One of those injured was Woodward, who was wounded by shrapnel during a grenade attack. The news was reported widely back in Britain. "If it is true that both his thighs have been seriously pierced by shrapnel," said the *Star Green 'Un* sports paper, "then we are afraid that his footballing days are over."

Woodward was evacuated back to England, where he made a remarkably swift recovery. By August, he was back on the front line, at the Somme. He survived the war, but many of his pals – including Walter Tull – did not. According to Frank Buckley, who was seriously wounded during the Somme offensive, 500 of the Football Battalion's original 600 men were killed in action during the war or died later as a result of their injuries or the effects of gas.

The news of Woodward's injury represented a double blow to the morale of the footballers in Ruhleben. First, there was distress that a friend and teammate had been badly wounded. Second, there was frustration that fellow footballers were fighting for their country while the Ruhlebenites were stuck behind fences. Many of those in Ruhleben were desperate to get out and fight against the forces that had incarcerated them. They felt entirely useless. A notice was placed on the football page of the camp magazine: "The hand of sympathy from everyone in Ruhleben will go out to Vivian Woodward, the fine gentleman and brilliant footballer."

Although football remained important in Ruhleben, the multitude of other activities now available meant it was perhaps less vital than it had been during the earliest months of the camp. "The players are not taking the same keen interest in football that they did when the game was first introduced here," wrote Fred Pentland in the camp magazine, noting that the men could occupy their time "in much more useful channels". "A year ago it was different," he wrote. "Sport was then practically everything to us, but at present sport just fills its proper function among us, which is the provision of healthy exercise."

The same issue of the *Ruhleben Camp Magazine* – newly-renamed from *In Ruhleben Camp* after being placed under the control of the Education Committee – provided multiple examples of alternative activities organised by the school, the theatre, the musical society, the debating society, the YMCA, the chess club, the arts and science union, the horticultural society, the history circle, the nautical circle and more. The renamed magazine retained its stiff-upper-lip humour and remained extremely popular, selling several thousand copies of each edition, with some prisoners buying multiple copies at 30pf each to send home.

A set of magazines was sent to George V, prompting a response from Buckingham Palace: "These have been laid before the King, who has received them with deep interest, but with increased feelings of sympathy for those of his subjects who, during their internment, are displaying such pluck and cheerfulness."

Eventually, the magazines came to the attention of the British press, who reported on the camp's myriad of activities and seemed to take the ironic humour presented in the magazine at face value. In February, the *Daily Mail* reported that the prisoners were "featherbed heroes" enjoying an easy life in Ruhleben while their fellow countrymen suffered at home and on the fronts. Then the *Daily News* criticised the "lazy interned Britons" who "sit in deck chairs and listen to concerts, attend the cinema and theatre" and refused to do any work.

The prisoners were furious. While conditions had undoubtedly improved – due largely to their own hard work and ingenuity – Ruhleben remained a prison camp and not a holiday camp. The captains immediately banned camp magazines from being sent home to Britain. The anger over how the Ruhlebenites were perceived back at home would continue to simmer for the remainder of the war.

Ironically, newspaper tales of the idyll that was Ruhleben appeared at a particularly difficult time for the prisoners, because winter was once again squeezing its grip on the camp. The pond was entirely frozen, and so were the playing fields – causing further suspensions of football. The game eventually resumed on 3 March 1916 with another exhibition match, Bloomer's XI v Cameron's XI. Bloomer's team, featuring Pentland and Brearley, beat Cameron's team, with Hartley and Wolstenholme, 4-3 in front of a big crowd. "Many people I spoke to consider it was the best game ever seen in Ruhleben," said Pentland.

In the league, leaders Barrack 9 won 2-1 in a hard match against Barrack 4, then won 7-3 against Barrack 5, with Harold Owen starring in front of goal. A 1-0 win over Barrack 7 followed before, finally, Barrack 9 dropped their first point of the season when they drew 0-0 with Barrack 8. But few football enthusiasts believed Barrack 9 could be caught in the race for the title. The only other team that had a chance was their next opponent – Wyndham Richards' Barrack 10.

"The Great Match of the Ruhleben Footer Season" – according to Richards – was played on Sunday 2 April between top-of-the-league Barrack 9 and second-place Barrack 10. It was a "terrifically exciting game" played in front of almost the whole camp. It was goalless at half-time, but in the second, Barrack 10, playing into the wind and sun, took the lead. Then Barrack 9 equalised with a penalty, "wrongly given against us for hands" – again according to

Richards. But, five minutes from time, McGill scored for Barrack 10. "Must have heard the shout in Berlin!" said Richards. "We won 2-1. Everyone delighted."

Unfortunately for Richards, Barrack 10 lost their next two games, ending any semblance of a title race. They slipped down the league and finished fourth. It was Sam Wolstenholme's Barrack 9 who were crowned champions of the second Ruhleben Football League. That meant Bobby Slade, George Treseder and Jimmy Quinn had all won the league twice in consecutive seasons – first with Bloomer's Barrack 1 and now with Wolstenholme's Barrack 9.

Barrack 9 also won the second Ruhleben Cup competition, to claim a unique "double". Baron von Taube presented the team with a silver cup bearing the inscription: *"Camp for Britishers interned in Ruhleben, Germany. Cup presented to Barrack 9 team, 1915-16."*

Following the league and cup campaigns, there were several friendly matches, including Ruhleben v Mercantile Marine, and Parcel Office v Pentland's XI. To Richards' delight, the Parcel Office won the latter game 5-3. But it was another friendly match against another set of prisoners that really captured the attention of Ruhleben's footballers – although it would not go as they had planned.

Döberitz was a prisoner of war camp located around six miles west of Ruhleben that held British, French, Russian and Polish POWs. Most of the British prisoners were members of the Royal Naval Division who were captured at Antwerp in 1914. Like the Ruhlebenites, the "Doberidgers", as they called themselves, had attempted to shape a society within the confines of their camp, albeit with fewer freedoms and resources than their civilian counterparts.

Döberitz had carpenters, cobblers, tailors, a post office, a theatre, an orchestra and a camp magazine – *The Link*. The prisoners spent their time playing cards, knitting and, of course, playing football. The game in Döberitz was not as well organised as it was in Ruhleben, and was played with "anything kickable... ranging from misshapen footballs to empty tins". "Sporting challenges are frequent," reported *The Link*, "even if most have to be played out on the fields of the imagination."

One day, "by some mysterious means", news reached the Ruhleben FA that the prisoners at Döberitz had got together a good football team. "It was immediately suggested by someone that a crack team from our camp should be chosen and make the journey to play them," said Steve Bloomer. The idea was passed to Captain Powell, who approached Baron von Taube, who, in turn, applied to the authorities in Berlin. "To give the old man credit, he must have placed the proposition in a favourable light," said Bloomer. Permission was granted for a 16-man squad to travel from Ruhleben to Döberitz for a "Civvies v Tommies" football match.

Preparations began immediately, and a representative squad was selected. It included all seven of Ruhleben's playing professionals – Bloomer, Brearley, Cameron, Dutton, Hartley, Pentland and Wolstenholme – plus the most highly-rated amateurs, including "crack goalkeeper" Gordon Nicoll, Bob Stewart, Bobby Slade, Oates Lithgow and Clem Burnill. The Ruhleben FA made contact with their counterparts at Döberitz, and received "highly gratifying letters expressing their joy at the prospective match".

It was swiftly arranged that the match would be played on the following Sunday. However, on the day before the match, the "Civvies" squad were training on one of the football pitches when Captain Powell approached, "his mouth drooping at the corners". "Boys," he told them, "tomorrow's game is off. Berlin have put their foot on the scheme." There was huge disappointment among the Ruhleben footballers, and no doubt even greater disappointment in Döberitz, where alternative distractions were much fewer. "Berlin never volunteered any reason for cancelling this fixture," said Bloomer, "and I have no idea why they did so."

The idea of a prisoner of war football team leaving their camp to play an exhibition match is somewhat reminiscent of the plot of the 1981 movie *Escape to Victory* (known as *Victory* in the US). Directed by John Huston, the bank holiday TV favourite stars Michael Caine, Sylvester Stallone and Pelé – plus numerous other real footballers – as Allied prisoners of war in a German prison camp during the Second World War. In the movie, the prisoners stage an escape attempt while playing a match against a German Wehrmacht team. With the escape planned for half time, the Allies postpone the attempt and go back on the pitch in an effort to win the match. Featuring British prisoners of war playing football surrounded by armed guards, *Escape to Victory* does have several parallels with the true story of the Ruhleben FA. But, back in 1916, the Ruhleben team did not get to go to Döberitz and did not have the opportunity to stage a real *Escape to Victory*.

Ruhleben's second football season closed on 30 April 1916 with a match between Brearley's XI and Pentland's XI. Richards played for Brearley's team and said he played "quite well", but Pentland's team won 5-3. Unfortunately, the back end of Ruhleben's second football season was overshadowed by an incident that proved a big blow to camp football – and explained why it was "Brearley's XI" and not "Bloomer's XI" that played in the closing match.

In one of the final games of the season, Steve Bloomer suffered a bad knee injury. While Pentland and Cameron were the main organisers of the Ruhleben Football Association, Bloomer was its inspirational leading man, driving its success through his brilliance and enthusiasm. He was, undoubtedly, Ruhleben's biggest star, and he drew players and spectators to the game, expanding its remarkable popularity. As one unnamed prisoner wrote in a letter home: "Whenever Steve Bloomer appeared in a football match at Ruhleben the attendance was always greater than at any other time." Without him, camp football would surely suffer.

News of the injury soon reached Britain. "*Steve Bloomer Hurt*," read one newspaper headline. "*Steve Bloomer Crippled*," said another. According to one report, Bloomer had twisted his knee so badly that "his further appearance on the field is an improbability". Another said Bloomer had suffered an injury that "incapacitates him for the remainder of his life". That report quoted a letter from a fellow prisoner, who said the injury represented "a sad end for a man after such a remarkable career". However, like much regarding Ruhleben that was reported at home, news of Bloomer's demise was grossly exaggerated.

10

Unpleasant Moments

It was the summer of 1916, and Count Schwerin was guiding an American visitor on a tour of Ruhleben Camp. In the manner of a proud parent, Schwerin pointed out the many improvements that had been made. The barracks were warmer and less crowded, there were new latrines and wash houses, and the kitchens and canteens had been improved. The parcel office was bustling (it had recently distributed its 500,000th parcel), Bond Street's multitude of traders were doing brisk business in all manner of goods and services, and the YMCA and other communal huts and halls were full of activity. On the playing fields, men played tennis on the sandy courts, cricket on the matted pitches, and golf on the five-hole course.

Ruhleben seemed a remarkably civilised and contented place in the middle of a tumultuous war, and the visitor was suitably impressed, but Schwerin told him: "You mustn't suppose that the camp was always like this. When the men were first brought here, the place wasn't fit to keep pigs in. All that you have admired in the camp they have themselves created."

Steve Bloomer returned to camp sport following his knee injury in August in a three-day cricket match. "I have not been too grand lately, but am picking up again now," he wrote in a letter home. "Our games make us for a while forget our troubles." Bloomer's side won the match and he scored 129 not out. "The crowd simply went mad and gave me a rare reception," he wrote. "You will see by my score that my knee is now all right again." That wasn't quite true. Bloomer was fit enough for cricket, but not yet for football – the return of which was already being anticipated.

Although so many of the Ruhlebenites loved football, and the game had proven to be an invaluable tonic, the approach of a new season was a disheartening reminder of the passing of time in what was becoming a seemingly endless incarceration. Jack Cameron expressed this sentiment in a letter he wrote to friends. "Our constant cry is 'How Long?' and we get utterly sick of each other," he said. "Must we be here for another football season? Surely not..."

The prisoners were not unaware of events outside of the barbed-wire fences. German newspapers arrived each day, and were translated into English for the *Ruhleben Daily News*, a one-sheet publication known in the camp as the *Daily Daily* for the regular morning sales call of *"Da-i-ly, Da-i-ly..."* yelled by its vendor, a popular little fellow called Tommy. But the men were wary of trusting news from the German media, particularly if that news was bad.

English newspapers were still banned, but they did reach Ruhleben, usually a week or two after publication. German guards purchased the English papers in Berlin for 1 mark, then sold them to prisoners in the camp for 10. Those prisoners then rented out their newspapers by the hour, and it was common to see men splitting the pages of borrowed papers between their barrack mates to ensure everyone got a read within the allotted time.

The men were able to read about the ferociously protracted Battle of Verdun – the longest battle in military history – and the dreadnought-led Battle of Jutland – the largest sea battle of the war. They also read about the death of Lord Kitchener, the Secretary of State for War (as depicted on the "Lord Kitchener Wants You" recruitment posters), who was killed alongside 736 others when the HMS *Hampshire* was sunk by a German mine. "War news still seems blinking bad," noted Wyndham Richards in his diary.

Then came news of the Battle of the Somme, which began on 1 July 1916. On the first day of the Somme offensive, Britain suffered 57,470 casualties, including 19,240 fatalities. Among those killed was Lieutenant Evelyn Lintott, the England international footballer who had played as a half-back for Queens Park Rangers, Bradford City and Leeds City. The Battle of the Somme would go on for another 140 days.

The muddy, bloody reality of what was happening some 500 miles west caused excitement, anxiety and depression in the camp, and there remained frustration from many that they were not able to participate in what was becoming an interminable struggle. Instead, they absorbed themselves in camp life with a mixture of guilt and relief. Flowers bloomed in the barrack gardens, frogs leapt around the pond on the playing fields, and swallows, storks and wild geese flew overhead. Men reclined in their deck chairs, reading novels and listening to gramophone records. The only shots they could fire were driven with golf clubs, tennis racquets or cricket bats.

All of the camp's distractions – football, cricket, plays, concerts – were very welcome, but they could not entirely insulate the prisoners from the miseries of war. "Although we prisoners in Ruhleben kept our spirits high and dry by sports and entertainments, our life was not all beer and skittles," said Bloomer. "There were many unpleasant moments."

One such unpleasant moment involved Alf Maw, a friend of Bloomer and one of the most popular footballers in the camp. Maw was a Londoner who had been working in France as a pharmacy manager. He was on honeymoon in Germany with his French bride when he was arrested. On his arrival in Ruhleben, he was described as inconsolable. "But my wife, what is to happen to her?" he asked Bloomer. "She is left out there all alone with no one to look after her." Bloomer and others pointed out that no amount of worrying would make her situation any better, but Maw remained in despair until the morning he received the glorious news that his wife had been allowed to leave Germany and return to France.

"Then he began to buck up and take an interest in life," recalled Bloomer. "He blossomed into a good footballer, playing outside left for Barrack 5, and gradually developed into one of the liveliest boys in the camp." Maw played for Wyndham Richards' "The Rest" team in the exhibition match held to mark the opening of the playing field and starred for Jack Brearley's Barrack 5 team when they won the first Ruhleben Cup. Bloomer had previously named Maw as one of the players he would select in a Ruhleben team that could give an English league reserve team a run for their money.

Then, in the summer of 1916, tragedy struck. Maw slept in the top of three bunks in one of the horseboxes in Barrack 5. One night, he turned over in his sleep and fell out of the bunk. "The distance from the floor to the third bunk was considerable," said Bloomer, "and, as he had fallen on to his head, he was knocked out altogether."

Maw's box-mates picked him up and hurried him to the Convalescent Barrack, where he was placed under the care of Mr Lambert. Maw remained in the hospital for eight weeks, and it was hoped he would make a recovery. He was seen to be walking about, but was cursing and ranting, and was described as having "went mad". It seemed he had sustained a serious head injury that could not be treated in the confines of the camp. Maw died on 4 July 1916, leaving his new wife as a widow. His death was a huge blow to the morale of Ruhleben's football community. And more deaths would follow. By the end of 1916, 50 prisoners had died in captivity in Ruhleben.

Another of Bloomer's "unpleasant moments" began with the arrival of Captain Charles Fryatt and around 36 members of the crew of the merchant navy vessel SS Brussels. Back in March 1915, the Brussels had encountered the German U-boat U-33 off the coast of the Netherlands. The submarine surfaced, and its commander hailed Captain Fryatt to stop. But Fryatt, expecting to be torpedoed, ordered the Brussels to proceed full steam ahead and rammed U-33, which was forced to crash-dive. In ramming the U-boat, Fryatt was obeying direct instructions issued to merchant navy captains by First Lord of the Admiralty Winston Churchill. Although he remained a civilian, Fryatt became regarded as something of a war hero.

Over a year later, on 25 June 1916, the Brussels was again off the coast of the Netherlands when it was surrounded by five German destroyers. Fryatt and his crew were arrested, and his ship was scuttled. The captain and his crew were sent to Ruhleben. They arrived early one morning and were taken to the canteen for food and hot coffee, before being distributed around the barracks.

"Unfortunately, I was not brought very much into contact with the heroic captain," said Bloomer. Fryatt kept himself to himself and spent a quiet month in the camp. Then, one evening, a rumour began to circulate that Fryatt was going to be tried for attempting to sink the German submarine. The camp's seamen, in particular, were furious, and they began to congregate in "angry little groups".

Early the next morning, before most of the prisoners were awake, Fryatt and six of his crew were paraded through the square towards the gates, escorted by heavily armed guards. Bloomer was one of the few prisoners who was out of bed and could see what was happening. Bloomer and the others rushed to the gates and cheered Fryatt and his men as they were led out of Ruhleben. "There was no sign of the white feather about Captain Fryatt," said Bloomer. Fryatt turned to acknowledge the cheers, then told Bloomer and the other prisoners: "Goodbye boys. I don't think you will see me again." And they would not.

Fryatt was tried at a court-martial in Bruges on 27 July 1916 and was found guilty of attempting to sink the submarine as a *franc-tireur* (a civilian combatant). According to German press reports, Fryatt was convicted as a result of having in his possession a watch inscribed with a tribute to his attempt to sink the sub. But the British Foreign Office said Fryatt had neither a watch nor any document with any such tribute. His six crew members, who were taken along as witnesses, were unable to save his life. He was sentenced to death – a sentence confirmed by the Kaiser. At 7 pm that evening, Fryatt was taken out onto the harbour and executed by firing squad.

"We only heard of his fate when a copy of an English newspaper was smuggled into the camp," said Bloomer. "And that night there was very nearly a riot. The two thousand seafaring men who were in the camp went looking for the Hun guards, who fortunately for themselves had been drawn to their own quarters. Our men swore they would have their revenge, but whilst they were searching the camp, several of the less emotional prisoners went among them and pointed out the futility of mutiny, and eventually succeeded in quieting them."

According to Davidson Ketchum, the death of Captain Fryatt changed the perception of many in the camp who had come to think of the war as occurring in another world. Ketchum wrote: "The judicial murder of a man who had lived in Ruhleben, if only for a month, caused deep shock and anger, and brought the war home to the camp as nothing had done before."

In September 1916, before the football resumed, the camp was shocked by the sudden departure of Baron von Taube. His belongings were hurriedly packed into biscuit tins and cardboard boxes, and he was bustled out of Ruhleben in a "most undignified" manner. None of the prisoners knew exactly why the hot-tempered *Lageroffizier* left. Wyndham Richards spoke to one of the guards, Janzen, who told him the Baroness was the cause of the Baron's departure. It seemed the Baroness had somehow upset the other officers, who told von Taube he must leave, or they would quit. Whatever exactly happened, it seemed the Baron was punished by the authorities in Berlin. Von Taube, despite his advancing years, was sent to Belgium and ended up on the Western Front.

Von Taube was replaced as camp officer by his former assistant, Rittmeister von Brocken. A thin, stooping figure in his late 50s, von Brocken was described as having "a stern and soured visage, and a harsh voice". He had previously worked in two other prisoner of war camps and had a reputation for brutality. However, Captain Powell regarded von Brocken as the most straightforward of the camp officers. When he said "no" he meant "no".

Count Schwerin remained as camp commandant for several months before he departed, too. Schwerin retired due to ill health and subsequently died following a throat operation. Although his management of the camp had often been incompetent, the Count was regarded on the whole as a fair and decent man. According to Captain Powell, Schwerin's death was "genuinely regretted in the camp". Schwerin was replaced as commandant by Lieutenant-Colonel von Reichenbach, who advised Powell on his arrival that he was happy for camp life to continue as it had before, as long as it was quiet and orderly.

After about a year, Rittmeister von Brocken left the camp, and von Reichenbach appointed as his deputy the "Young Count" Schwerin, Count Schwerin's son. The Young Count was generally as sympathetic to the prisoners as his father, although Powell said he was not as dignified and used "violent language". According to Powell, "his father had implored him, on his deathbed, to do his best for the interned".

Ruhleben's third football season began on 7 October 1916 with a now-traditional exhibition match. Cameron's XI, with Fred Pentland, George Treseder and Jimmy Quinn, beat Brearley's XI, with Percy Hartley, Bob Stewart and

Clem Burnill, 4-1. There was no place for Bloomer, whose injury would leave him frustrated on the sidelines for another few weeks. The league began on the following morning with a match between Barrack 4 and Barrack 10, but heavy rain caused the afternoon's match to be cancelled. Once again, winter weather played havoc with the Ruhleben FA's fixture list.

Barrack 9, the reigning league champions, made a strong start to the season. They were "easily the best team in the camp" according to Pentland. "They are strong in every position, and with Sam Wolstenholme's brilliant play and masterly tuition they are and deserve to be the outstanding team."

Elsewhere, Barrack 2 emerged as a "surprise team" who "only beat the good 'uns". Barrack 3 were regarded as the fastest side in the league. And Jack Brearley's "tireless energy and great ability" made Barrack 4 a team to be feared. Wyndham Richards' Barrack 10 made a winning start to the season although, as Pentland noted, "their jam has been in", including in a match with Barrack 7, where they luckily won 2-1 when their opponents had an equaliser dubiously ruled out for offside.

The biggest game of the season was a grand exhibition match played on 25 November to "welcome and honour" Bishop Herbert Bury, who was visiting Ruhleben from England. The match saw the return to football after injury of Steve Bloomer, who captained Bloomer's XI against Wolstenholme's XI. There were five professionals on the field. Pentland and Brearley played with Bloomer, and Hartley played with Wolstenholme. The Bishop reluctantly performed the kick-off, worrying he might have "rather let down the dignity of the Anglican Episcopate".

"It was a great day – perfect weather, beautiful blue sky flecked with white clouds and sunshine – with nearly the whole camp present," wrote the Bishop. "The play was very fast and very excellent, for the two teams were wonderfully matched. Steve Bloomer was said to distinguish himself even beyond his usual form and some of the younger players played with remarkable zest and rapidity." Bloomer scored the opening goal of the game in the first half, but Wolstenholme's team equalised in the second, "which brought the match to a very even and satisfactory end."

Bishop Bury also visited the men in their barracks, ate with them, and attended a chamber music concert, and said he thoroughly enjoyed the experience. "Never in all my life have I been so thankful, so happy and so proud of being an Englishman as I was with those men," he said on his return home. "We know what they have passed through, and now to see what British character, grit and determination, with the aid of people at home, have made of the camp, is one of the most wonderful things that an Englishman can witness."

Although Bishop Bury was popularly received in the camp, his subsequent written report was not. On the face of things, the Bishop did seem to describe the camp as he found it. He marvelled at the improvements the prisoners had made and the mini-society they had built, but he also noted the camp's failings, such as the inadequate rations and poor winter shelter. Parcels of food and clothing from home were essential, he said, and the men would "starve or freeze to death" without them. He also noted the mental effects of incarceration on the Ruhlebenites. "Two years of strain and restraint are beginning to tell on the strongest of prisoners," he said.

But many in Ruhleben baulked at the Bishop's descriptions of the positive aspects of camp life, which were highlighted in newspapers before the prisoners go to see the full report. The men had been stung by previous criticism and did not want people at home to think incarceration at Ruhleben represented an easy life. "I hear he painted the camp in glowing colours," wrote one prisoner, named Ewing, in a letter home. "We haven't had a copy here, but saw some of the English criticisms. Many have been down on him here for it, for their 'sufferings' are the men's most prized possessions and they'll give them up to nobody. There will be some terrible yarns told when we get home by some of our would-be martyrs."

Part of the problem was that the Bishop's visit coincided with a campaign by Sir Timothy Eden, the brother of future Prime Minister Anthony Eden, for the Ruhlebenites to be released in a wholesale prisoner exchange. Timothy Eden had spent 18 months in Ruhleben before being released in an individual exchange for a no doubt prominent German. Now he wanted the British and German governments to agree to exchange all 4,000 remaining prisoners held at Ruhleben for German civilians held in Britain.

Eden said the prisoners in Ruhleben were housed in "shanties" and fed "mangy potatoes", and the hospital conditions for sick prisoners were "shocking". "The confinement is beginning to seriously affect the people, and they ought to get out without delay," he told *The Times*. "Physically, they are moderately well, but from a mental point of view, there is occasion for alarm. Many of them could scarcely pass another winter in those quarters."

The positive spin surrounding the Bishop's visit somewhat undermined Eden's campaign, as did multiple contradictory reports from Germany. The British welfare campaigner Emily Hobhouse, who visited Ruhleben under the auspices of the German War Office, said the barracks were delightful, the food was excellent and the hospital was so nice that it almost made her wish to be ill. The American ambassador to Berlin, James Gerard, who had previously condemned Ruhleben, now spoke of the many improvements and said the authorities were doing all they could to ensure the welfare of the prisoners.

German newspapers, perhaps unsurprisingly, dismissed claims of harsh treatment and hardships. According to the *Vossische Zeitung*, tales of suffering were being circulated in order to increase sympathy and to encourage food and gifts to be sent from home. The Ruhlebenites dismissed these claims as fatuous and disingenuous. One former prisoner, the aptly-named Stephen Grimm, wrote to *The Times* and said of Ruhleben, "Hell could not be worse." "People who have not been there cannot realise the misery in that camp," he said.

In truth, while there had been many improvements, some aspects of life in Ruhleben had deteriorated – most notably the food. Germany had suffered from food shortages since the beginning of the war and, by 1916, staples such as flour, milk, potatoes, eggs and butter were severely rationed. Food shortages were worst in big cities such as Berlin, where citizens marched and rioted in protest at the lack of provisions. The people of Berlin were on the verge of starvation, and they were not about to give up precious supplies for British prisoners.

So the food in Ruhleben became even worse. One man

found a dog's claw in a meatball. When he complained to the authorities that it was made from dog meat, he was told that it was actually made from *good* dog meat. When the meat was withdrawn, the prisoners were served nothing more than boiled cabbage in water. Fortunately, many of the prisoners no longer relied on camp rations, and were fed via the parcel office. One prisoner remarked: "What the deuce will happen to us should the parcels from home fail, blessed if I know."

Then, in a stark illustration of how bad the food shortages were becoming in Berlin, the camp was invaded by a swarm of rats. The prisoners believed the hungry rats had "disloyally left their German homes for the well-fed enemy camp". Scores of stick-wielding men fought a campaign to wipe them out, assisted by a ferret and a terrier. Hundreds of rats were chased down and destroyed, while the frightened camp cats kept a wary distance.

The situation in Berlin was made clearer to the prisoners from mid-1916 when wives, mothers and children of interned men were allowed to visit for two hours every month. The prisoners and their loved ones had not seen each other for more than 18 months, and the first meetings were rather awkward. According to one prisoner, husbands and wives "seemed unable to talk at all for a long while, they felt so strange together". The wives brought distressing tales of the food shortages in Berlin. One prisoner went to one of the officers, Lieutenant Gliech, and asked for assistance for his young wife, who was practically starving. Gliech, described by Captain Powell as "a typical Prussian bully", refused the request and cruelly told the prisoner there was "no need for any young and pretty woman to starve in Berlin".

In December, Wyndham Richards' Barrack 10 played Sam Wolstenholme's league leaders Barrack 9. Wolstenholme's team scored an emphatic victory. "Got simply wiped to the tune of 5-0," wrote Richards. "All played badly." Richards was fed up. "I'm heartily sick of football and most other things," he wrote. He was working long hours at the parcel office in order to earn money to eat properly. And, in a depressing blow, Jessie James, the young woman who had been sending him letters and pictures from home, had written to tell him she was engaged. "You must find me someone else," he wrote to his brother.

Richards' diary entries, which had been daily rituals, became less regular. Then, on 15 December, he described an "event of great importance". Richards and fellow Tilly's boy DH Lee were allowed out of the camp to deliver parcels to the sanatorium in Charlottenberg. They were escorted by two guards, Strachmann and Glatter. When they got there, Richards left Lee and went with Strachmann and Glatter to a pub. There, they met two women, one of whom was called Trütchen. Richards and Trütchen got on very well. "Had a simply gorgeous time!" said Richards. "Oh, it was just grand to kiss again. Next time was promised something better." When Richards got back to Ruhleben he was "pretty drunk" and he had spent 45 marks. He immediately wrote home to ask for more money.

On Christmas Day, a seemingly-rejuvenated Richards played football, for a Land Lubbers team against the Seamen, and lost 2-1. Afterwards, he drank and ate, listened to the gramophone, sang and danced, and drank some more. In a great boost to morale, the sale of beer had now been authorised – perhaps in an effort to add some nutrition to the men's diet, given the lack of food. And a "wine line" was established, presumed to be for the purpose of disposing of cheap wine that had been accumulated during the war. That night, as he had been on the previous Christmas, Richards was "violently sick". "A splendid day," he wrote.

The New Year brought another boost to morale. US Ambassador Gerard visited the camp to announce that the British and German governments had arranged an exchange of prisoners over 45 years of age. Timothy Eden's campaign had apparently prompted some action and some of the Ruhlebenites, it seemed, would be going home.

Around 400 of the prisoners – ten per cent of the camp's population – were over 45, including the footballer Wattie Campbell. Unfortunately, the majority of them, including Campbell, would have to wait a little longer for their release. Sixty-five of them were released in January before the arrangement broke down and the American ambassador was withdrawn, with the US having broken off relations with Germany.

A couple of weeks later, during another parcel office trip to the sanatorium, Richards went with Strachmann to the house where Trütchen lived with her landlady. "Trütchen had everything on offer but I was being careful," he said. "We kissed to madness. It was wonderful. This Trütchen is a pretty girl and I really like her." The visit cost 96 marks, and Richards later paid Trütchen 5 marks for a photograph, suggesting that she charged for her services, perhaps professionally or perhaps, as Lieutenant Gliech had suggested, so that she would not starve. What happened on his next few visits is unknown, but in the following month Richards was complaining of "terrible pain in my 'tail'" and was using Boracic Powder on his genitals.

The winter months in early 1917 were the coldest the Ruhleben prisoners had experienced. The temperature plunged from minus 12 degrees celsius in January to minus 25 in February. Pipes froze and burst, and water and heating were cut off. The pond froze, and ice skating became the camp's most popular pastime. All other outdoor activities – and some indoor ones – were cancelled. Football was suspended until late March.

One freezing cold January night, the men were woken by a loud smash. Two goods trains had collided on the railway line outside of the camp, with sub-zero blizzard conditions likely to have been a factor in the accident. Russian prisoners of war were brought in to clear the wreckage. Then, later that same night, there was a huge explosion at the Spandau munitions works on the other side of the Spree. A cloud of dust billowed across the river, and debris showered the camp. The prisoners had to clear rubble and pieces of shrapnel from the playing field before football resumed.

Richard's first game back after the big freeze was for Barrack 10 against Barrack 2. "We won 2-1," said Richards, "but the forwards played a putrid game, and I was one of the worst." Richards lost 40pf by betting he would score. "Never looked like scoring," he wrote. "Was absolutely awful." In addition to the league, cup fixtures also resumed. Holders Barrack 9 were knocked out in extra time by Percy Hartley's Barrack 7, so there was set to be a new name on the cup.

The cup final was played on Easter Sunday, 8 April, between Barrack 8 and Barrack 20. Spring had very quickly sprung, and the match was played in "perfect" weather, and in front of more than 3,000 spectators. Lionel Warner's Barrack 8 were favourites, and they dominated the first half but failed to score. Barrack 20 "played like a different team" in the second, and five minutes from the end a mistake at the back allowed Mills to score for the underdogs. A wild cheer from the spectators greeted this success," wrote Fred Pentland, "because a British crowd dearly loves to see a weaker side conquer."

However, just before full-time, Nappin equalised for Barrack 8. "Again there was a mighty cheer as a tribute for Barrack 8 for pulling off what appeared to be a forlorn hope." Extra-time – 10 minutes each way – was played, but there were no more goals. The replay was played on the following Wednesday. "In comparison with the first game it was very disappointing," said Pentland. "Barrack 20 were by far the best team and eventually won by 3-0."

During the last few weeks of the football season, Steve Bloomer suffered the worst of his "unpleasant moments" in Ruhleben – worse than his knee injury, worse than the death of his friend Alf Maw, worse than the crushing realisation that the war might have no end. It was 5 May, and Bloomer was sitting in a deck chair reading a book and enjoying the spring sunshine. Fred Pentland approached and cheerfully tossed a letter into his lap. "From home, Steve," he smiled. Letters were generally a welcome tonic for the prisoners. But this one was not. Bloomer opened the letter, and his face – always pale – went completely white. "The shock," he said, "as the import of the message dawned upon me, just about put me out."

The letter, from Sarah, advised Bloomer that his beloved second daughter, Violet, was dead. Violet, "a dear, loveable girl" was just 17 years old. She had been ill for some time and had succumbed to kidney disease. "Although Mrs Bloomer had several times written and said that she was ill," recalled Bloomer, "I was quite unprepared for the shock of the news of her death."

Bloomer, for so long a talisman of resolve and resilience for his fellow prisoners, began to succumb to the deadly depression known as barbed-wire disease. "I got rather low spirited, and a sort of hopeless feeling that I should never survive the ordeal of captivity began to get a grip on me," he said. "I shunned everyone and everything, and was drifting to a fatal state of melancholy when my football chums intervened."

"One thing is sure," Percy Hartley told him, "and that is that you must start playing."

"I protested, but it was of no avail," Bloomer recalled. "The whole bunch would hear of nothing else but that I must turn out again, and I was simply forced to do it. Now I am glad that those real pals of mine were so insistent, because had I cut myself adrift from all interests I feel certain now that my reason would have gone."

Bloomer returned to football 11 days after receiving his devastating letter in what was the final league game of the season. The match, between Bloomer's Barrack 11 and Richards' Barrack 10, was played in "tremendous heat", with the weather having flipped from arctic to tropical. Bloomer lined up alongside his great mate Edwin Dutton, who had finally recovered from his broken arm. Bloomer and Dutton's Barrack 11 won 6-3, and Richards blamed his team's defeat on "poor back play and goalkeeping". "We were all over them but had rotten backs," Richards wrote.

Ultimately, the match did not have a bearing on the

league championship, but it was very significant for Steve Bloomer, and it demonstrated in no uncertain terms the power of football to combat the agonies and distresses of Ruhleben. But football was not a miracle cure. Football would not bring Violet back. Bloomer remained stricken with grief and would need to fight to pull himself out of his state of hopelessness.

At the end of the season, the league champions for the second consecutive time were long-time leaders Barrack 9. So Bobby Slade, George Treseder and Jimmy Quinn – who had all previously played for Barrack 1 – had now won the league in all three seasons in Ruhleben. George Rogans, the former Garston Gasworks footballer, paid tribute to his Barrack 9 captain. "We have had a long run of successes, and Sam Wolstenholme is the key to the whole machine," he said. "His coaching and advice to all of us has proved of great value. We are all very fond of the old Evertonian, both on and off the field."

In the aftermath of the football season, Wyndham Richards made several more diversions from the sanatorium into Berlin. Others tried to make a more permanent diversion. At the end of May, several prisoners attempted to escape. DP Hall went missing during a trip to the sanatorium. He reappeared two days later claiming to have been left behind by the guards. Fromm and Cressell from Barrack 2 "leapt it" – as the prisoners called climbing the fence – and managed to cross much of Germany, but were caught near Düsseldorf. Two other prisoners, Armstrong and Kaufmann, got out of the camp on what was their second escape attempt but were captured three days later. Then JE Norton went missing from the Tea House. Like the other escapees, he was captured and punished with 14 days in the Stadtvogtei – the municipal prison in the Molkenmarkt square in Berlin.

The flurry of escape efforts prompted a clampdown from the camp authorities. Appells or roll calls were increased to three times a day, at 7 am, 2 pm and 9 pm – which greatly annoyed the prisoners. The number of sentries at the top end of camp was increased from three to five. And any soldier catching an escaping prisoner was promised a reward of 20 marks plus 14 days leave.

Escaping from Ruhleben had become much more difficult and risky, but not everyone was deterred. "It's simply horrible, trying to get out," said Wyndham Richards. "But I am going to get out."

11

Bloomer's Hard Lot

While on a visit to London in the summer of 1917, a Swedish sports journalist "of strong pro-entente sympathies" met with the British football writer George Wagstaffe Simmons, who was also a member of the English FA council. During their conversation, the two men discussed the subject of Steve Bloomer's incarceration in Ruhleben. Bloomer was well known to the Swedish journalist, who suggested that it might be possible to secure the footballer's release into neutral Sweden by getting him a job there as a coach. On his return to Stockholm, the journalist approached the Swedish FA and the country's foreign office, and an urgent request for Bloomer's release was made via the Swedish ambassador in Berlin. Unfortunately, the request was refused.

"Every guarantee that the Huns might wish for was ordered through the Swedish office, but in vain, and poor Bloomer will have to go on languishing in his camp," wrote *Manchester Evening News* football columnist "JRC", under the headline *"Bloomer's Hard Lot"*. "If we had not shed so many of our illusions of Germany we might have thought that a sense of gratitude would have prompted the Huns to grant the request, for all Bloomer had done was teach their young men how to excel in one manly game."

Bloomer was still suffering. He was trapped in a black cloud of grief, in helpless mourning for Violet while separated from Sarah and the rest of his family by more than 600 miles of war-torn land and sea. The strain was showing. After a photograph of Bloomer surrounded by a group of Ruhleben footballers appeared in Liverpool's *Football Echo*, sports columnist "Bee" noted his "excessive sombreness". "Never altogether happy-looking, Bloomer looked very ill," wrote Bee.

With the changing of the season, the camp's focus switched once again from football to cricket. One of the highlights of the sporting summer was a "sensational" cricket match between Barrack 5 and The Rest of the camp. The latter team, featuring footballer Jack Brearley and sporting all-rounder John Masterman, was expected to win but did not – to the disappointment of spectators. The absence of Ruhleben's most popular sportsman caused further disappointment. It was noted on the teamsheet for The Rest that Edwin Dutton played "instead of Bloomer". Sport, it seemed, was no longer enough to raise Bloomer's spirits. He needed to get out of Ruhleben, which itself was beginning to fall apart. Then the camp caught fire.

The fire bell began to ring at 8.15 pm on 14 July – and it was not signalling an appell. Men rushed out of the barracks, the grandstand and the YMCA and saw thick clouds of black smoke billowing up from the western end of the camp. A prisoner ran towards the gathering crowd leading a horse. The wooden stables were on fire, he yelled, and the other horses and the camp's cows were still inside. The men rushed to the stables, behind Barrack 4 and right next to Barrack 22 – the Boys' Barrack. Another prisoner hurried past leading two horses. One of the horses was horribly, fatally burnt.

Wyndham Richards was among the first of the crowd to reach the stables. The timber building was engulfed in flames and impossible to save. Nevertheless, Richards and the others began “working like mad”, pouring buckets of water on the burning stable, and soaking the fire-threatened Barrack 22. Someone brought the hose used by the prisoners to maintain the tennis courts, but the camp’s water pressure was so weak that Richards said the pathetic stream of water that was produced “could be stopped with the finger”. The lack of water pressure also made it difficult to refill the buckets, and the fire continued to rage.

The guards did nothing to help the situation. They stood around with loaded guns, seemingly expecting to have to prevent a mass escape attempt as a result of the chaos. “They understand the English so little,” said Richards. Then part of the stables collapsed onto Barrack 22, which quickly caught alight. Barrack 4 was also under threat, so men climbed onto the roof to douse it in water. Barrack 4 could be saved, but Barrack 22 could not. The firefighting effort became a rescue mission, as a chain of men – Richards and Captain Powell among them – rushed to carry beds, bags and belongings out from Barrack 22 and then, as the fire spread, from the adjacent Barracks 20 and 21.

After about 15 minutes, the fire brigade arrived. The prisoners commandeered the fire carts and took charge of the hoses, much to the displeasure of one of the fire officers, who struck Powell with the butt of his rifle. Then the soldiers – around 500 of them – arrived and pushed the prisoners back away from the barracks and onto the playing fields. The fire was now under control and, eventually, the fire brigade’s hoses put it out. The stable was destroyed and Barrack 22 was ruined. The other barracks were saved. It was found that the fire was caused by a failure in the camp's heating system. Three horses and four cows died, but none of the prisoners were hurt. They were fortunate. "Thank God there wasn't a breath of wind," said Richards. "Otherwise the whole camp might have gone."

The fire acted as a warning of the fragility of camp life and was symbolic of the changes that Ruhleben was undergoing. The boys from Barrack 22 were distributed around the camp, their beds and belongings squeezed into any available gaps in the horse boxes. Everything from appells to football teams were affected. Even small changes had the potential to disrupt and unsettle the men's routine. And much bigger changes were on the way – changes that would affect life in Ruhleben through to the end of the war.

In August, the prisoners organised another sports day. Bloomer was not among the competitors, although he did act as a judge alongside Tom Sullivan and John Masterman, with Fred Pentland in charge of the organisation. Events included a three-legged race and an obstacle race – the latter won by jockey Freddy Winter. Jack Brearley beat the likes of Captain Powell and the "Pearl of Earth" in the veterans' race. The new football season – Ruhleben's fourth – began a few weeks later. On the opening day, Barrack 2 beat Barrack 10 2-0.

Now Bloomer was persuaded to put his boots back on, and he returned to camp football in familiar style. "Bloomer nowadays is naturally not the speedy man he was," noted prisoner Walter Butterworth in a letter, "but all the old accuracy remains and whenever he turns out there is always sure to be a big crowd, not so much perhaps to witness his adroit methods but to listen to his comments audibly expressed, and sometimes in words not discoverable in a respectable dictionary."

Butterworth's news of Bloomer was received with relief. "I am delighted to hear [Bloomer] is still keeping his 'pecker' up and, what is more, helping others to do so," said JRC in the *Manchester Evening News*. The columnist said he had heard from several sources that football had been the "salvation" of the prisoners and that Bloomer had played a central role and had become an inspiration to the younger men at Ruhleben. "Some of his old friends will smile when they read Mr Butterworth's references to the famous player's language," said JRC. "In his eagerness, Bloomer was always more forcible than polite, and the few words he once addressed to a well-known goalkeeper are almost historic."

Barrack 9 continued their formidable form with another winning start to the season. But their successes were not recorded in the camp magazine, which had abruptly ceased publication in June. Davidson Ketchum, in his written study of Ruhleben, was unable to find a reason for the end of the popular *Ruhleben Camp Magazine*, although he did mention rising production costs, which might have become too much to bear. Another popular magazine, the French-language *La Vie Française de Ruhleben*, published by the camp's French Circle primarily for the several hundred prisoners who were taking French lessons, also folded.

Football was still written about in letters home and talked about in the barracks and on the grandstands. But football had a new challenger as the most talked-about diversion in Ruhleben. Those who were not preoccupied with football spent their time thinking about escape.

There were several escape attempts, one a "mass escape" involving five men. The escapees threw boxes over the fence to break their fall as they went to "jump it", but made "a hell of a noise". Three of them were caught on the fence. The other two were captured by a patrol several miles away. The escapees were brought before Lieutenant-Colonel von Reichenbach, who told them, "I expected better from you."

In response to this latest escape attempt, the commandant placed guards back in each of the barracks – until the camp captains protested, and they were once again removed. But he also implemented a much harsher punishment for attempted escapees. Previously, they were sent to the Stadtvogtei municipal prison in Berlin for 14 days. Now they would be sent to the Havelberg prison camp for an indefinite period. Havelberg, located around 60 miles north-west of Ruhleben, was described by the British government as "a very bad camp used mainly for criminals".

Steve Bloomer was aware of several escape attempts, even if he did not attempt to "jump it" himself. One evening, while sitting in the grandstand "enjoying a last fag before turning in", he was approached by a young man from Newcastle called Tom Roxburgh.

"Well, Steve," Roxburgh told him. "Tonight's the last night."

"What's it to be?" asked Bloomer, misunderstanding Roxburgh's meaning. "Poison, a bit of cold steel, or a length of rope?"

"Not any of those yet," laughed Roxburgh. "But it might finish up with a little firing practice in the cold, damp hours of some chilly morn. We're going to jump it."

Roxburgh explained that he and two other men had bribed a guard to help them get out of the camp. They had obtained a marked-up map and a compass, and planned to follow a safe route to Roscoe in Denmark.

"Well, best of luck, Tom," said Bloomer. "Success to the venture."

Bloomer kept the matter to himself but, on the following afternoon, he went around the camp searching for Roxburgh, who could not be found. Later, Bloomer noticed "feverish activity" behind Barrack 7. The guards had discovered a mysterious hole in the barbed wire. A head-count was ordered, and it was found that three prisoners had escaped. Bloomer admitted that he laughed to himself. But the escape was short-lived.

Two days later, Roxburgh and his two friends were marched back into the camp looking "very depressed, muddy, wet and hungry". Bloomer hurried over and asked what had gone wrong. It transpired that the men had got out of the camp relatively easily, then crossed the Spree by footbridge, and went into the forest, where they came across a small cottage. There, they were cornered by a large dog, which started barking, making "enough noise to waken the dead". A light went on in the cottage, and a woman stuck her head out of the window and proceeded to unleash an "unearthly yell", which she kept up for around 15 minutes – with the men unable to flee due to the attention of the snarling dog – until a policeman arrived to arrest them.

"I just had time to sympathise with him when the guards marched him off to the punishment camp," said Bloomer. Another of the attempted escapees – Bloomer reckoned there were around 100 of them – was John Halpin, better known as "Bicycle Billy". An actor and comedian, Billy was regarded as a "laugh merchant" in the camp and could always be relied upon to spin entertaining yarns. He brought his bike to Ruhleben and allowed his fellow prisoners to ride around the camp for a small fee. Unfortunately, the German guards took Billy's tyres for one of their own bicycles. Unable to ride the bike, Billy turned it into a "wheel of fortune", placing numbers around the wheel rim to run gambling games.

Billy was an itinerant soul and struggled with captivity. "Any sort of confinement was torture," said Bloomer, "and he made several attempts to escape. On most of these adventures he never seemed to succeed in getting out of sight of the camp." On one occasion he did get a little further after feigning pneumonia, then escaping from the hospital. He took a train to Magdeburg, where he was challenged by officials. "I protested that I was an American, but the officials maintained I was English," Billy told Bloomer. "The argument was clinched, however, when they searched me and found a Huntley & Palmers biscuit in my pocket." Billy was sent to Havelberg.

In October 1917, Wyndham Richards made his attempt to escape. Bloomer described Richards' story as a "very hard case". Richards had been planning to escape for more than a year, although he did not record the plans in his diary or letters home for fear of being discovered. First, in the autumn of 1916, he made contact with a British man in Hanover via notes wrapped in old clothes and hidden inside sticky fruit. Richards arranged for the man to meet him outside the camp, provide him with papers, and smuggle him out of Germany. He bribed a guard to let him out of the camp but, on the night of the planned escape, the guard changed his mind. Instead, Richards attempted to climb the fences, but he struggled to get past the barbed wire and sentry patrols and ended up returning to his barrack. He wrote to his accomplice to arrange another attempt but, "owing to a careless mistake on my part", the note was intercepted, and the man and his wife were arrested and imprisoned. The note was unsigned, so was not traced back to Richards.

His second attempt was in the spring of 1917. Richards and a friend bought German passports and military leave papers from a "German Socialist friend" for 500 marks. However, it was a set-up. The friend was arrested but Richards, who had passed the documents to someone else to hold, was not. Despite interrogation and "terrible punishment" – six weeks in dark cells on bread and water, during which he was driven to attempt suicide – the friend refused to give up Richards' name. And Richards did not name the friend in his diary or other written accounts, but he seems to have been Wallace Ellison, the former captain of Barrack 13, who made multiple attempts to "jump it".

Then came Richards' final attempt to escape. On the morning of 23 October 1917, he left the camp with a group of prisoners, under escort and in work overalls, to unload a parcel truck at a nearby railway siding. Climbing into the back of the tarpaulin-covered truck, he changed out of the overalls and put on an overcoat. Then he slipped out of the side of the truck and walked brazenly away from the prisoners and the guards down the road. The plan was almost sunk when he passed an officer who recognised him, but Richards turned back towards the camp, then doubled back along the road, passing five more guards on the way.

Richards walked five miles to the Berlin Zoological Gardens, where he boarded an express train for Dortmund. He intended to travel on by train through Düsseldorf to Mönchengladbach, then cross the border on foot into the Netherlands. Richards had a carriage to himself and was beginning to feel safe when the train reached Bielefeld, almost three hours from Berlin. However, between Bielefeld and Hamm, a man came into his carriage and asked for identity papers. "Realising the game was up, I gave him my particulars," said Richards. The escape had failed.

Richards was taken off the train at Hamm and placed in the custody of a soldier who could not understand why he had left Ruhleben. "He said he would rather be three years interned [in Ruhleben] than three weeks in the trenches in Flanders," recalled Richards. "There, he said, is hell. He was there six weeks ago." Richards was held in Hamm for several days until a guard came from Ruhleben to escort him back. But he wasn't returned to the camp. Instead, Richards was taken to the Stadtvogtei, where he expected to spend 14 days in solitary confinement. But the Stadtvogtei was now just a staging post for punished prisoners.

Richards wrote to his brother, Frank, from the Stadtvogtei advising him of his failed escape and capture. "I cannot say how the Barrack 10 football team are doing without their captain," he wrote. "Trust they've won them all, but I greatly fear that I left them in the lurch, somewhat. Still, it had to be done..."

Two weeks later, while expecting to be returned to the camp, Richards was informed that he and 28 other captured escapees in the Stadtvogtei would be transferred to

Havelberg. Primarily, Havelberg was an internment camp for non-British military and civilians. At its busiest, like Ruhleben, it housed around 4,500 prisoners. These included French and Russian soldiers, Polish women and children, and around 350 Indian civilians. Now they were joined by prisoners from elsewhere who were being punished for disobeying rules, refusing to work or attempting to escape.

Richards was one of 50 British prisoners in Havelberg, alongside the likes of Tom Roxburgh and John "Bicycle Billy" Halpin. The contrast between the civilised and relatively comfortable Ruhleben and the wretched and run-down Havelberg could hardly have been starker. Arriving in Havelberg was like going back to the worst days of Ruhleben, before Richards and the others had worked so hard to improve it. The barracks were damp, dirty and infested with rats. The food was pathetically meagre, and there were no kitchen facilities. Post and parcel deliveries were infrequent and unreliable. "Hell of a place," wrote Richards. "No. Worse than that. I feel more depressed than I have for years – than ever – during my captivity."

Back in Ruhleben, Richards' barrack mates were dismayed by his escape attempt. Their football captain had left without telling them and was at least in part responsible for the entire camp being punished with extra appells and increased security. But while the disappearance of Richards shocked Barrack 10, the departure of another figure rocked the entire camp and shook the bedrock of Ruhleben's civilian society.

At the end of October 1917, Joseph Powell was confined to Dr Weiler's Sanatorium after suffering what was described as a "nervous breakdown". The camp captain, it seemed, had succumbed to the danger he had previously identified as barbed-wire disease.

The importance of Powell in the transformation of Ruhleben can hardly be overstated. It was Powell who bargained with the authorities to gain everything from relief payments to the use of the playing fields. Under Powell's leadership, the camp moved from military rule to civil administration. This allowed Ruhleben to grow into what was effectively an autonomous British town within a fenced-off corner of Germany, and an oasis of order in the middle of a chaotic war.

It was a remarkable achievement, but it was also an arduous task and a burdensome responsibility. The former sales manager had taken on the needs of 4,500 men while dealing with his own individual worries – about the war, his incarceration, and the well-being of his family. It had apparently become too much. Although he was not universally liked – as few in authority are – he was pretty much universally respected. Captain Powell's departure left a hole that could not be filled. Ruhleben had lost its leader.

As Christmas approached – the fourth the men would spend in Ruhleben – a group of prisoners including Steve Bloomer received a consignment of parcels from supporters in England containing sweaters, gloves, caps, mufflers, slippers and underclothes, plus football boots, shirts, stockings and leather ball cases. But the present they most desired – the end of the war – did not arrive. There were contradictory reports from the Western Front. The Battle of Passchendaele cost both the Allied and German sides hundreds of thousands of casualties. The battle was described in Britain as "one of the great disasters of the war" and in Germany as having brought the country "near to certain destruction".

Rumours of release swirled around the camp, although most prisoners, worn down by constant speculation, steeled themselves for disappointment. According to Davidson Ketchum, "The rumours did not alter the steady pulse of Ruhleben life." The men continued to play football, to attend lectures and plays, and to complain about the heating boilers, which once again failed under the strain of winter. That December, Bloomer wrote a letter home to Sarah. "I am not building my hopes too high," he told her, "but do not be surprised if I walk into the house some fine day."

In the week before Christmas, league leaders Barrack 9 beat Barrack 7 in a cup match 3-1, and a football concert was held with presentations made to some of the Ruhleben FA officials, including Steve Bloomer and Jack Cameron, who each received a silver cigarette case. With the temperature hovering just above zero, the camp's heating system broke down. Then, on Christmas Eve, it was announced that the exchange of prisoners aged 45 and over would resume. A batch of 370 "45ers" would be repatriated on 2 January. Among them was Cameron, who was 45 years and eight months old at the time of the exchange.

Cameron would be the first of the professional footballers to leave Ruhleben. Bloomer was just about to turn 44, so was ineligible for exchange on grounds of age. Another of the footballers, Wattie Campbell, was almost 51, but he wasn't included in the initial batch of repatriations. Campbell would be released in a further batch of 120 prisoners in March. The other professionals – Pentland,

Brearley, Dutton, Hartley and Wolstenholme – would remain with Bloomer in Ruhleben.

At 6 am on 2 January 1918, a bitterly cold morning, the entire camp gathered together, some climbing on stairways and roofs, to give their friends a rousing send-off. The 370 fortunate men were marched with their luggage across to the railway station and boarded onto a train. But their departure was delayed because the engine driver couldn't get the train moving. As the leavers sat on the train, the remaining prisoners sang and cheered – for more than three hours. But there was sadness as well as joy in the air. The long goodbye, one prisoner wrote, "seemed something like standing on a wreck and saying goodbye to those the lifeboats could hold." When the train finally pulled away, at 9.30, the remaining prisoners yelled, *"Are we downhearted? No!"*

"They gave us a fine send-off, poor devils," said one of the 45ers. The unnamed former prisoner was interviewed on his return to London by a reporter from the *Evening News*, and he spoke mostly about football, which he said was by far the most popular game in the camp. He spoke of Bloomer and Cameron, and the league and cup matches, and also mentioned "ragtime matches" – not the games that were played with a rag-ball before the establishment of the Ruhleben FA, but "a loose kind of game for the elderly prisoners". He explained how the camp authorities were amazed by the enthusiasm for football. "The German guards could never understand the constant cheerfulness of the British," he said.

Another returnee described sports as "a medicine for the prisoners". "It was the remedy which was applied as a prevention against sickness as well as for maintaining cheerfulness and good humour," he said. "Sport it was that enabled many of the interned to bear their imprisonment without breaking down in health." This former Ruhlenbenite mentioned golf, hockey, rugby, cricket, baseball, lacrosse and skating, but made it clear that football was key. "With such as Bloomer, Wolstenholme, Pentland and Cameron in the camp, it was not to be wondered that 'soccer' should be the most popular of all the sports," he said. "Bloomer was always a great favourite with the crowd."

Another released prisoner, the Scottish footballer Tommy Miller, who had been plying his trade in Germany before the war and was highly rated by Steve Bloomer, said the game had brought him enjoyment and improved his well-being in the camp "I don't believe we could have stood it out but for this recreation," he said. "This year's league is not finished yet, and I feel quite anxious to hear how the contest will end. Barrack 9 were at the top when I left and looking like likely winners again, but the teams were excellently matched, and there might be surprises."

One of the first duties of a released prisoner on his return to Britain was to visit the friends and family of the comrades he had left behind, to pass on messages and to reassure them of their loved ones' well-being. So, after his return home, Jack Cameron began to travel around the country on behalf of some of his many friends. During his travels, he met with several newspaper reporters, one of whom said he looked "wonderfully fit considering the hardships he and his compatriots have had to endure".

Cameron, of course, put his good condition down to playing football and other sports "on the limited scale permitted". He explained to reporters how he had helped form the Ruhleben FA, and then "had a busy time" arranging fixtures, so they didn't clash. But, while he highlighted the scale of the organised football in Ruhleben, he also said that players would take off their coats and join in friendly games "just for the love and the sport of the thing, and for helping others along".

He spoke about the conditions in the camp and urged people at home to continue sending parcels to sustain the men as "a few potatoes and a little soup" was all the Germans provided. And he said conditions outside of the camp were bad, too, with Berlin on the verge of starvation. According to Cameron, people in England were "a hundred or even a thousand times better off" than the Germans, so he was surprised to hear grumbling when he got home. He was very happy to see that German reports about starving conditions in England were not true. The English should consider themselves happy to be so well off, he said, compared with people in the "enemy countries".

Ultimately, Cameron said, "the football played at Ruhleben probably saved the reason of the majority of prisoners". His one hope was that the "big scrap" would soon be over. And he proudly showed one reporter the silver cigarette case he had received just weeks before his release. It was engraved with the words: *"Presented to John Cameron by the football players of Ruhleben, December 1917."*

Several of the reports concerning Cameron's release carried similar footnotes for concerned readers with variations on the same words: "Steve Bloomer is still interned." Bloomer was still playing football, too, although sport – like everything in Ruhleben – seemed less important. In a short period of time, the camp had lost its commandant and its captain. In addition to the 50 or so Ruhlebenites who had been removed to Havelberg, almost

500 45ers had left or were about to leave, many of them senior figures in camp committees and administration. Each of these men had been a building block in the construction of the prison camp society. Each of them had been comrades and friends. Their removal changed – and in many cases damaged – almost every aspect of camp life. "Ruhleben was not yet a wreck," noted Davidson Ketchum, "but the loss of a tenth of its population was a blow that could not be repaired."

While the outcome of the Great War remained uncertain, it was clear that 1918 would be a climactic year, and the Ruhlebenites became preoccupied with war news. At around 8.30 each morning, the prisoners would hear the familiar cry of "*Da-i-ly, Da-i-ly*" from Tommy, the newspaper vendor, as he made his rounds. "It is the herald of the Ruhleben dawn," said prisoner Percy Brown. "As soon as the cheery, raucous voice strikes through the heavy air of the barrack gloom disappears and spirits rise. There is something of a humorous sob and a chuckle in those tones that is irresistible and infectious even to the surliest of men." However, one winter morning, there was no cry to be heard.

Tommy, "a little shrivelled man with wizened features" who had apparently been a jockey, described the *Ruhleben Daily News* in his sales patter as "the most important paper in the camp". In fact, the one-sheet publication, with its translations of stories from the German newspapers, was not considered as reliable as the "ordinary papers". But it was the vendor rather than the content that made the *Daily Daily* a Ruhleben institution. Tommy moved "like a human whirlwind" around the barracks, dispensing "sharp quick patter" as he exchanged his papers for 5pf pieces, enlivening the prisoners' "drab and weary existence" and leaving behind "a fresher and livelier air". This made his sudden disappearance all the more perplexing.

"'Bout time Tommy was here with the rag," said one prisoner as 8.30 came and went.

"No paper this morning," said another. "Tommy died last night."

The shock was devastating. According to Percy Brown, "If a shell had burst on the roof of the barrack the effect could not have been more startling."

The news quickly travelled around the camp, and the "old gloom" settled over the camp. *The Ruhleben Daily News* would continue to be published, and a new young vendor would be appointed. But the *Daily Daily* was no longer a vital part of Ruhleben life. "We realised why we bought the rag," said Brown, "in spite of the fact that it rarely contained news which was pleasing or apt to cheer us up."

Then, a few weeks later, there was a commotion near the grandstands. A cheering mob of prisoners came charging around the corner, and they were carrying someone on their shoulders, someone who was waving sheets of newspaper. "Suddenly," recalled Brown, "above the noise and commotion, there rings out the dear old voice of Daily Daily!" Tommy had spent several weeks in the hospital, but he was alive. His "resurrection" was celebrated across the camp. "Although we feel that in spite of numerous rumours to the contrary we have many months before us," said Brown, "we look forward more optimistically since we have our dear old Daily Daily back again with us."

More good news arrived in Ruhleben that January courtesy of a postcard that was received from the Netherlands. It was from a friend of Wallace Ellison, the serial escape artist, advising that he had safely crossed the border. After being punished so brutally that he was almost driven to suicide and lunacy, Ellison had finally escaped from Ruhleben and reached freedom at the fourth attempt. According to Bloomer, "The whole camp silently rejoiced." The news also reached Havelberg, where Wyndham Richards noted in his diary that he was pleased to hear of his friend's escape.

More prisoners would be leaving Ruhleben – without having to go over the fence. On 6 March, Wattie Campbell and the rest of the second batch of 45ers were released. Among the 120 prisoners repatriated alongside Campbell were Tom Sullivan the rower and Andries Ventner the remarkably tall circus performer, who was cheered by the crowd at the docks as he disembarked after arrival at the port of Boston, Lincolnshire. One released prisoner, named Phillips, died on the voyage home.

Following his return, Wattie Campbell was interviewed by his old Moffat FC teammate Jimmy Niven, a former Scotland international who was now a football journalist. "His long confinement at Ruhleben has not improved his health by any means," said Niven, "but Scotch grit and stamina has stood him in good stead, and all the abuse, hunger and provocation has not killed Wattie Campbell. He does so love the Germans!" Campbell told Niven he thought "old footballers and men used to a seafaring life" were best equipped to survive in Ruhleben. It was in this interview that he said football had "kept them alive".

Tom Sullivan, meanwhile, was another who attributed

his good physical condition to camp sport. "Some of our well-known footballers are interned there," he said, mentioning the names of Bloomer, Brearley, Pentland and Wolstenholme. "These old professional footballers have devoted no end of time to coaching and helping younger men in the great winter game and always taking part in the play themselves." Sullivan made particular mention of Pentland, who he said gave up much of his time to his duties as secretary of the sports committee. "Great praise is due to him," said Sullivan, "for the energy which he has displayed in every way to make the men's internment as endurable as possible, as well as to promote their physical well-being."

Back in Ruhleben, the fourth football season was stuttering to a close, with Barrack 9 at the top of the league. While previous seasons had ended in exciting climaxes, this one was petering out amid dwindling interest and enthusiasm. With repatriations unpredictable and the war on a knife-edge, the camp seemed consumed by frustration and anxiety. Morale was weakening and many prisoners were becoming demoralised. Their frustration boiled over in an incident in March at the camp's cinema under the grand-stand.

The prisoners were expecting to watch a Charlie Chaplin picture, but this was substituted at the last moment for a 12-minute propaganda film following the exploits of the German auxiliary cruiser SMS *Wolf*, a 440ft, 11,000-ton merchant raider equipped with naval guns, torpedoes and mines. The film was shot at the end of a 15-month tour during which the *Wolf* sunk or captured 27 Allied ships. Bloomer was among the men in the cinema who watched as the cruiser fired on ships and captured prisoners. "As each vessel was attacked and sunk, jeers and boos went up from all the seafaring men in the audience," recalled Bloomer, who said a riot was narrowly averted. Many prisoners were so affronted that they declared an intention to boycott the cinema. However, the moving picture shows were so popular that the boycott would not last very long.

In late March 1918, five months after Wyndham Richards was sent to Havelberg, four months after Joseph Powell went to the sanatorium, twelve weeks after Jack Cameron was repatriated and two weeks after Wattie Campbell and the other 45ers were released, it was announced that Steve Bloomer would be leaving Ruhleben. Bloomer had been incarcerated for three years and five months. He was beaten-down but not broken by his incarceration. His release was more than welcome, but he would not be going home.

Bloomer's release was orchestrated by the Dutch FA rather than the Swedish FA. Since the Americans had broken off relations with Germany and entered the war, the still-neutral Dutch had taken on a representative role for the prisoners of war. So the Dutch FA, via its nation's ambassadors, was able to exert some influence in Germany. Still only 44, Bloomer was not eligible for repatriation to England. Instead, he would be transferred from Germany to the Netherlands, where he would take up a role as a coach for FC Blauw-Wit Amsterdam. The conditions of his release would not allow him to leave the Netherlands, but at least he was leaving Ruhleben. "The full meaning of what it meant to me took some time to soak in," he said.

Ruhleben's most popular celebrity could not leave

without a celebration, and Pentland and the other footballers swiftly organised a grand farewell match, "as a sort of memento and a send-off to Steve".

For this game, played on 20 March, all of the remaining pros played on the same side, so Bloomer lined up alongside his great pals Pentland, Dutton, Brearley, Wolstenholme and Hartley. Also in Bloomer's team were some of his most highly-rated amateurs – goalkeeper Gordon Nicoll, David Owen, Oates Lithgow, Bob Stewart and Bobby Slade.

The opposition team was made up of more of Ruhleben's best amateur players, many of them coached and improved by Bloomer and his fellow veterans. Photographs were taken of the two teams, lined up in one of the goalmouths, in slightly mismatched shirts, shorts and stockings. In the photos, Bloomer's team wear plain coloured collared and laced jerseys, while their opponents wear stripes. In a combined photo of both teams, Bloomer stands among his comrades with his arms folded across his chest. His relief seems palpable. It is one of the few photos taken of Bloomer in which he is smiling.

The occasion of the farewell match was more important than the result, and Bloomer's team lost 5-3 after a "rousing game". According to spectator George Rogans, "The younger side were value for their win, too." Rogans, the former Garston Gasworks player, paid tribute to Bloomer, who received takings of £30 from the match as a parting gift. "He has been a wonder, has Steve," said Rogans, "and although well over 40 years old he used to run about the field like a young man. He really was a treat to watch, and also a devil to stop – I know because I played against him."

Bloomer left Ruhleben two days later, following a stirring send-off. "The party we had will always be memorable," he said. As he boarded the train for the Netherlands, he was shocked to see women and children begging for scraps of food. "There seemed even less food on the outside than there was in the camp," he said. Bloomer and his fellow prisoners generously gave as much as they could, despite their treatment at the hands of their German captors.

When the train arrived in the Netherlands, Bloomer was greeted by thousands of cheering fans. "Much to my surprise a lot of them seemed to know me, and there was such an enthusiasm there for football as I had never imagined." British newspapers reported that Bloomer was waiting in the Netherlands for a boat to England and was expected to return home at the earliest opportunity. But that was not the case. Bloomer wrote to Sarah saying he expected to remain in the Netherlands for the remainder of the war.

12

Forgive and Forget

An epic story of the triumph of the British spirit of sportsmanship in a German prison camp." That was how the *Sunday Chronicle* newspaper billed an exclusive article by Steve Bloomer following his release to the Netherlands. "The great goal-getter of Derby County and international fame has written an exceedingly picturesque and interesting account of the horrors of prison life at Ruhleben," said the paper, "of the way in which the spirit of British sportsmanship relieved the otherwise insupportable misery and tedium of captivity in the hands of the Huns."

When not recounting his experiences to journalists, Bloomer threw himself into football. Within days of his arrival in the Netherlands, he played for a team of British soldiers against a team of Belgians in front of 13,000 spectators in The Hague. The soldiers were prisoners of war who were being held in the Netherlands under peace conventions. Bloomer's team won 4-0, and he scored twice.

One of the soldiers who played with Bloomer in The Hague was his former England international teammate Dicky Bond, the Bradford City outside-right. Bloomer and Bond had lined up together for England twice in 1905. Sergeant Bond was a machine-gunner with the Bradford Pals battalion, which fought in Egypt and then on the Western Front and suffered heavy casualties. Bond was captured during a German raid and spent two years in a prisoner of war camp before being transferred to the Netherlands.

After being cleared through The Hague, Bloomer went to Amsterdam to take up his position as coach of Blauw-Wit who, unsurprisingly, played in blue and white. Bloomer reckoned his team had some good players, although he would need to give them a bit of "tuning up". None of the players spoke English, so Bloomer relied on one of the club directors for translations.

Although Bloomer was still not a free man, he was no longer confined to a camp. Instead, he stayed in a comfortable apartment above a chemist's shop on the Leliegracht (Lily Canal) in the Jordaan neighbourhood of Amsterdam. Bloomer liked Amsterdam and enjoyed mixing with the numerous other British internees who were interned in the city, although he found it very expensive and complained that he struggled to get English cigarettes. He recognised, though, that these were minor gripes given the ordeal he had previously been through. And, importantly, he could continue to play and coach football.

Blauw-Wit's stadium was the Nederlandsch Sportpark, known in Amsterdam as the Stadion. It had a large capacity of 29,000, but its most interesting features were its floodlights, which would not be common at British football grounds until the 1950s. Bloomer played in several exhibition matches at the Stadion, including night matches under the floodlights. But he struggled with the "dazzling brilliance" of the electric lights and kept losing sight of the ball. "I seriously doubt if football matches at night will ever become popular," he remarked.

Bloomer slipped back easily into life as a football

coach. During his time in Ruhleben, he had never really stopped working with players, inspiring them and schooling them, following his principle that football was something that could be taught. But he had gone from playing football on a makeshift pitch inside a ring of barbed wire to playing in one of the grandest football stadiums in Europe. And when he wasn't working, he could sleep in his own room, eat regular meals, and stroll along Amsterdam's canals at his leisure. Life was much more comfortable, but he remained separated from home by more than 300 miles and the North Sea.

Back in Ruhleben, football continued without its star player. Barrack 9 topped the league for the third consecutive time, and then a series of friendly matches were held to mark the end of the season and to celebrate Easter. Fred Pentland and Edwin Dutton played for a Land team against a Sea team that included Bobby Slade and Clem Burnill. Percy Hartley was the referee. Then Jack Brearley played in a "representative match" for the Greens against the Stripes. David Owen and JA Falck also played in that game. Then summer arrived, and football was replaced by cricket and tennis.

By then, two more Ruhleben footballers had left. Sam Wolstenholme and Edwin Dutton were both released to the Netherlands, alongside Bloomer. Like Bloomer, they were to remain in the Netherlands and could not return to Britain. But it meant they could continue to play and coach football outside of the confines of barbed-wire fences. Of the Ruhleben professionals, there were now just Pentland, Brearley and Hartley left in the prison camp.

Also still in the camp was a star of Ruhleben's summer

sports, John Masterman. However, Masterman did not intend to remain in the camp for long. He had decided to escape. Another prisoner, WF Mackenzie, who had been released to the Netherlands, had made contact with a Dutch people-smuggling gang who specialised in getting prisoners from other camps out of Germany. Mackenzie wrote to Masterman and offered to arrange passage over the border for him and two friends if they could find their own way out of the camp and into Berlin.

To get out of the camp, Masterman and the others followed Wyndham Richards' lead and used the parcel cart as their distraction. They reached Berlin and hid out in a brothel until the evening, when they boarded a train. After travelling for around five hours, they reached Lohne, less than 50 miles from the Dutch border. However, all passengers were told to leave the train, and the men were ordered to show their papers – which they were unable to do. They were surrounded and arrested. "Escape was impossible," said Masterman, "and we were taken under armed guard to jail in Hanover."

Masterman deeply regretted his escape attempt and said he had been shamed into "jumping it" when he felt he could easily have sat out the war in Ruhleben. But he was by no means the only prisoner to attempt to get out in the summer of 1918. Almost every few days the men would hear that someone else had "gone over the wire". The increase in escape attempts was partly due to demoralisation and a growing fear that the war might never end. But a change in camp personnel had created new opportunities to get out. The younger and fitter camp guards had been sent to the battlefronts where they were desperately needed to bolster the German forces. They were replaced by elderly and "doddering" guards who posed a less than formidable obstacle for potential escapees.

Another reason so many prisoners were at least thinking about escape, if not actually attempting it, was the general deterioration of camp conditions. Many of the improvements that had been made to the camp were now three or four years old. These improvements – the accommodations, the heating system, the latrines, the kitchens – had been knocked together as quickly as possible using basic supplies by men who, in most cases, were not competent tradesmen. This DIY camp hadn't been built to last this long, because no one had expected the prisoners to still be in Ruhleben in 1918.

The accommodations were falling to pieces. The heating system regularly broke down, and coal deliveries were increasingly unreliable. The latrines were backed up after years of use from thousands of men. And the kitchens were starved of supplies, with the bulk of Germany's nutritious foods being diverted to feed the army. The prisoners continued to rely almost entirely on parcels from home for sustenance and, while these still arrived regularly, there were reports of parcels being stolen by German civilians who were becoming increasingly desperate for food. If the parcel delivery service stopped, the prisoners feared starvation.

Meanwhile, the population of Ruhleben was gradually decreasing as more 45ers and the ill and infirm were gradually repatriated. Small groups of men were released intermittently throughout the first half of 1918. By July, there were 2,336 men in Ruhleben – a reduction of almost 50 per cent compared to its largest population. Although the release programme was good news for the men who went home, it inevitably affected the morale of those left behind. The remaining prisoners were losing not only close friends but also officials, tradesmen, entertainers and other men who played key roles in camp society. Without them, that society began to collapse.

The camp's civil administration system had also begun to break down since the departure of Captain Powell. Thankfully, he returned to the camp from the sanatorium in May, and he appeared to be fully recuperated. "I gather, from the minutes of the captain's committee, which I have since read, that I was worse than I knew and that my recovery was for some time doubtful," he wrote. "I did recover, however."

In his absence, the captain's committee had restructured and expanded, and had become, in Powell's view, disorganised and "too large for convenience". According to Powell, the camp's administration had fallen into "crisis". At the end of July, he resigned as camp captain. Then he began to push for a new, more democratic system of administration, and a constitution was drawn up. Powell regarded Ruhleben's constitution for prisoners of war to be "a unique thing in the history of war".

Meanwhile, the prisoners became increasingly obsessed with news of the war. Through the translated *Daily Daily* and smuggled English papers – and through the guards, who were not always well-informed – the prisoners were able to piece together the narrative of the war, which was now entering its final few months. Maps, which were previously prohibited, began to appear on barrack walls, and the men plotted the movements of the Allied and German armies with coloured flags. The camp guards and officers would come into the barracks to study the maps, which often gave a clearer picture of the conflict than the Germans could obtain from their own sources.

During the first half of 1918, the prisoners' coloured flags retreated on the Western Front as Germany's Ludendorff Offensives pushed the Allies back towards Paris and the Channel ports. But, from July, the flags began to advance, as the Allies' fierce counterattack, utilising hundreds of tanks and heavy guns, plus hundreds of thousands of men, drove the Germans back to the French and Belgian borders. In August, the Allies launched the Amiens Offensive, the opening phase of the Hundred Days Offensive that would ultimately lead to the end of the war.

"A good deal of information" about the war came from a German visitor to the camp who had been one of the crewmembers of the raider *Wolf* – the ship featured in the propaganda film that almost caused a riot. He came to Ruhleben to visit a British sailor who had been captured by the German vessel. The two men had become friends following the capture. The German sailor said he did not think he would sail aboard the *Wolf* again and expected to be transferred to a submarine. But the German navy was on the verge of mutiny. "They won't get any of us to sail," he said. "You've beaten the submarines, and we're sick of the whole business."

Meanwhile, the prisoners heard tales of failing morale in the German trenches. It was said that the only way officers could get their men to go over the top was to tell them there was food in the Allied trenches. Nearer to home, civilians from Berlin arrived at the gates of the prison camp begging for food. Camp guards failed to appear for roll call. Some went on leave and didn't come back. There was talk of revolution. The German people, it seemed, wanted their government to accept a ceasefire agreement offered by the Americans.

Then, in September, Allied forces launched a series of attacks between the Argonne forest and Flanders. On 29 September, British troops smashed through the Germans' strongest defence position, the Hindenburg Line. There was now little doubt that the war was coming to an end.

On 1 October 1918, Wyndham Richards was returned to Ruhleben from Havelberg. He was initially placed in Barrack 14 but, after a couple of weeks, he was transferred back to be with his old friends in Barrack 10, and they appeared to forgive him for his escape attempt. In many ways, life in Ruhleben continued as usual. A fifth football season commenced – although it would not be completed.

The camp administration was now in much better shape following the return of Joseph Powell. Under the terms of the prisoners' constitution, an election was held for camp captain. Powell was nominated by Fred Pentland and won by a landslide. Ruhleben's de facto leader had taken back control. But it was now obvious that Powell's main duty would be to prepare for the end of the war. Two weeks after the election, Powell formed a committee to supervise the breakup of the camp, and also to defend it in case of invasion from marauders from Berlin.

The war reached its climax at the beginning of November. Saturday 9 November 1918, was known as "Red Saturday" because it was the day of the German Revolution when the Kaiser abdicated and the Chancellor resigned. In Berlin, Social Democratic Party leader Philipp Scheidemann stood on the balcony of the Reichstag and announced the formation of a Free German Republic. The revolution swept its way into Ruhleben. The guards formed a soldiers' council and deposed the camp officers. Before the officers left, Young Count Schwerin, the late commandant's son, came to see Powell. Sobbing, the Young Count told Powell he was glad his father had not lived to see this day or he would surely have "blown his brains out" rather than submit to such degradation.

The soldiers' council gave up their ammunition, and camp security was handed over to Captain Powell and 60 special constables, including Wyndham Richards. Many of the prisoners wanted to visit Berlin to experience the revolution, and there was little to stop them from doing so. The camp administration issued 150 leave passes, but so many hundreds more left that the pass system was quickly abandoned. According to Richards, Berlin became occupied by British civilians. "In all the main streets, cafes, hotels and theatres one met Englishmen and heard English being spoken," said Richards. "How did Berlin take this invasion? Very well. Englishmen were brothers. They had helped make the German nation free."

In the early hours of the morning on 11 November 1918, in a railway carriage at Le Francport near Compiègne, representatives of the Allied forces, led by supreme commander Marshal Ferdinand Foch, and their German contemporaries, led by politician Matthias Erzberger, signed the armistice. It came into effect from 11 am that morning, halting fighting on land, sea and air, and ending the Great War for Civilisation. The total number of military and civilian casualties was estimated at around 40 million.

In Ruhleben, those prisoners who wished to remain in Germany were immediately released. The others eagerly awaited repatriation. The process of obtaining paperwork and arranging transport would take almost two weeks. So the men continued to while away the hours. They played football right up until the end. And they enjoyed new-found freedoms. On one particular day, it was recorded that half of the camp went to Berlin. Many Ruhlebenites were seen arm-in-arm with German women, and some brought women back to the camp. In the morning, the women could be seen leaving with bundles of food and clothing to take back to Berlin. Meanwhile, wives and children in Berlin and further afield were allowed into the camp, and many stayed for the last few days.

And these really were, after four long years, the last few days of Ruhleben. Bags were packed, and everything that had been built and made was dismantled and put away. Men went around the camp saying farewells and seeking souvenirs. Handshakes and home addresses were exchanged. Photographs and sketches were removed from barrack walls. Autographs were collected, and camp magazines and other ephemera were bundled away. Then Captain Powell and his committee handed out passports. It was all over. The men of Ruhleben were finally going home.

The first batch of prisoners left Ruhleben on 22 November. Including wives and children, around 1,400 civilians travelled via Sassnitz to Copenhagen and on to Hull aboard the Danish liner *Frederick VIII*. When they arrived in Hull, every ship in the port sounded its horn in welcome. The returnees were taken to Ripon for "mental decontamination", then to London for administrative processing. The second batch of around 1,200 left Ruhleben on 24 November and sailed from Copenhagen to Leith.

Captain Powell was among the last to leave Ruhleben,

at 10.30 am that Sunday morning. As he stood on the railway station platform, ready to board the train to Denmark, he turned back to take one last look at the camp. "Not a soul was to be seen," he said. "Trafalgar Square was absolutely deserted." Then he spotted a single figure, a German guard, staggering under a huge load of food and other items that had been scavenged from the empty barracks. "While his colleagues were at the railway station seeing the prisoners off," said Powell, "he was taking advantage of their absence to have the first pick of what had been left behind without disturbance or competition."

Powell and the others arrived in Leith on 30 November. Many of the Ruhlebenites carried a card that had been handed to them as they left the camp. It bore a message asking the prisoners to leave without ill-feeling or hatred, and without holding the German people responsible for the actions of its former leaders. "We congratulate you on your bearing," said the card, "that nothing ever broke your spirit or made you lose your faith." The message ended: "Peace and conciliation, forgive and forget."

Fred Pentland had been among the first batch of returnees. Shortly after his arrival home, Pentland visited the *Sports Argus* offices in Birmingham. "His many football friends will be pleased to know that he looks in the pink of condition," the paper reported, "and while returning thanks to those who remembered him in captivity hopes to thank all personally."

Pentland told reporters there how he had "made the best of a bad job". In the absence of anything else to do, he said, he and the other professionals had encouraged the "other unfortunates" to play football. According to Pentland, “no one can say what sport meant to the weary occupants of that camp.”

Steve Bloomer was already home. Within days of the armistice, Bloomer, Wolstenholme and Dutton had travelled to Rotterdam, where they boarded a ship for Hull. The ship carried 2,000 repatriated prisoners of war – 200 civilians and 1,800 military. As the ship departed, Bloomer noticed a Scotsman standing at the rails waving a sad goodbye to a pretty young woman on the shore. “Leaving the missus behind,” one of the man’s friends explained. “It’s been a bit of a war romance. They met one another when he was sent to Leeuwarden. She was a Dutch girl, and, as they both fell in love with one another, Jock fixed up things, and they got spliced.”

“Its hard luck that they’ve got to be parted,” said Bloomer.

“It is,” said the friend. “They tried to get her on board, but the authorities wouldn’t hear of it. There’s no sentiment about government departments.”

Due to the presence of German mines, the ship had to take an evasive route and anchor at night, and it took almost four days to cross the North Sea. “We spent the last night in the vicinity of the Humber, and were actually within sight of Blighty, but could not land,” recalled Bloomer. “Many of the chaps took it keenly to heart, and very few slept that night.” On the following morning, the returnees were given a warm welcome and a “jolly good” meal at the city’s American Hostel. Then they said their goodbyes.

As he was leaving the hostel, Bloomer was recognised by a reporter from the *Hull Daily Mail.* “Steve Bloomer, by all that’s wonderful!” said the reporter as he shook Bloomer's hand. "And how have you fared out yonder?"

"Rotten," replied Bloomer. "Absolutely rotten, and I don't ever want to see or hear of Germany ever again. Am I glad to be back? Yes, but don't let them know at Derby I am on my way home. I have wired the wife and want to get home to my family quietly for a good rest before the boys find out. I am tired but thankful." Although Bloomer reiterated that he would never return to Germany, he said he would consider returning to the Netherlands once everything was settled. For the time being, though, he wanted to go home.

"I got the first train to Derby, and that night I was safe in the family circle with my wife and daughters," recalled Bloomer. "My first few days at home were a perfect paradise, when all the horrors of life in the hands of the Germans seemed dim and part of the experiences of a man other than myself. It was difficult to realise that I had come safely through them all and that my efforts to keep myself in fairly decent health had been successful, despite the endeavours of the German authorities to kill us all off by bad food, monotony and inhumane conditions."

Of course, Bloomer's family circle was no longer complete. He admitted that the absence of Violet, who had died during his captivity, prevented him from fully enjoying his homecoming.

Local newspaper reporters soon arrived to interview Bloomer. "He is looking and confesses himself very fit, notwithstanding the hardships he has experienced," wrote one of the reporters, "a fact which he attributes largely to his lifelong devotion to athletics, and also in no small measure to his having received food from home."

"We lived on parcels from home, and on sport,"

Bloomer told them. He explained how he had promoted football among his fellow prisoners and had built a strong team from "tin-can dribblers". And he proudly showed off his Ruhleben league championship medal, his engraved silver Ruhleben FA cigarette case, and the cup that he won in the veterans' sports day race.

Despite his good condition, with his 45th birthday approaching, Bloomer said he would not be making a playing return to professional football. "I am done with serious football," he said. "I intend to go in for training." The coaching job in Amsterdam remained open to him, he said, but he had made no definite plans for the future. Instead, he would take time to be with his family and to reflect on and try to process his time in Germany.

"Now that my experiences at Ruhleben are over, I cannot help wondering how so many of us have survived the treatment which the Huns meted out to us," said Bloomer. "To live for three and a half years in captivity, controlled by men whose one desire was to make life unbearable, to be compelled to eat food which was not fit for dogs, and to endure sheer monotony for that period, is a future which few men would like to contemplate."

But he retained positive memories of comradeship and resilience – and football. "In Ruhleben we were all brothers, and we made a life for ourselves out of nothing," he said. "There were some terrible times. Make no mistake that boys became men in Ruhleben. But it is far more pleasant to recall the good times when we went out to play football. Myself and many others would not have survived without it."

Epilogue

The Inevitable End

It was a dull, cloudy day, and a mist of drizzle was drifting across the football field. The muddy pitch was surrounded by banked terraces and a grandstand, and butted between rows of red-brick terrace houses and a strip of billowing smokestacks. This was the Baseball Ground, the footballing home of Derby County and the club's returning hero Steve Bloomer. It was 7 December 1918, and Bloomer had only been back in the country for a couple of weeks. But he was keen to get back to football and, as he stepped out onto the pitch in front of his many fans and friends, he was "cheered to the echo".

Bloomer was playing for a "Pick of Derby Wartime League" team against the 1st Royal Engineers in a match organised to benefit the Football Association War Charity Fund. The Derby team was made up of players from local amateur sides that had helped fill the void during the suspension of professional football, including the Midland Railway Carriage and Wagon Department, and the Derby YMCA. Before kick-off, Bloomer received a "very flattering reception from old friends" and was serenaded by the Derby Town Band, who played *Auld Lang Syne* – for old times' sake.

Once the game got underway, Bloomer "displayed much of his old artistry, although his long captivity in Germany had taken its toll on his energies". The Royal

Engineers – whose original highly-influential football team had won the FA Cup back in 1875 – boasted several Football League players and were a stronger proposition than Bloomer's amateurs. Although the Derby team scored the first goal, the "Sappers" won 2-1. There were 6,000 spectators, and newspapers reported that the charity would receive "substantial gain" to the value of around £200.

Two weeks later, on 21 December, Bloomer played in front of a much larger crowd for Newcastle United against Sunderland at St James' Park in a match to raise funds for the Comrades of the Great War. Newcastle won 4-0, with Bloomer scoring a left-footed drive and receiving a great ovation from the 20,000-strong crowd. "While the match as a game proved thoroughly interesting," noted one newspaper, "chief attention centred on the doings of Bloomer, who has recently returned to England with a party of repatriated prisoners. He played with much of his old skill, and there was quite a demonstration when he worked through and shot a goal."

Over the next few months, as Bloomer settled back in to family life in Derby, he continued to play and enthuse about football, albeit in somewhat reduced circumstances. He began to turn out for the works team of the British Cellulose chemical plant in Spondon, near Derby, and may have been employed by the plant, although it seems unlikely that any work he did strayed far beyond the realms of football. He also began to write columns for the *Derbyshire Advertiser*, providing comments on the current state of the game while offering coaching tips for players.

When the Football League resumed for its first post-war season in August 1919, Bloomer returned to Derby County – or at least to Derby County Reserves. Bloomer played several matches and captained the reserve side, and also did some coaching. He was effectively back where he had been before his move to Germany five years earlier. But it wasn't quite the return to football he might have dreamt of. He was now 45, and beyond the age most footballers could rely on their bodies. But, as Bloomer would no doubt have pointed out, he was only six months older than Billy Meredith, who was still playing for Manchester United in the First Division. (Meredith would continue to play at the top level until he was almost 50.)

Realistically, Bloomer knew his future was in coaching, but opportunities remained scarce. In November 1919, Bloomer received an offer to go to Warsaw to coach the Polish Olympic team. The appointment would have lasted six months and, despite the lack of opportunities in Britain, Bloomer decided to remain at home. "I prefer to stay in Derby," he said. "They are still scrapping up there in Poland, and I don't want to run into any more of that... The Old Mother Country's good enough for me."

Nevertheless, there was a feeling that the Old Mother Country was beginning to forget its greatest footballer, and newspaper columns began to suggest that Bloomer's waning career should be commemorated. "There never was such a player [and] there never will be such another in our time," wrote a *Derby Daily Telegraph* football columnist. "Now he is quitting the scene where so long he ruled supreme and unapproachable there appears to be a danger that he may walk off the stage unobserved. The idea to us is intolerable."

The columnist proposed that the FA should organise an international testimonial match on his behalf. "Bloomer's wonderful record for his country and the game generally... is worth recognition," he wrote, "but above all, during his long internment, he was the life and soul of the camp at Ruhleben, and was the means of brightening the lives of his compatriots."

Derby supporters backed the proposal. "I am afraid we shall never see another Steve," wrote one longstanding supporter, who had first watched Bloomer when both men were boys. "Like WG Grace at cricket, so Steve stands out alone in the football world." Another supporter wrote: "It does not seem right that this idol of the crowd should be allowed to sink into oblivion without some special effort being made on his behalf." But Bloomer would not get his testimonial match. Instead, he continued to scrap around for opportunities that were largely beneath his talents.

The 1920-21 season was disastrous for Derby County, who finished second-bottom of the First Division and were relegated. In the following summer, the club appointed Bloomer as first-team coach on a full-time basis, working under the manager, his former Derby teammate Jimmy Methven. "No better choice could have been made," said the *Telegraph*. But Bloomer struggled to work miracles. Derby finished in mid-table in the Second Division.

At the end of the season, in April 1922, Bloomer left England for the first time since the war to take up a summer coaching role in Canada with Montreal's Grenadier Guards FC. As he sailed from Liverpool on the Canadian-Pacific liner *Minnedosa*, he must have reflected on the events that transpired the last time he left his country and his family to pursue his coaching career. Thankfully, this foreign assignment would be less complicated than the last.

His new club was named for the Canadian Grenadier

Guards reserve regiment, but it was not a military team. Most of the players were British emigrants. Football in Canada was still an amateur pursuit and was played in the summer to avoid the winter weather. Although he struggled a little with the heat, Bloomer enjoyed the experience. He found there was not much football outside of Montreal, Toronto and Ottawa, and that baseball and lacrosse were more popular. But he said the younger generation was taking to football "with great enthusiasm".

By the end of the summer season, the Grenadier Guards had won their league and the Quebec Cup – beating Beloeil 4-0 in the final. Bloomer declared himself "highly pleased" with his Canadian adventure, and the Canadians seemed pleased with him. "If I don't go back, they say they will come and fetch me," he said.

Unfortunately, things were not well at Derby County. Jimmy Methven had been sacked during Bloomer's trip abroad. Bloomer resumed duties as first-team coach under new manager Cecil Potter, but Derby continued to struggle and racked up big debts. Financial troubles meant Bloomer's contract would not be renewed.

Bloomer's association with Derby County as a player ended in May 1923 when he turned out for an Old International team against a Derby team at the Baseball Ground, raising £374 for the Mayor's War Memorial Fund. Billy Meredith and former England captain Bob Crompton were among the old internationals. Bloomer scored two goals, including one from the penalty spot, and his team won 5-3. It was the last hurrah for Britain's greatest footballer.

Afterwards, during a gathering of players, officials and friends at Ramsden's Restaurant, a toast was raised to Bloomer, and he was called upon to make a speech. He thanked those who had helped make the day a success, and made an announcement. "Today's match has been my last," he said. "I shall never play any more. I have had enough." If he was younger, he said, he might have played in more charity matches. But he was now approaching 50 and was suffering severely from "shortness of wind". The crowd laughed, but Bloomer wasn't joking. He would never play football again.

"I am no longer a youngster, although my enthusiasm for the game is as great as ever," he subsequently explained. "I feel that the years of internment at Ruhleben in Germany have hastened the inevitable end and so I have decided that my last game in public has been played. I have not come to this decision without many pulls at my heartstrings, for the game has always had an irresistible fascination for me, and it is with a pang that I realise my playing days are over."

Like Bloomer, Fred Pentland also struggled to get back into football following his return from Ruhleben. He declared himself to be "keen on a game", and played several times for Queen's Park Rangers Reserves. But he never made the first team, and he accepted that he had spent the last of his playing days in the prison camp. "Years may bring experience," he said, "but a man doesn't become any faster after he has passed the 36-year mark." Instead, he began working in an office while waiting for a suitable opportunity in coaching that he knew might never come. When an opportunity did arrive, it came from a familiar source.

In September 1919, Walther Bensemann, on behalf of the German football association, posted a notice in British newspapers asking for the addresses of Bloomer, Pentland

and Sam Wolstenholme. Bensemann wanted to persuade these and other British footballers to return to Germany and resume their coaching duties. But the English FA had broken off relations with its German counterpart and declared there should be no future dealings between English and German clubs. One newspaper called Bensemann's approach a "German trap for footballers", and said that no footballer would be stupid enough to be lured to Germany by the promise of "an easy time and high wages".

Nevertheless, Pentland seriously considered the proposition and asked the FA for advice. "Will he go back?" asked the *Star Green 'Un*. The answer was "no". Pentland wrote to Bensemann and said that unless the German authorities were prepared to make an offer of compensation for broken contracts, their long incarceration in Germany, and four years' of lost income, there was little prospect of any British players returning to Germany.

One footballer who did return to Germany after the war was William Townley, who resumed his engagement as coach and manager at Bayern Munich – and won the Southern Bavarian championship in 1919-20. But those who had been in Ruhleben chose to pursue their careers elsewhere. For Pentland, that initially meant Strasbourg in France, just across the Rhine from Germany and disconcertingly close to Karlsruhe, where he had been arrested and imprisoned before being sent to Ruhleben.

Pentland became coach of AS Strasbourg in March 1920, on the recommendation of FA secretary Frederick Wall. During his year there, he also took charge of the French Olympic team at the Antwerp Games. It wasn't a great tournament for Pentland. The players complained about his rigorous training methods, and France were well beaten by Czechoslovakia in the semi-finals. But while he was in Antwerp, Pentland was approached by a Spanish player who asked if he could help find a coach for Racing de Santander. He had always wanted to go to Spain, he said, so "I decided to take the post myself".

This was the beginning of a remarkable Spanish adventure for Pentland that would help him banish the memories of Ruhleben. After one season in Santander, Pentland moved to Athletic Bilbao. It was at the Basque Country club that Pentland helped revolutionise continental football and became one of the most influential coaches in football history. He instigated an innovative training programme, drilled his players in short-passing and shooting, and focused on improving their technique. Soon, he had a skilful passing side that was a clear precursor of many Spanish sides that would follow.

His style of football became known as *lo de Pentland* – Pentland's way. And he had instant success. In his first season, 1922-23, Athletic won their regional championship, then won the Copa del Rey – which was then a national championship contested by the regional champions. For Pentland, there would be many more trophies to come.

Just as he had followed Fred Pentland to Germany in 1914, Steve Bloomer followed his friend to Spain in 1923. Bloomer was offered the position of coach at Real Unión of Irún, around 50 miles from Bilbao. While he was initially reluctant to leave England for the continent, his release by Derby County and the continuing dearth of coaching opportunities in Britain left him little choice. "Many Derby people will wish Steve Bloomer every luck in his new coaching job in sunny Spain," said the *Derby Daily Telegraph*, "for after all there is only one Steve, and Derby regards him as their own."

Bloomer must have noted Pentland's instant success in Spain, and it seems probable it was Pentland who alerted Bloomer to the availability of the role or recommended him for it. Pentland had previously recommended Bloomer to the English FA for the role of Olympic football coach, but this recommendation had been ignored. Almost immediately after his arrival in Irún, Bloomer went to Bilbao to see Pentland, who he said already spoke perfect Spanish and "looked like a real 'Don'".

In Irún, Bloomer was pleased to find that Real Unión played in the black and white of his beloved Derby County. And he was thrilled by the enthusiasm the locals had for football, with big crowds ranging from 25,000 to 30,000. The team was mostly comprised of local Basque players, but several of them were internationals. Bloomer reckoned he had at least four players who were "the real goods", including Spanish international half-back Francisco Gamborena and French international centre-half René Petit. His new charges, he said, were "born ball-players" who were ripe for his still-radical method of training with the ball at their feet.

Like Pentland, Bloomer enjoyed immediate success. In his first season in charge, Real Unión won the Guipúzcoa regional championship, ahead of Real Sociedad, and qualified for the climactic Copa del Rey. Unión beat Sevilla and Barcelona on the way to the final. (The Sevilla manager was former Ireland international Charles O'Hagan and the Barcelona manager was former England international Alf Spouncer.) Their opponents in the final were Real Madrid. José Echeveste scored the only goal of the game as Real

Unión won 1-0 to become the Spanish champions. Bloomer was now a hero in Spain, just as he had been in England.

That summer, Bloomer went to Bilbao to see Pentland and to watch a touring Newcastle United side lose 1-0 to a Spanish Select XI in front of 45,000 spectators. "The Spaniards went mad – literally mad – and they will celebrate the event for a week," said Bloomer. Football was making "vast strides" on the continent, he said, and particularly in Spain. What he was perhaps too modest to say was that those vast strides were largely due the presence and influence of men like himself and Pentland.

The Spanish called Bloomer "Mister Bloomer" and Pentland "Mister Pentland". It is because of them and the other British managers who went to Spain during the country's footballing dawn that even today the Spanish colloquial term for a football manager is "mister". Bloomer and Pentland paved the way for Mister Toshack, Mister Venables, Mister Robson and others. More than that, it could be argued that they helped teach a nation to play and helped shape its football philosophy. If their methods and techniques had been honed during their years of internment, then they could perhaps claim to have taken something positive from Ruhleben.

"There are no hard and fast rules by which men may be taught to play," Pentland had written back in 1915 in the *Ruhleben Football Association Handbook*. "Careful coaching and practice will teach a man much, but all this is absolutely useless unless the player himself is capable of creating ideas and putting them into instant practice in the field of play when the occasion arises. Matches are won on the playing grounds, not in the barracks... And that's the secret of football."

Steve Bloomer saw out his two-year contract in Spain, then returned to England. During his second season in Irún, Real Unión beat Real Madrid 3-0 and 7-0 in friendlies, but finished second to Real Sociedad in the regional championship, and failed to qualify for the Copa del Rey. Meanwhile, Bloomer was complaining about the heat and the olive oil. He thought the latter should be used for massages but not as a foodstuff. Reading between the lines, he was homesick. Back in Derby, he resumed his scouting and coaching duties, mostly with schoolboy teams, and wrote about football for the *Derbyshire Football Express*.

In 1929, Bloomer went back to Derby County, where he was employed as a groundsman at the Baseball Ground. In October 1931, he made a final "comeback" of sorts, at the age of 57. The occasion was a benefit for the Orphan Children's Fund, and Bloomer scored a penalty with his "customary accuracy".

It was after the death of his wife that Bloomer's health began to decline. Sarah Bloomer died in 1936, at the age of 61 following a short illness. Within a few months, Steve was "indisposed" due to bronchitis and asthma, and was hardly eating or sleeping. The "shortness of wind" he had complained about some years earlier could now be explained. The Derby County manager George Jobey issued an appeal for donations to send Bloomer on a trip to Australia and New Zealand to recuperate. Donations were received from football associations, clubs, players, and fans from as far afield as his antipodean destinations on the other side of the world. The fund raised £558.

One fan who contributed to the fund was James Dale, formerly of Ruhleben's Barrack 5, who sent a postal order for 10 shillings "collected from a few football enthusiasts in

Rochdale". "I knew Steve when he was a prisoner in Ruhleben," wrote Dale, "and I have the liveliest and happiest recollections of his football artistry and his boundless enthusiasm for the game – revealed by his amazing vocabulary when things went wrong. He was a wonderful trainer at that time. Out of what was mostly the rawest materials, he made the finest football team in the camp – and it *was* a team."

Bloomer left for Australia in November 1937. He was waved off from Derby train station by his daughter Doris, George Jobey and several Derby players, and his old England teammate Fred Spiksley, who was visiting Derby for the races. "I shall be glad to get away from the damp and fog of the winter here," Bloomer told a reporter. And the trip seemed to go well. Bloomer wrote in a letter that he was feeling much better and was managing to eat and sleep. He returned from New Zealand in March 1938, and it was reported that he looked better. However, within a day of his arrival, he was taken ill. He would never recover.

On 16 April 1938, the front page of the *Derby Daily Telegraph* broke the sad news: "The *Telegraph* announces with regret the death early today of Steve Bloomer, one of football's greatest personalities, and the finest inside-forward in the history of the game." Bloomer died at Doris's house. He was 63 years old. His funeral, at Derby Cathedral, was attended by hundreds of mourners, including scores of footballers. Many were unable to gain entrance, and stood outside the cathedral with their hats in their hands in silent acknowledgement. Well-wishers left more than 60 wreaths.

The tributes were fulsome. "There was only one Bloomer," said the *Telegraph*, "whose name and fame will never die in football annals, and those who remember his brilliant play declare there will never be another." Sir Frederick Wall, the former FA secretary, called Bloomer "the greatest of the old-timers". FA president William Pickford said he was "incomparable". Vice president Fred Rinder called him "the Prince of Football". And former Derby director PO Francis said, "There was only one Steve Bloomer, and there could never be another such a player. He was, in my opinion, the most outstanding man who ever played football."

In 2009, a bronze bust of Bloomer by the sculptor Andrew Edwards was unveiled on a plinth of red bricks next to the dugout at Derby County's Pride Park stadium. The red bricks were taken from the old Baseball Ground, which was demolished in 2003. Underneath the bust is an old metal tablet that was originally fitted to the Baseball Ground's brick wall. It reads: *"In Memory of Steve Bloomer 1874-1938. This tablet was erected by many of his friends and admirers as an appreciation of his services to Derby County Football Club and his country. Also as a tribute to one of the greatest players the game has ever produced."*

Fred Pentland managed Athletic Bilbao, Atlético Madrid and Real Oviedo during a 15-year career in Spain through to the outbreak of the Spanish Civil War. It was during a second period at Athletic Bilbao, between 1929 and 1933, that he cemented his legend, winning the Copa del Rey in four consecutive seasons and winning the league and cup double twice. In 1931, he led Bilbao to a 12–1 victory over Barcelona, which remains the Catalan club's worst-ever defeat. Pentland became forever linked with Athletic Bilbao, shaping the club's philosophy and future. Rarely seen without a bowler hat, or *bombín*, “Mister Pentland” was regarded as the distinguished English gentleman of Spanish football.

In 1959, Athletic Bilbao invited Pentland to return to their San Mamés stadium for a tribute match against Chelsea. The white-haired Pentland was presented with a commemorative medal for his service and invited to perform the kick-off. The crowd chanted his name, and he thanked them over a loudspeaker and told them that he could now “die happy”. He passed away three years later, in March 1962, at the age of 78. He is still revered in Bilbao. References to Pentland and his *bombín* can be found around the San Mamés, and his name is remembered by supporters of all three clubs he managed. The London branch of the Athletic Bilbao supporters’ association is called the “Mister Pentland Club”.

Jack Cameron returned to football before the end of the war, in July 1918, as manager of Ayr United. The former Ruhleben FA secretary held trial matches in Ayr and built a team that finished fifth in the Scottish First Division in 1918-19 – regarded as “an astounding finish” considering they had been 18th and last in 1917-18. But he gave up management after a single season and reverted to working as a referee and linesman in the Scottish League and Scottish Alliance.

In 1921, Cameron attended a 20-year reunion for Tottenham’s 1901 FA Cup-winning team, which he had player-managed. According to *Athletic News* editor Jimmy Catton, Cameron had not changed much since the glory days. “His face is furrowed here and there,” said Catton, “but in spite of his long detention at Ruhleben – ‘where we had some good football,' he said – his hair is dark and his body is 'soople'." Cameron died in April 1935, aged 63.

Edwin Dutton, who Steve Bloomer called "one of my biggest chums", returned to England and Newcastle after the war rather than going to his parents in Berlin. The reason for this was his relationship with Mary McPherson, the daughter of Newcastle United trainer Jimmy McPherson, which had survived his four-year absence. Dutton married Mary in Newcastle in early 1919. After that, he remained connected with Newcastle United Reserves, as an occasional player and an assistant trainer, alongside his two new brothers-in-law, Robert and James McPherson Jnr. (James Junior went on to coach the Norwegian Olympic team before succeeding his father as Newcastle's first team trainer.)

Dutton went back to Germany in 1924 and spent a season coaching Stuttgarter Kickers. But, probably for family reasons, he was soon back in England, on Tyneside. In 1925, Dutton was appointed assistant trainer of South Shields FC in the Second Division of the Football League. Two years later, he became the trainer of Ipswich Town in the Southern League. He then returned to Newcastle, where he became a partner in a chiropody and massage practice in the suburb of Jesmond. He later moved to Wilmslow in Cheshire, where he died in 1972, at the age of 82.

Sam Wolstenholme was another Ruhlebenite who decided not to return to his coaching position in Germany and instead followed Pentland and Bloomer to Spain. The three-time Ruhleben Football League champion coached RS Gimnástica de Torrelavega for two seasons from 1924.

During his tenure, Gimnástica beat Germany's Freiburg 3-1 in what was Gimnástica's first international club match. But Wolstenholme couldn't quite emulate Pentland's or Bloomer's success in Spain. Wolstenholme died in hospital in 1945, aged 68.

Jack Brearley, the captain of Ruhleben Cup-winning Barrack 4, does not seem to have gone back to football following his return from Ruhleben. In later life, he lived at Thorpe Bay in Southend-on-Sea. Tragically, Brearley was killed after being thrown from a bicycle in Southend in 1944. He was 68.

Percy Hartley married Jessie Archer in Bolton in March 1919, then went back to Belgium, where he resumed his role at CS Verviers and then coached Standard Liège in the country's top division for more than a decade. He continued to coach in Belgium for another decade after that. He said continental football had "suffered considerably owing to the war" but the players continued to work hard.

Hartley was interned for a second time during the Second World War, with his son Harold, following the German invasion of Belgium in 1940. He was still working as a football coach. He died in Horwich, Lancashire in 1954, at the age of 69.

Wattie Campbell, the former Evertonian who struggled to play due to injury in Ruhleben but helped organise the football league, resumed his work as an engineer in the merchant navy after the war. He retired due to ill health and died in June 1930, aged 63.

Wyndham Richards, the amateur footballer and unsuccessful escapee, returned to teaching after his internment. He had never stopped writing to his sweetheart Jessie James, even after she told him she was engaged. And in Cardiff in July 1923, almost five years after his release from Ruhleben, Wyndham Richards married Jessie James. Richards died in March 1966, a few days before his 75th birthday.

Joseph Powell, Ruhleben's determined captain, resumed his work in Berlin as the European sales manager for the Eclair film company. In 1919, he co-wrote a book, *The History of Ruhleben*, and presented an exhibition about the camp at London's Westminster Central Hall. The exhibition was attended by George V, and Powell presented the King with a Union Flag bearing the Ruhleben coat-of-arms and the inscription: *"Although unable to fight for our King and country on the battlefield, we endeavoured to maintain the British ideal of patriotism, patience, courage, and usefulness through four years."*

Powell was awarded the OBE for his services to the Ruhlebenites. The man who "did so much useful work as captain of the camp" died of pneumonia in Berlin in January 1925. He was 50 years old. His body was repatriated for burial at Highgate Cemetery, London, where his gravestone reads: *"Leader of the Internees at Ruhleben POW Camp 1914-18."*

Geoffrey Pyke, Ruhleben's first successful escapee, gained further fame following the Second World War for his work as a spy in Nazi Germany and for his military inventions, including a proposed ice ship – a giant aircraft carrier made out of a mixture of wood pulp and ice – which he demonstrated in a bath for Winston Churchill. However, most of his inventions came to nothing. His biography, by David Lampe, was titled *Pyke: the Unknown Genius*. Pyke died from an overdose of sleeping pills in 1948, aged 54.

John Masterman was another Ruhlebenite who became a spy. Before that, he resumed the sporting career that had blossomed in the camp, playing tennis at Wimbledon, hockey for England, and first-class cricket for the MCC. He was also more than decent at golf, squash and the high-jump. He became a novelist, writing murder mysteries, but it was his role during the Second World War as an MI5 official in charge of the Double Cross System, which turned Nazi spies into British double agents, that brought him most notoriety – particularly after he wrote a book about it. He was knighted for his service to his country. Sir John Cecil Masterman OBE died in 1977, aged 86.

Alex Bodin, the former Rangers player who would not take part in any game played on a Sunday, entered the Divinity Hall of Glasgow University following his return from Ruhleben and subsequently became a minister in the Church of Scotland. In 1937, the "exceedingly popular" Reverend Bodin suffered a relapse of "an unfortunate breakdown". Newspaper reports linked his illness to his internment in Germany. He died in Biggar, South Lanarkshire, in 1948, aged 60.

Israel Cohen, the journalist who was arrested in Berlin at the same time as Bloomer, was released from Ruhleben in the summer of 1916. A correspondent for *The Times* and *The*

Guardian, and also the general secretary for the World Zionist Organisation, he investigated and reported on anti-Semitism in Germany and elsewhere through to the start of the Second World War. He wrote several books, including *Ruhleben Prison Camp: A Record of Nineteen Months' Internment.* He died in 1961.

Tom Sullivan, the New Zealand rowing and sculling champion who turned his hand to land-based sports in Ruhleben, became a highly-regarded rowing coach. Echoing the career paths of some of his footballing friends from Ruhleben, Sullivan coached rowing in the Netherlands before returning to Germany with the Berlin Rudder Club. He also coached the German coxed four to a gold medal at the 1932 Olympics. Sullivan ended his career in Austria and died in Vienna in 1949.

Sam Heapy, the Derby jockey and old friend of Bloomer, returned to Belgium after the war to ride and train horses for Baron Brugmann. He rode 3,260 winners over the course of his career, breaking the world record for career wins and making him one of the most successful British jockeys of all time. Heapy died in Brussels in 1963, aged 82.

Harry Edward, the teenage sprinter who dominated the first Ruhleben sports day, moved to London after the war and went on to become the first black athlete to represent Great Britain at the Olympic Games. He won bronze medals in both the 100 metres and 200 metres at the 1920 Olympics in Antwerp. He later immigrated to the US and New York, where he worked for the United Nations. He died back in Germany in 1973, aged 75.

John "Bicycle Billy" Halpin got back on his bike, because he "got fed up of standing in dole queues", and cycled from London to Edinburgh and back, then from Land's End to John O'Groats, stopping off at various army garrisons to entertain troops along the way. In April 1920, he pleaded guilty to stealing a miner's bicycle from a shed at Grassmoor Colliery in Derbyshire and was sentenced to 15 months' hard labour. Halpin confessed he had "a mania for cycle stealing". Newspapers reported on his previous incarceration in Ruhleben with Bloomer, and, further to his failed attempts, said Halpin had successfully escaped, then joined the army, serving in France, where he was wounded.

Ruhleben was used to house 3,000 Russian prisoners of war after the departure of the British. The Russians faced a lengthy wait for repatriation due to the post-war chaos in both Germany and Russia. An American Red Cross worker who visited the camp in the spring of 1919 to check on the prisoners noted seeing the faded white lines of former football pitches in the centre of the racetrack. Traces of football, he said, were "always an indication of occupancy by the British".

Eventually, Ruhleben was restored to its original purpose and became a trotting track once again. Its final race was held in October 1955. In the following year, the Ruhleben *Trabrennbahn* was demolished to make way for the new Ruhleben *Klärwerk* – or sewage works. Today, Ruhleben is at the end of the line of the Berlin U-Bahn transit system. There is nothing left of the prison camp. Walking from the U-Bahn towards its former site, there is a McDonald's restaurant, an Aldi supermarket, the sewage works, and then – pretty much where the prisoners' wholly inhospitable barracks would have been – a modern, glass-fronted 4-star hotel. The road that runs alongside the hotel, and alongside the former Ruhleben camp, is called *Freiheit* – Freedom.

Footballers in Ruhleben

There were eight former professional footballers in the Ruhleben prison camp:

Steve Bloomer; Jack Brearley; Jack Cameron;
Wattie Campbell; Edwin Dutton; Percy Hartley;
Fred Pentland; Sam Wolstenholme

During their playing careers, the eight professionals played for three national teams and at least 20 different clubs:

England (3); Scotland; Germany

Blackburn Rovers (2); Blackpool; Brentford; Chester City; Crystal Palace; Derby County; Everton (4); Exeter City; Halifax Town; Huddersfield Town; Middlesbrough (3); Millwall Athletic; Newcastle United; Norwich City; Notts County; Preston North End; Queens Park Rangers; Small Heath (Birmingham City); Stoke; Tottenham Hotspur (2)

There were also several amateur or semi-professional footballers in Ruhleben who had played at various levels. Some had played in the top regional divisions in Germany.

The following catalogue of prominent footballers in Ruhleben presents the eight professionals followed by the amateurs, semi-professionals and others who emerged as the most notable players in the camp.

Stephen "Steve" Bloomer

Born: Cradley, West Midlands, 20 January 1874
Position: Inside left / inside right
Career: Derby County, 1891-1906 (375 apps, 238 goals); Middlesbrough, 1906-1910 (125 apps, 59 goals); Derby County, 1910-1914 (98 apps, 53 goals)
International: England, 1895-1907 (23 apps, 28 goals)
Management: Britannia Berlin, 1914
Occupation in 1914: Football coach
Arrested: Berlin, 6 November 1914 (aged 40)
In Ruhleben: Barrack 1 (captain), later Barrack 11; "Tottenham"; "England" (captain); Ruhleben (captain); Bloomer's XI (captain)
Released: To Netherlands, March 1918
After Ruhleben: Managed/coached: Blauw-Wit Amsterdam, Netherlands; Grenadier Guards, Canada; Real Unión, Spain. Assistant trainer: Derby County
Died: Derby, 16 April 1938 (aged 64)

"Everywhere football is played Steve Bloomer's name and fame are known. He is the most famous English inside-right the world has ever known, and his brilliant record is never likely to be equalled by another player... Those who have seen the manner in which he has taught the game to his colleagues in Barrack 1 can imagine what he would have done for his club in Berlin." – *Ruhleben FA Handbook*

John "Jack" Brearley

Born: Liverpool, 8 November 1875
Position: Forward / right half
Career: Millwall Athletic, 1899-1900 (51 apps, 13 goals); Notts County, 1900-1901; Middlesbrough, 1901-1902; Everton, 1902-1903 (24 apps, 8 goals); Tottenham Hotspur, 1903-1907 (133 apps, 24 goals); Crystal Palace, 1907-1909 (71 apps, 3 goals); Millwall Athletic, 1909-1911
Management: Millwall Athletic (player-coach), 1909-1911; Viktoria 89, Berlin, 1911-1914
Occupation in 1914: Football coach
Arrested: While in hospital, Berlin, 19 November 1914 (39)
In Ruhleben: Barrack 4 (captain); "England"; Ruhleben; Cameron's XI; Brearley's XI (captain)
Died: Thrown from bicycle, September or October 1944 (aged 68)

"To those people who are ever ready to decry professionals in sport the character and spirit of the captain of the cup-winning team are eloquent testimony of a sport being fortunate in having such a man in its ranks." – *Ruhleben FA Handbook*

John "Jack" Cameron

Born: Ayr, 13 April 1872
Position: Inside right / inside left / centre-forward
Career: Queen's Park, 1895-96; Everton, 1896-1898 (42 apps, 12 goals); Tottenham Hotspur, 1898-1907 (111 apps, 43 goals
International: Scotland, 1896
Management: Tottenham Hotspur, 1899-1907; Dresdner SC, 1907-1914
Occupation in 1914: Football coach
Arrested: Dresden, 6 November 1914 (aged 42)
In Ruhleben: Barrack 10; Ruhleben; The Rest; Cameron's XI (captain); Secretary of Ruhleben FA
Released: 2 January 1918
After Ruhleben: Managed Ayr United, became referee
Died: Glasgow, 20 April 1935 (aged 63)

"We were wonderfully fortunate in having the old Tottenham Hotspur manager as our secretary. With his expert knowledge and charming tact, the success of the affair was a foregone conclusion." – *Ruhleben FA Handbook*

Walter "Wattie" Campbell

Born: Moffat, Dumfrieshire, 1867
Position: Left half / left back
Career: Moffat; Bootle, 1888-1890; Everton, 1890-91 (17 apps, League Championship winner)
Occupation in 1914: Marine engineer
Arrested: Hamburg, 31 July 1914 (aged 46 or 47), held on hulks
In Ruhleben: Barrack 3 (non-playing manager / chairman)
Released: 6 March 1918
After Ruhleben: Returned to sea, but suffered from ill health
Died: Liverpool, 12 June 1930 (aged 63)

"His long confinement at Ruhleben has not improved his health by any means, but Scotch grit and stamina has stood him in good stead, and all, the abuse, hunger and provocation has not killed Wattie Campbell. He does so love the Germans! He thinks old footballers and men used to seafaring life stood the test best." – *Liverpool Echo*

Edwin Dutton

Born: Mittenwalde, Germany, 8 April 1890
Position: Inside left
Career: Britannia Berlin, 1906-1908; BFC Preussen, 1908-1910; Newcastle United (touring/reserves), 1910-1912; Britannia Berlin, 1912-1914
International: Germany, 1909
Occupation in 1914: Sports outfitter / Semi-pro footballer
Arrested: Berlin, 6 November 1914 (aged 24)
In Ruhleben: Barrack 1, later Barrack 11; "Tottenham"; Ruhleben
After Ruhleben: Returned to Newcastle United as reserve team player, 1918-1924; Coach, Stuttgarter Kickers, 1924-1925; Assistant trainer, South Shields, 1925; Trainer, Ipswich Town, 1926-1927
Died: Wilmslow, 24 May 1972 (aged 82)

"Excellent form was displayed by Dutton, a son of an English athletic outfitter in business in Germany, who came over from the Fatherland specially for the game and showed excellent form at centre, shooting with splendid accuracy" – *Hull Daily Mail*

Percy Wilding Hartley

Born: Bolton, January 1885
Position: Left half
Career: Preston North End 1906-1908; Huddersfield Town 1908-1909; Exeter City 1909
Management: CS Verviers, Belgium.
Occupation in 1914: Football coach
Arrested: 1914 (aged 29)
In Ruhleben: Barrack 7
After Ruhleben: Returned to manage CS Verviers, then Standard Liege, Belgium. Interned for a second time, with his son Harold, following German invasion of Belgium in 1940.
Died: Horwich, Lancashire, 1954 (aged 69)

"Of splendid physique, he is a clever tackler, capable feeder, and a better shot than many forwards." – *Manchester Courier*

Frederick "Fred" Beaconsfield Pentland

Born: Wolverhampton, 29 July 1883

Position: Outside right

Career: Small Heath, 1900-1903; Blackpool, 1903 (8 apps, 5 goals); Blackburn Rovers, 1903-1906 (51 apps, 9 goals), Brentford, 1906-1907 (36 apps, 12 goals); Queens Park Rangers, 1907-1908 (37 apps, 14 goals); Middlesbrough, 1908-1912 (92 apps, 11 goals); Stoke, 1913 (12 apps, 6 goals); Halifax Town, 1913-1914

International: England, 1909 (5 apps, 0 goals)

Management: Germany Olympic team

Occupation in 1914: Football coach

Arrested: Karlsruhe, 6 November 1914 (aged 31)

In Ruhleben: Barrack 10, later Barrack 11; "England"; Ruhleben; Bloomer's XI; President of Ruhleben FA

After Ruhleben: Managed France Olympic team, 1920; Racing de Santander, 1920-21; Athletic Bilbao, 1922–25; Atlético Madrid, 1925–1926; Real Oviedo, 1926–1927; Atlético Madrid, 1927–1929; Athletic Bilbao, 1929–1933; Atlético Madrid, 1934–1935; Barrow, 1938–1940

Died: Lytchett Matravers, Dorset, 16 March 1962 (aged 78)

"A very smart and alert forward, and readily adapts himself to almost any forward position." "He possesses an abundance of speed, and his crosses are of the best type." – *Lancashire Evening Post / Edinburgh Evening News*

Samuel "Sam" Wolstenholme
Born: Little Lever, 16 March 1877
Position: Right half / centre-half
Career: Everton, 1897-1904 (160 apps); Blackburn Rovers, 1904-1908 (97 apps, 1 goal); Croydon Common, 1908-1909; Norwich City, 1909-1913 (138 apps, 7 goals); Chester City, 1913
International: England, 1904-1905 (3 apps)
Management: Norddeutscher Fussball-Verband (North German Football Association) XI, 1914
Occupation in 1914: Football coach
Arrested: Hamburg, 6 November 1914 (aged 37)
In Ruhleben: Barrack 9 (captain); "Tottenham"; "England"; Ruhleben; Cameron's XI
After Ruhleben: Managed / coached Gimnástica de Torrelavega, Spain, 1924-1926
Died: In hospital, October 1945 (aged 68)

"No one who saw Sam play during our past season would have imagined he is in his 39th year. From start to finish of every game he displayed such stupendous energy and speed as would make anyone think he was nearer 20 than 40. He always has been a great half-back... The writer could tell many stories of Sam's good advice and kindly thoughtfulness when they played together for Blackburn Rovers years ago."
- *Ruhleben FA Handbook*

AS Belmont
Born: Australia, 1896
Career: Eton (wall and field games, rugby)
Occupation in 1914: Language student
In Ruhleben: Barrack 10 (captain of second team); "Oldham Athletic"

"His side owe him much, not only for his actual playing ability, but for the splendid spirit he infused everywhere. Until he came to Ruhleben he had never before played association football, having always favoured the rugby game." – *Ruhleben FA Handbook*

Alexander Hastie "Alex" Bodin
Born: Govan, 24 May 1887
Position: Half-back
Career: Rangers (as an amateur), 1906-1912
Occupation in 1914: Assistant Professor of Logic at the University of Glasgow
Arrested: While on holiday, Aschaffenburg, 5 August 1914 (27), held Aschaffenburg, Rastatt, Plötzensee, Berlin
In Ruhleben: Barrack 11 (captain); "Scotland"
After Ruhleben: Became a minister in the Church of Scotland
Died: Biggar, South Lanarkshire, January or February 1948 (aged 60)

"It was quite evident from Bodin's skill on the football field last season that he had experience in a class far above the usual amateur standard." – *Ruhleben FA Handbook*

Richard Clement "Clem" Burnill
Born: Holton-le-Clay, Lincolnshire, 1891
Position: Forward
Occupation in 1914: Ship's stoker
Arrested: 2 August 1914, Hamburg, held on hulks
In Ruhleben: Barrack 9; Bloomer's XI; Brearley's XI; "England"; Sea

"A clever player who was up to all the moves." – Bloomer

James Cant
Born: Alloa, 9 June 1884
Career: Played in Germany in Ratingen

Occupation in 1914: Fireclay presser
Arrested: Ratingen, 1 September 1914
In Ruhleben: Barrack 12 (co-captain)

"Like Miller in the same barrack, Cant is a Scotsman. They came to Germany at about the same time, played for the same teams in this country, and so it is quite in the order of things that they should share the captaincy of their barrack team here." – *Ruhleben FA Handbook*

Alexander Davidson Garden
Born: Aberdeen, 19 February 1894
Career: Robert Gordon College
Arrested: While on holiday, Hamburg, 1 November 1914
In Ruhleben: Tea House (captain), later Barrack 3; Brearley's XI; Cameron's XI; "Scotland"; The Rest

"The captain of the Tea House is further example of a good player only being able to show his real ability when playing with men of experience who are capable of bringing out the best... In the representative matches when his colleagues were picked men of the camp, he showed skill much superior to his barrack games" – *Ruhleben FA Handbook*

Horace Morgan Davies
Born: San Angelo, Texas, USA, 9 July 1888
Career: Gelligaer Old Boys, 1905-07; Sale (rugby union), 1907-12
Occupation in 1914: Engineer
Arrested: Berlin, 11 November 1914
In Ruhleben: Barrack 2 (captain); The Rest

"Although for most of his playing life he has been connected with the rugby code, and further, has a decided preference for it, he has shown such splendid form in the association games in the camp as would make us think he had played it always." – *Ruhleben FA Handbook*

Hugo Norton Dixon
Born: Southport, 23 November 1892
Position: Forward / inside right
Career: Charterhouse; Old Carthusians; possibly Southport FC

Occupation in 1914: Employed by US cotton firm in Bremen
Arrested: Bremen, 11 October 1914 (aged 21), held Bremen
In Ruhleben: Barrack 7 (captain); The Rest; Brearley's XI
After Ruhleben: Moved to US, founded successful cotton firm in Dallas, Texas, became philanthropist
Died: Following car accident, Memphis, Tennessee, 25 November 1974 (aged 82)

"Earnestness is a keynote of Dixon's play on the football field, and apparently no man in the camp enjoyed the games more than he. Tall, strong, fast, and possessing splendid technique, he was one of the most prominent players in Ruhleben. There is no doubt many amateur football honours would have fallen his way had he remained in England." – *Ruhleben FA Handbook*

William "Billy" Dixon
Born: Dunston, Tyneside, 1894
Position: Centre-forward
Occupation in 1914: Ship's clerk
Arrested: Hamburg, 1914 (aged 20), held on hulks
In Ruhleben: Barrack 2; "Scotland"; Wolstenholme's XI, Sea

"He was an exceedingly versatile player, and could ably occupy any position. If any first-class team manager approached Billy in the right way, providing of course, the FA make football worth a man's while, I believe that he might be captured." – Bloomer

John Arthur Falck
Born: Huddersfield, 8 November 1894
Position: Centre-forward / outside right
Career: Fartown Amateurs 1910-12; Huddersfield YMCA, 1912-13; Kölner FC 1899, Cologne, 1913-1914
Arrested: Wesel, 20 August 1914 (aged 19)
In Ruhleben: Barrack 14-15 (captain); The Rest; Cameron's XI
Died: Huddersfield, 1972 (aged 78)

"Another striking example of a good player not having sufficient support from his team to give him the opportunity of showing his real ability. In one of the representative games Falck gave evidence of what he can do and was voted one of the best forwards in the camp." – *Ruhleben FA Handbook*

Bradley Heath
Born: Macclesfield, 13 March 1894
Position: Left half-back
Career: Macclesfield Grammar School Old Boys
Arrested: 6 November 1914, Lubeck
In Ruhleben: Barrack 6 (captain)

"Every man in [Barrack 6] played with a stupendous energy and never spared themselves a jot. None played better, keener or fairer than their captain. The writer had a slight shock when Heath informed him he was only 21 years of age, for he is a splendid specimen of an athlete." – *Ruhleben FA Handbook*

Richard Frampton Kindersley
Born: Radley, Oxfordshire, 1887
Career: Eton, Cambridge University
Occupation in 1914: Engineer
Arrested: Berlin, 6 November 1914 (aged 26 or 27)
In Ruhleben: Barrack 1; "Oldham Athletic"
Died: 1960

Son of former England rugby international and Oxford University rower RS Kindersley.

Oates Lithgow
Born: Middlesbrough, 1885
Occupation in 1914: Marine engineer
Arrested: Hamburg 16 October 1914, held on hulks
In Ruhleben: Barrack 1, later Barrack 10; Bloomer's XI; Cameron's XI; "England"
Died: 15 February 1948 (aged 62)

Selected by Bloomer as one of the best players in the camp.

Alfred "Alf" Maw
Born: London, 1887
Position: Outside left
Occupation in 1914: Pharmacy manager
Arrested: While on honeymoon, Cologne, 6 September 1914

In Ruhleben: Barrack 5; "England"; The Rest
Died: In Ruhleben after falling from bunk, 4 July 1916

"He blossomed into a good footballer, playing outside left for Barrack 5, and gradually developed into one of the liveliest boys in the camp." - Bloomer

Thomas "Tommy" Miller
Born: Dreghorn, Ayrshire, 23 January 1882
Position: Full-back / right-half
Career: Kinghorn; Lochgelly; Ratingen Viktoria, Düsseldorf, 1903-1906; Düsseldorfer SC 99, 1906-1909; Ratingen Viktoria, 1909-1914
Occupation in 1914: Seaman
Arrested: Düsseldorf, 1 September 1914 (aged 32), held Sennelager, Düsseldorf, Friedrichsfeld, Münden
In Ruhleben: Barrack 12 (co-captain), later Barrack 8; "Scotland"; "Tottenham"
Died: 1946 or 1947 (aged 64 or 65)

"When Tom Miller came to Germany, Scotland lost a man who with very little coaching would certainly have developed into a first class full back. No man in this camp knows the game better than he, and this knowledge coupled with keenness unsurpassed by another player, place him in the first rank of Ruhleben FA celebrities." - *Ruhleben FA Handbook*

Alfred "Alf" Mills
Born: Hamburg, 1881
Position: Goalkeeper / full-back
Career: BFC Preussen, Berlin
Occupation in 1914: Trainer
Arrested: 6 November 1914 (aged 32 or 33), held on hulks
In Ruhleben: Barrack 11; "Tottenham"; The Rest; Cameron's XI

Selected by Bloomer as one of the best players in the camp.

Gordon Nicoll
Born: Dundee, 1897
Position: Goalkeeper
Occupation in 1914: Student

Arrested: 6 November 1914
In Ruhleben: Barrack 3; Brearley's XI; Cameron's XI, Land

"The camp's crack goalkeeper" - Bloomer

David Owen (also known as Dafydd French)
Born: 1885, Porthmadog, North Wales
Occupation in 1914: Seaman, *George Casson*
Arrested: Hamburg, 4 August 1914
In Ruhleben: Barrack 14, later Barrack 9; Bloomer's XI; The Rest

Selected by Bloomer as one of the best players in the camp.

James "Jimmy" Quinn
Born: Bootle, 1894
Position: Centre-half
Occupation in 1914: Civil engineer
Arrested: Hamburg 6 November 1914
In Ruhleben: Barrack 1, later Barrack 9; Bloomer's XI, Cameron's XI; "England"; The Rest

"Then there was Jimmy Quinn of Liverpool... All of these men are exceptionally fine amateur players. They improved even under the conditions imposed upon them at Ruhleben, and I have no hesitation in saying that if they were trained with First League players they would blossom out into fine, class men. If I were the manager of a club I would not have the smallest doubt of signing them up." – Bloomer

Thomas Wyndham Richards
Born: 11 March 1891
Position: Half-back
Football career: Newtown North End (Montgomeryshire and District League), St Albans AFC (Cardiff)
Occupation in 1914: Teacher
Arrested: Studying in Germany, 6 November 1914 (aged 23)
In Ruhleben: Barrack 10 (captain); "Oldham" (captain); The Rest (captain)
Escaped: October 1917, captured and sent to Havelburg, returned to Ruhleben

After Ruhleben: Continued to teach
Died: March 1966 (aged 74)

Selected by Bloomer as one of the best players in the camp. "Leads one the largest Cardiff clubs." – *Birmingham Daily Gazette*

George Rogans
Born: Workington, 10 November 1892
Position: Right half
Career: Garston Gasworks (amateur)
Occupation in 1914: Engineer
Arrested: During his first trip to sea, Hamburg, 16 October 1914 (aged 21)
In Ruhleben: Barrack 3 (captain); "Scotland"; The Rest
Died: Newton Le Willows, Lancashire, 1961 (aged 68 or 69)

"[Barrack 3] had a fast, young side, and were fortunate in having as a captain Rogans, whose keenness and wholeheartedness were given to his team." – *Ruhleben FA Handbook*

Robert "Bobby" Slade
From: Surbiton, London
Position: Outside left
Occupation in 1914: Seaman
Arrested: 4 October 1914, Brake on Weser
In Ruhleben: Barrack 9, later Barrack 10; Bloomer's XI; Cameron's XI; "England"; Sea

"He showed considerable promise. He would. I feel sure, train up into a first class man." – Bloomer

Robert "Bob" Stewart
Born: Fleetwood, 19 June 1894
Position: Left back
Career: Ilford North End (Essex and District League), 1909-1914
Occupation in 1914: Accountant
Arrested: While working in Germany, Elberfeld, 22 September 1914 (aged 20)
In Ruhleben: Barrack 5 (captain); The Rest (captain)
Died: 1940 (aged 45 or 46)

"As a football player I have a great admiration for Stewart... There is no doubt about it, he was one of the few men who are born football players." – Bloomer

George W Treseder
Born: Cardiff, 27 May 1893
Position: Left half-back
Occupation in 1914: Nurseryman
Arrested: Frankfurt
In Ruhleben: Barrack 1, later Barrack 9; Bloomer's XI, Cameron's XI; Land

"He played left half-back, and one would have to tramp a long way before coming up against an exponent quite so clever in that position." - Bloomer

Lionel Percy Warner
Born: Mansfield Woodhouse, Nottinghamshire, 6 August 1878
Position: Left half
Career: Mansfield Mechanics (Notts and District League); Hanau (German Nordkreis-Liga), 1907-1914
Occupation in 1914: Rubber salesman
Arrested: Karlsruhe, 4 August 1914 (aged 35), held Karlsruhe, Baden-Baden, Rastatt
In Ruhleben: Barrack 8 (captain); "England"; The Rest
Died: Mansfield, Nottinghamshire, 1948 (aged 69 or 70)

"Everyone who has seen the captain of the Barrack 8 team has been impressed by his earnestness. And this, added to an ability much above the amateur average, places him in the first rank among the camp players. He earned the soubriquet of 'unlucky' on account of always getting in the wars." – *Ruhleben FA Handbook*

Notes and Acknowledgements

I've long been fascinated by the Ruhleben footballers. I first wrote about them, briefly, in one of my previous books in 2006. Several years later, in 2014, I wrote a feature for *FourFourTwo* magazine, and realised their story should become a book. The feature was titled *The Real Escape to Victory*, but the story of the Ruhleben FA is not a fictional bank holiday TV movie. This story, of a remarkable group of men who used football as a tool to survive in the most difficult of circumstances, is entirely true.

As a student of Victorian and Edwardian football, I'm a big admirer of Steve Bloomer. I've no doubt, given the opinions of the most respected observers of the time, he was the greatest player of his generation. Above the desk where I wrote this book is a colour portrait of Bloomer by the artist EP Kinsella. My dad was born in Derby, and my great-grandad ran butcher's shops in the city during the era that Bloomer was banging in goals for Derby County. So perhaps I have some deep-rooted (meat-based) connection to Bloomer. Or, more likely, I'm just drawn to him as one of history's greatest working-class heroes.

My research for this book took me to London, Berlin and Amsterdam, and involved countless trawls through microfilm reels, bound and boxed newspapers, and blessedly searchable digitised archives. I read hundreds of newspaper articles, letters and other documents, and made full use of the resources of the British Library in London, Newcastle Library and Edinburgh Library. I'm grateful for our invaluable yet endangered public library system.

The camp magazines, published by the prisoners in extraordinary conditions, were a valuable resource, as was the Ruhleben FA handbook. Several of the most prominent footballers, including Bloomer, gave serialised accounts of their time in Ruhleben to newspapers – useful but full of mis-remembered and mis-transcribed names. I spent far too long trying to identify "Sammie Wilson-Holmes"...

Key books included J Davidson Ketchum's *Ruhleben: A Prison Camp Society*, a detailed – although truncated – study, Captain Joseph Powell's *History of Ruhleben*, and Israel Cohen's *The Ruhleben Camp*. Peter Seddon's *Destroying Angel* is a worthy biography of Steve Bloomer. And Rory Smith wrote about the British football managers, including Bloomer and Pentland, who took the game abroad in *Mister*. Of the many online resources used, I should particularly mention Chris Paton's *The Ruhleben Story* website, which contains details of more than 2,000 Ruhlebenites.

I was fortunate to obtain the diaries of Wyndham Richards, the leading amateur player, who recorded many details about football in Ruhleben and became a major character in the book. Wyndham's diaries were compiled and transcribed, and in some cases translated from French, by his son, Derek Richards. Sadly, Derek died before I was able to speak to him about Wyndham and Ruhleben. I was provided with a copy of the diaries by Derek's widow, Eira Richards, and I am extremely grateful.

I'm also grateful to Charlie Campbell for his assistance during the early stages of the project.

Final thanks go to Louise, who selflessly accompanied me on my short-haul research trips and provided encouragement during the book's long development, and also to everyone who has read and supported my previous books.

Cheers. – *Paul*

Bibliography

Camp publications

Handbook of the Ruhleben Football Association, JS Preuss, 1915
In Ruhleben Camp, 6 June 1915 - December 1915
Ruhleben Camp News, 27 January - February 1915
Ruhleben Camp Magazine, March 1916 - June 1917

Books

Anon., *In the Hands of the Huns*, Simkin Marshall Hamilton Kent, 1916
Bury, Herbert Right Rev., *My Visit to Ruhleben*, AR Mowbray, 1917
Catton, JAH, *Wickets and Goals*, Chapman & Hall, 1926
Cimino, Hugh, *Behind the Prison Bars in Germany*, 1915
Cohen, Israel, *Ruhleben Camp*, Methuen & Co, 1917
Gibson, Alfred & Pickford, William, *Association Football & the Men Who Made It*, Caxton, 1906
Ketchum, J Davidson, *Ruhleben: A Prison Camp Society*, University of Toronto Press, 1965
Mahoney, Henry C, *Interned in Germany*, Robert M McBride, 1918
Powell, Joseph & Gribble, Francis, *History of Ruhleben*, W Collins & Sons, 1919
Pyke, Geoffrey, *To Ruhleben and Back*, Constable, 1916
Richards, Derek, *Wyndham's War*, Vine Press, 2014
Seddon, Peter, *Destroying Angel: Steve Bloomer, England's First Football Hero*, Breedon, 1999
Sharpe, Ivan, *40 Years in Football*, Hutchinson, 1952
Sladen, Douglas (ed.), *In Ruhleben: Letters from a Prisoner to his Mother*, Hurst and Blackett, 1917
Smith, Rory, *Mister: The Men Who Taught the World*, Simon & Schuster, 2016
Stibbe, Matthew, *British Civilian Internees in Germany: The Ruhleben Camp, 1914-1918*, Manchester University Press, 2008
Talbot, Frederick A, *Sixteen Months in Four German Prisons*, Sampson Low, 1917
Wall, FJ, Alcock, CW & others, *The Book of Football*, Amalgamated Press, 1906

Newspapers

Aberdeen Daily Journal, Aberdeen Evening Express, All Sports Weekly, Athletic News, Birmingham Daily Gazette, Birmingham Daily Post, Birmingham Sports Argus, Bury Free Press, Coatbridge Express, Coventry Evening Telegraph, Daily Mail,

Daily Mirror, Daily Record, Darling Downs Gazette, Derby Daily Telegraph, Derbyshire Advertiser, Dublin Daily Express, Dundee Courier, Dundee Telegraph, Evening Dispatch, Fife Free Press, Folkestone Herald, Globe, Gloucestershire Echo, Graphic, Hull Daily Mail, Illustrated Police News, Illustrated Sporting & Dramatic News, Lichfield Mercury, Liverpool Daily Post, Liverpool Echo, London Standard, Malaya Tribune, Manchester Evening News, Motherwell Times, New York Times, Newcastle Chronicle, Newcastle Journal, North Wales Chronicle, Northern Whig, Nottingham Evening Post, Nottingham Journal, People, Portsmouth Evening News, Ripley News, Scotsman, Sheffield Daily Telegraph, Sheffield Daily Telegraph, Sheffield Independent, Shields Gazette, Shipley Express, Star Green 'Un, Suffolk Free Press, Sunday Chronicle, Sunday Echo, Sunday Mirror, Sunday Post, Surrey Mirror, Thomson's Weekly News, Times (London), Western Daily Press, Western Mail, Western Times, Yorkshire Evening Post

Key footballer accounts

Steve Bloomer in Germany, Sunday Chronicle, 14 July 1918; *Steve Bloomer's Experiences Among the Huns, Sunday Post,* 1 Dec 1918 to 9 February 1919; *John Cameron: My 3 1/2 Years in Ruhleben, Thomson's Weekly News,* 25 August 1918; *Fred Pentland: It Ain't All Lavender, All Sports Weekly,* 3 December 1921 to 28 January 1922; *Fred Pentland: My Four Years in Germany, Sports Argus,* 7 December 1918 to 4 January 1919

Online

11v11, 11v11.com

England Football Online, englandfootballonline.com

Hugo Norton Dixon Memoirs, Shelby County, bit.ly/hdixon

In Ruhleben Camp series, Harvard Law School Library blog, bit.ly/inruh

Jockeypedia, bit.ly/jockpe

John Masterman collection of Ruhleben British Civilian internment camp documents, Harvard Library, bit.ly/jmaste

Maurice L Ettinghausen collection of Ruhleben civilian internment camp papers, Harvard Library, bit.ly/mettin

MT9 Project, spw-surrey.com/MT9

Rec.Sport.Soccer Statistics Foundation, rsssf.com

Ruhleben Story, ruhleben.tripod.com

Ruhleben Transcriptions, Lincs Inspire, bit.ly/ruhtran

Ruhleben: A Digital Exhibit, Harvard Law School Library, bit.ly/ruhdigi

Steve Bloomer Website, stevebloomer.weebly.com

Index

About the Author

Paul Brown writes about football, history, true crime and adventure for publications including *FourFourTwo*, *When Saturday Comes*, *The Guardian* and *The Blizzard*. He is the author of several books, including *Savage Enthusiasm: A History of Football Fans*. He lives in the North East of England.

www.stuffbypaulbrown.com
www.twitter.com/paulbrownUK

ALSO AVAILABLE

Savage Enthusiasm

A History of Football Fans
By Paul Brown
Goal Post, Paperback, 9780995541221

Being a football fan is both a privilege and a burden. When you're winning, it's the best thing on Earth, and when you're not, it's the end of the world. And the thing about being a football fan is, whichever way fortune swings, you're stuck with the game and your team for life. We've come to accept the great hold football has on us. But how did this happen? How did we become so entirely wrapped up in the game? How did we become football fans?

"An important addition to efforts that seek to put a history of football fans on a par with the well-written histories of players, owners and administrators to form a complete picture of a sport that is so dominant in our culture" – Sports books of the year – *Irish Examiner*

"A very decent, impeccably sourced, primer on what has happened to fans down the ages" – *When Saturday Comes*

"An excellent read, rich in anecdotes and explanation" – *Game of the People*

"A splendid new book by an always exemplary researcher" – *Sports Journalists' Association*

"Predictably excellent" – *The Two Unfortunates*

ALSO AVAILABLE

The Rocketbelt Caper

A True Tale of Invention, Obsession and Murder
By Paul Brown
Superelastic, Paperback, 9780956227003

When three friends set out on a quest to build a real-life Buck Rogers-style flying machine, their obsession with the Rocketbelt 2000, or Pretty Bird, shattered their friendship and set in motion an astonishing chain of events involving theft, deception, a bizarre kidnapping, a ten million dollar lawsuit and a horrifically brutal murder. This book also reveals the secret history of the flying jetpack, involving Nazi scientists, James Bond, and the US Army. From sci-fi to reality, this is the true story of the amazing rocketbelt.

"A delight to read. Genuinely stranger than fiction. Recommended" – *Popular Science UK*

"The story has all the markings of a Hollywood blockbuster and is a bizarrely unforgettable read" – *The Crack*

"A can't-put-it-down murder mystery that shows how obsession and betrayal can lead people to commit dastardly deeds" – *General Aviation News*

"Reads like good movie material" – *BBC Focus*

"There's probably a Tarantino movie in this somewhere" – *Fortean Times*

Printed in Great Britain
by Amazon

51108400R10180